"Esterhammer creates laugh-out-loud moments of at times daunting or utterly embarrassing experiences. An energetic mix of wry humor and heartwarming moments, this engaging account will appeal to armchair travelers and memoir lovers alike." — *Library Journal*

"A lighthearted memoir of new friends, delicious food, and culture shock... A brisk chronicle of a family's (mis) adventures in Vietnam." — *Kirkus Reviews*

"Karin Esterhammer has artfully delineated what it's like to live outside your comfort zone. Her sharpshooter's eye for detail captures the Vietnamese people, their culture, and the pretzels an American family has to twist themselves into in order to adapt."

— Phil Doran,
author of *The Reluctant Tuscan*

"When life hands you financial ruin—as the Great Recession did to former *LA Times* journalist Karin Esterhammer—the answer might seem simple: Why not move to Vietnam? Along with her husband and child, Esterhammer did just that, facing her new life in Ho Chi Minh City with courage, wit, and an open heart, all the while examining one of life's biggest questions: What is it that truly makes us wealthy? It's an unforgettable—and important—adventure of the body, soul, and pocketbook."

— Alison Singh Gee,
author of *Where the Peacocks Sing:
A Prince, a Palace, and the Search for Home*

"A loopy adventure and charming cautionary tale for anyone who's ever dreamed of packing it in and starting over somewhere new—the perfect read for the armchair expat."

— Mark Haskell Smith,
author of *Naked at Lunch* and *Baked*

So
Happiness
to
Meet You

Foolishly, Blissfully Stranded in Vietnam

Karin Esterhammer

PROSPECT
·PARK·
BOOKS

Published by Prospect Park Books
2359 Lincoln Avenue
Altadena, CA 91001
www.prospectparkbooks.com

Distributed by Consortium Book Sales & Distribution
www.cbsd.com

Library of Congress Cataloging in Publication Data
Names: Esterhammer, Karin, author.
Title: So happiness to meet you: foolishly, blissfully stranded in Vietnam /
   by Karin Esterhammer.
Description: Altadena : Prospect Park Books, [2017].
Identifiers: LCCN 2016047486 (print) | LCCN 2016048366 (ebook) | ISBN
   9781938849978 (pbk.) | ISBN 9781938849985 (ebook)
Subjects: LCSH: Ho Chi Minh City (Vietnam)--Description and travel. |
   Vietnam--Social life and customs. | Americans--Foreign countries.
Classification: LCC DS556.39 .E87 2017 (print) | LCC DS556.39 (ebook) |
DDC
   959.7/7--dc23
LC record available at https://lccn.loc.gov/2016047486

Cover design by David Ter-Avanesyan
Book layout and design by Amy Inouye, Future Studio
Author photo by Marisa Cooper

For my mom
I miss you

DISCLAIMER

This book contains trace amounts of humor. Do not read while driving. Also, I changed the names of all but the main players to protect my neighbors' privacy. Otherwise, the story is all true. Really, you can trust me.

CHAPTER 1

Stranded

"Cake comes; cake goes."
(VIETNAMESE PROVERB)

IF YOU EVER GET THE CHANCE to become stranded in a foreign country with no money to get home, I recommend Vietnam. I say this because while you are boo-hooing and berating your rash decision to sell all your earthly belongings and move to this steamy hot Southeast Asian nation, like I did, you might pause long enough to ponder Vietnam's own history of hardships: back-to-back wars, colonization, famines, and those seventeenth-century Jesuit missionaries who couldn't make heads or tails of the writing system, so with a haughty, ethnocentric sniff, replaced the ideograms with the Roman alphabet, thus rendering the classics unreadable to future generations. The Vietnamese are philosophical about struggle: Don't look back; tomorrow will be better.

As I sat at the kitchen table in my sweltering, nine-foot-wide house in Ho Chi Minh City, my young Vietnamese teacher explained hardship this way: "Life *ee* like being on a boat and you have to drive you boat, but a *beeeg* ship go by you and make *beeeg* wave and you get trouble with you boat and you almost fall off boat. Then wave go back down and everything *ee* calm. But then there *ee* nothing to do."

I tried to decipher Tin Nguyen's point. Did he really believe that life is dull without adversity? I knew he was trying to
cheer me up. I'd been depressed lately about all that I'd lost in the
Great Recession, though I hadn't told him so specifically. Why say
anything? I'd already obliterated all chances for sympathy just by
flying to Vietnam. My neighbors needed only to apply a little in-
ductive reasoning: "The Americans purchased airfare to Vietnam.
It takes a lot of money to fly to Vietnam. Therefore, they have a
lot of money."

I knew that Tin, who was a born-again-and-again-and-again
Buddhist, would be mystified by my Western worldview that the
Joneses were viable opponents, that satisfaction with the hand life
dealt was a character flaw, and that frequent spending was a lovely
way to stave off the unhappiness that always threatened to engulf
me if I thought or felt *too* deeply. In fact, the insidious cycle of
always wanting more and more (which seems to be part and par-
cel of the American Dream), and then precariously tying those
material possessions to my identity, had worn me down physically
and emotionally. I hadn't realized how exhausted I was until I'd
lost it all. By the time I got to Vietnam, I nearly stumbled—wearied, worn, and whimpering—into the arms of my new neighbors,
who smiled sweetly and intoned, *"Trời ơi. Thôi đừng có than nữa!"* I
didn't know what it meant, but I thanked them for their kindness.
(Loosely translated: "Oh, for the love of God, stop complaining!")

My attention shifted to a noisy fly that alternately attacked
a basket of sweet, oozing mangoes on the table and the drops of
moisture on my brow. Annoyed at the zzzz-ing around my face, I
inadvertently swatted myself. My sweat glands shifted into over-
drive and I felt a rivulet of water drip down my back, soaking the
waistband of my skirt. It was only 10 a.m. and odor already wafted
up from my armpits. *Holy crap, Vietnam is hot.*

Tin (pronounced Din), twenty-five years old and runway-
model gorgeous, also focused on the fly. He stood up suddenly

and whapped it senseless in mid-flight. The obnoxious creature fell to the tile floor, its black, thread-thin legs curled up. Dead. *Wahoo!* Tin's quick reflexes astonished me. He normally moved like an astronaut out for a Sunday spacewalk. My gentle tutor, sliver-thin in his neatly pressed slacks and short-sleeved dress shirt, languidly sat back down and wagged one of his long, slender fingers at me. "*Ee* time to pay attention." I looked back at him. He flashed his straight, white teeth, framing them with a gentle smile. "You wasting *ow-ah* lesson time."

I was indeed. And for good reason. These Vietnamese lessons weren't going very well and I felt embarrassed. Unbeknownst to me up till now, I had the language facility of a Cheez Doodle. My husband, our eight-year-old son, and I had been living in Vietnam for more than a month already and I hadn't even mastered the alphabet. It wasn't so much the twenty-nine Roman letters, but the six tonal inflections that changed the sounds of those letters. If you raised your voice, lowered it, wiggled your voice box, or warbled like you were choking on a frog, the meaning of the word changed. Swallow too-hot coffee and you might well be in danger of telling your neighbor that his mother looks like a pork chop.

The language was only a small part of my adjustment to life in Vietnam. We were there to live cheaply, save up a bundle of money, and return home in a year. However, did that mean I was planning to morph into a Buddhist monk and renounce all comfort? Lord no! Such a concept didn't fit my red-blooded American sensibilities. Yet, on this little alley in a threadbare section of the city, we were indeed living that way.

When I grew up, my family stood several notches below the middle class, but at least we enjoyed hot water and 24/7 electricity, both missing from this skinny house. Instead we had legions of ants and cockroaches as big as rats (oh, dear God, those *were* rats). What cheapskate's dumb idea had it been to rent a house in one of the city's poorest neighborhoods? Okay, mine, but what choice had there been?

Now, sitting in our sultry front room (southern Vietnam being a measly ten degrees from the equator), I struggled to count to fifty in Vietnamese while dear, dear Tin, my unwitting mentor, listened with nothing less than the singular patience of a spider on its web waiting for pizza delivery. It was all too apparent that my head-on collision with the Great Recession had damaged the left side of my brain for language, the right side of my brain for attention span, and turned everything in between into marshmallow fluff.

Tin glanced up at me and noticed the constipated look on my face. He closed his notebook, reached over to close mine, and sat back. "Ms. Karin, tell me, why you come to Vietnam?"

CHAPTER 2

Travel Solves All Problems

"Raising bees in your sleeves."
(VIETNAMESE PROVERB: YOU GET STUNG BY YOUR OWN DOING)

WE HAD TO MOVE. It was September 2008. Lehman Brothers had just filed for bankruptcy. Fannie Mae and Freddie Mac had to be bolstered by the Fed. China had its chopsticks poised over America's plate, ready to gobble up our deep-fried debts, sweetened with interest.

The US's financial free fall served as a metaphor for my own life. Just six weeks before, I'd lost my awesome job, the first to which I wasn't required to wear a hairnet. The *Los Angeles Times*, where I'd been an editor/writer for fifteen years, laid off a few hundred journalists, including—and this made no sense—me. I woke up from the American Dream, saddled with credit-card debt, a self-employed (read: non-earning) husband, two car loans, and a house with a mortgage as big as the GDP of Liechtenstein. This was no time for clear thinking or careful planning.

On a sunny day in August, as our son, Kai, played with the garden hose, my husband, Robin, and I sat on chaise lounges in the backyard of the Los Angeles house we could no longer afford, staring up at the blue sky as if the answer to our jobless crisis would fall out of it.

We had no clue what to do next. The only certainty was that we couldn't stay put and ride out the recession. Newspapers and magazines were a dying industry, and journalism was all I'd ever done and all I'd ever wanted to do. Neither had I any hope that Robin's let's-not-rush-things approach to job-hunting would produce a job fast enough or lucrative enough to sustain us. His focus and passion were all spent on his own home-based company. *Do what you love and the money will come.* (Whoever coined that phrase owes me tens of thousands of dollars.) Robin's vocation—producing and selling CDs of soundtracks from older films—had a niche audience in the first place. Now his customers were sitting on their wallets watching CNN to see how far the economy was going to tank.

"What are we going to do now?" Robin said after several minutes of an uneasy silence. For a guy who practically aced his SATs, spoke four languages fluently, could read Latin, and did math in his head faster than a calculator, he had ZERO ideas.

I sighed, flattened the back of my chaise lounge, shoved a pillow under my neck, and turned onto my side. I faced the tall, vinyl privacy fence we'd recently put up on the street side because I'd been sure passersby (if they were at all snoopy like me) could see through the slats and knotholes of the old wood fence. I hated being in the limelight, even if it was just someone peeking through a knothole. Serenity to me meant staying hidden—away from prying eyes and judgmental snorts. Solitude was vital to my well-being. Ironically, within six weeks I'd be living on a crowded alley where housewives unabashedly peered through my front windows, clucking and chirping about every move I made: "What's she cooking tonight?" "Why is she wearing shoes *in* the house?" "Look! She just threw out old bananas! They're still edible!"

I pulled the pillow down and hugged it as tears filled my eyes and the straight edges of the fence panels began to blur and arc.

The brick-and-mortar foundation of the family and everything we'd built up for so many years had crumbled so fast and so completely, I couldn't imagine our world would ever right itself again. I looked over at the house. *All that work!* We'd refinished furniture, planted fruit trees, spread peat moss, painted, buried pets, and hosted barbecues. Now, my life was over, and all I wanted to do was run away, step off the grid.

So I did what I always do to ease existential pain. I bought airline tickets.

I was both shattered that life had blown up in my face and wildly excited that Plan B involved travel, the major culprit for much of our debt in the first place. I had dipped too often into one of those—oh, shoot, what do you call them? —emergency savings accounts. Not that I was inept at saving money. It just depended on what I was saving *for.* If it was for an upcoming trip, I could stretch my paycheck like nobody's business. It was no sacrifice to wear ragged underwear or lengthen the life of my sneakers by wrapping duct tape around the loose soles. But save money for rainy days and global financial meltdowns? Why would I do *that?* I wasn't happy unless I was either on a trip or planning the next one. I lived for the morphinelike high I felt when I could suspend reality in some oh-so-foreign enclave.

I justified travel to my friends and family by insisting the excursions were mind-expanding cultural journeys. I scoffed when I heard a radio psychologist say that people who traveled obsessively were using their trips as a substitute for personal growth and transformation. But inside, I knew the psychologist wasn't talking about normal people who go on vacation to relax and refresh themselves. He was talking about me, someone blatantly discontented with her life.

And like any other addict, over the course of the last several years, I'd been needing ever more expensive, exotic, and lengthy itineraries to trigger that euphoric rush. Vietnam, for instance. We had visited Vietnam two years before on a weeklong scratch-and-sniff tour that had left us wanting more. My recollection from our trip there in 2006 was that it was a place of friendly people and prices so low that tightwads could spend lavishly. A bowl as big as a motorcycle helmet of *phở*, the aromatic noodle soup quickly becoming popular in America, cost eighty-five cents; parking a motorbike all day in a city lot cost eleven cents; and a gorgeous linen blouse could be had for a mere three bucks. I had loved our tour of Hanoi (the capital), Hue (the ancient capital), and Ho Chi Minh City (the former capital of South Vietnam, Saigon). Unlike any other place on earth—and I'd been to some forty countries—Vietnam had left me in a choke hold of infatuation.

In 2008, Vietnam's economy was burgeoning with a GDP growth rate of 6.5 percent and, with it, the number of people clamoring to learn English. While America was closing up shop, it seemed perfectly reasonable to leave the country and head to Southeast Asia. The plan spun out quickly in my head. Robin would take over the bread-winning duties and teach at a language school. It would be my turn to stay home with Kai, who had autism-spectrum behaviors and would need homeschooling.

Kai was excited to move because it meant he could get out of school. Robin, too, eagerly agreed with my impulsive decision to relocate. As always, he was pliable, unruffled, and ludicrously happy, personality traits that had appealed to me ever since our first date fourteen years earlier. He was the perfect antidote to…well, me. I walked the planet compulsively anxious about 1) money, 2) what people thought of me, and 3) why didn't they think of me more often? I had hoped Robin's easygoing nature would rub off on me. It hadn't.

So I arranged for us to sell nearly everything we owned, throw the rest in a bag, and move to a significantly cheaper place on the planet to start our lives over again.

It hadn't completely escaped my attention that the solution to our financial demise bore an uncanny resemblance to its cause. I felt somewhat sheepish when, one night soon after making my decision, I called my parents, who lived on the Oregon coast, to tell them we'd be moving to a foreign country in a month.

My coupon-clipping, don't-touch-the-nest-egg, wash-and-reuse-aluminum-foil parents had retired years earlier: Dad from teaching and Mom from mom-hood followed by a career in real estate. Asking them for a financial bailout was out of the question. They would know better than to throw their carefully saved money at their frivolous daughter who should have been satisfied all these years with the kind of camping vacations that my older sister, younger brother, and I had taken every summer with them when we were kids. Back-to-nature trips within two hours of my Portland, Oregon, home were all my parents could afford (a campsite in a lush forest was just two dollars a night). And we loved it.

Now here I was, impatient to blow my severance pay on yet another global hop. Ach, such guilt! I dialed my parents late at night—9 p.m.—to tell them of our prospective move and, with each unanswered ring, I took a deep breath and steeled myself for the inevitable lecture. "Little sister," I could already hear my dad say, "I told you this would happen. You should have been putting money away for your future instead of jet-setting all over the world." (Uh, Dad, it was more like backpacking all over the world.)

Luckily, it was my mother who answered the phone. I pictured her sitting in her favorite recliner wearing her twenty-year-old rose-colored robe, worrying and wondering why the phone was ringing so late.

"Sooooo, Mom…," I began, trying to sound as if what I was about to tell her was something I'd put a lot of thought into, which it wasn't, and something she should really get on board with, which I knew she wouldn't. My voice squeaked as I explained that we couldn't afford to stay in our house due to the recession, and it was probably a good idea to sell everything and move somewhere a whole lot cheaper than Los Angeles.

"Oklahoma?" my mother asked, half-jokingly.

"No. Vietnam."

"*Where?*"

I didn't repeat it. My pause confirmed her fears.

"What will you do for work? Will the Communists even let Americans live there? More important, will they let you out?"

"It's perfectly safe, Mom. They need Westerners to teach English so Vietnamese students can hear proper pronunciation. This is a great opportunity to earn a lot of money quickly while living cheaply."

I could nearly hear her eyeballs darting from side to side in her head. She hadn't been too happy about us vacationing in Vietnam two years before, and now here we were preparing to move there. I understood her fear about 'Nam. Her generation remembered all too well the horrific TV news stories of the Vietnam War, especially US involvement during the 1960s and early 1970s. She knew sons and husbands of neighbors who'd been drafted and didn't return. I was sure she was picturing us living in some sort of concrete bunker with landmines in the backyard.

Indeed, even today, forty some years after President Nixon brought back all the troops, if you played a word association game with countries, it would go like this: Italy—pasta, France—wine, Jamaica—reggae, Brazil—Carnival, Vietnam—war.

"What will you do with your house?" my mom asked, still sounding unconvinced that this was a wise decision.

I was standing in the kitchen leaning against the counter. At her question, I looked wistfully at the matching stainless-steel appliances and shiny hardwood floors.

"We'll have to rent it out," I said, suddenly feeling subdued at the thought of someone else living in it. "Nothing is selling around here. Besides, we'd lose money if we sold it."

"What do the girls think of your move?"

The girls. My babies. My best friends and the joys of my life. I'd been putting off telling them, not ready to face my sorrow or theirs. My elder daughter Marisa, twenty-seven, lived an hour south of LA and had a full-time job designing beach bikes. Talia, twenty, was studying marine biology in college an hour north. Many years before, my first husband—their father—had died of brain cancer. The tragedy had brought the three of us closer. We called ourselves the Three Risskateers—from Marisa's nickname, Riss—and after the girls were off to college, we still saw each other as often as possible, and talked or emailed each other daily.

Discussing my decision with them would be difficult. I already had a plan to mitigate the sadness for everyone. I was going to surprise them with tickets to Vietnam for Christmas. (I guess I really was medicating emotional pain with travel.)

My mom was still waiting for my answer.

I sighed. "We'll be back in a year, Mom. I promise. We just need to get back on our feet. I mean, how long can this recession last?"

CHAPTER 3

8,000-Plus Miles from Home

*"A day of traveling will bring
a basketful of learning."*
(VIETNAMESE PROVERB)

ONE MID-SEPTEMBER MORNING, Robin, Kai, and I hauled ten boxes and four suitcases into an airport shuttle to LAX. Three hours later we boarded our flight to Vietnam.

"Well, we're finally off!" I said to Robin as I fastened my seat belt.

"When we are airborne, with Germany behind us, *then* I will share that sentiment," he said, quoting a line from *Indiana Jones and the Last Crusade*. A passionate movie buff, Robin often peppered his conversations with dialogue from films. To him, life was one big adventure movie and he was its director. He was excited for this trip. No place on the planet was too scary or gritty or risky to him. No person was on his do-not-talk-to list. He could just as easily start a conversation with a drunk whose head was flat against the bar as he could with a corporate suit. He treated everyone as if he'd known them for years. Robin always jumped into new experiences with complete abandon, as if there was nothing to lose. Funny how that expression was so apropos in this moment.

Kai sat between us studying the diagrams on the safety card. He bent over to look under the seat for his life vest.

"Mom, is this plane going to crash?"

"No."

"How do you know?"

"I just know. It's not my time to die."

"But what if it's that man's time to die?" he said, watching an elderly man across the aisle try to jam his bags into the overhead compartment.

"Why don't you pull out a granola bar," I said, redirecting this line of questioning, as parenting experts suggest. "It will be at least an hour before they feed us."

I looked around at the other passengers. How many other Americans on the plane were also ditching a sinking ship and looking for job opportunities abroad? As the plane gained speed and took off, I looked out the window at the frayed white ribbons of waves that framed the California coastline and watched them until the clouds obscured the earth.

I contemplated all that we were leaving behind. It already felt like a lifetime ago. Flying has that effect on me—a complete detachment from everyday life, as if all below me was only a dream and my seat in the airplane to somewhere exotic was the whole of existence. That's what I love about travel: Reality stops.

Robin unfolded the thin airplane blanket and began to drape it over his head. I frowned. He knew I needed him to assist me with Kai, who would most certainly chatter and squirm the whole flight. Robin looked back at me, and I gave him my woman-scorned look. "Don't worry," he reassured me. "I'll share Kai duties. I'm just closing my eyes. I can't sleep on airplanes."

"You do nothing BUT sleep on airplanes!" It was always the same argument and it was always fruitless. While Robin sat corpse-like for hours, Kai wiggled, talked to himself, talked to me, talked to the flight attendants in the galley, talked to the old man across the aisle, bumped Robin's elbows playing video games, climbed over him to go to the bathroom, and even once brashly yanked the headset from Robin's ears when his own set had become too tangled. Did Robin react to any of it? No. He was asleep.

Twenty-four hours and one international dateline later, I woke up from the last leg of our flight with a pat of butter from dinner smeared on the edge of my shoe and my hair matted down on the side of my head where I'd fallen asleep against the airplane window. The pilot had just announced we'd be on the ground soon at Ho Chi Minh City's Tan Son Nhat International Airport.

"Robin, we're landing," I said loudly as I tapped him on the shoulder. Kai had finally stopped wiggling and fallen asleep an hour before.

"I know," Robin muttered from underneath his blanket. "I heard the announcement. I'm wide awake." He yawned and lifted his arms to stretch. "I wish I could sleep on planes," he said, pulling the blanket off his head, the static causing his fine, straight hair to stand on end like a lightning-zapped Chia Pet.

As I began to clean up the mess around my seat, I accidentally brushed against Kai, who bolted up, instantly awake and completely refreshed from his one hour of sleep. One of the not-so-endearing behaviors of kids on the autism spectrum is that they don't need much sleep. His incessant chatter-mouth revved up again. "Which one is our house?" he asked as he leaned across me to open the shade and look out.

"We'll pick one out together," I said, giving him a kiss on his soft cheek and combing back his curls with my fingers. Stretched out to the horizon was a flat landscape with the Saigon River and its many veins and arteries snaking through the city. Like many large cities with fast, unchecked growth, hardly a green patch was left—just miles and miles of concrete and asphalt topped with shops; office buildings; apartment complexes; and houses built back to back, side to side, leaving no space for yards or gardens.

"Look, Kai, see how long and skinny the houses are?" I said, pointing down to a typical neighborhood. "The houses are built that way because they have to pay property taxes based on width, not depth or height."

But Kai wasn't interested. His fluffy little head was off in the clouds, thinking about pilots.

"Never shine a flashlight in a pilot's eyes," he said.

I nodded. I began to wonder how he would fare away from his normal routine of occupational therapy, remedial academics, and socialization-skills classes. I'd be on my own now without the help of experts who could structure an education plan around his learning disabilities, which were further complicated by Fetal Alcohol Effects and Attention Deficit Hyperactivity Disorder. I felt relatively prepared. I had observed the techniques of his therapy since we'd adopted him from the Crimea as a malnourished eighteen-month-old. Plus, I was armed with stacks of workbooks his teacher had given me to help him keep current with his school curriculum. She had generously proffered her services as an adviser via email or Skype during our year abroad.

Kai's autism was not marked by stereotypical "Rain Man" behaviors. He didn't become easily agitated if his schedule was interfered with. Nor was he the type to retreat to a corner to study his pant leg for hours. And unlike many people with his diagnosis who are overly sensitive to being touched, you could hug Kai and he'd hug back, which we valued immeasurably. Just don't try to clip his toenails or clean his ears. He was a happy kid with a sense of humor all his own. Because he understood only the literal meaning of words, he couldn't understand idioms and missed a lot of jokes. Or he'd laugh at situations that weren't funny to anyone else. You could have a conversation with him, but as the wheels in his head would quickly run in contrary directions, the conversations became…well, creative.

"If you eat a rubber band, it will destroy your body," he said to everyone within earshot as we stood in the aisle waiting to get off the plane. There was wisdom in there somewhere, but at that moment I was too travel-weary to find it.

Still, we were here. *We were here!* After going through customs, we were met by a lithe young woman in a purple silk *áo dài*, the traditional long tunic top and blousy trousers that the Vietnamese wear so beautifully. She'd been sent from the language school where Robin was to start his four-week teacher-training course. Miss Ha smiled warmly when I pointed to the sign she held up with our name on it. Robin and Kai were right behind me.

"Welcome in Vietnam. I take, you go, your hotel, yes?"

She looked at Kai and reached over to feel his wavy, blond hair. "How *owed* you?"

Kai looked at me. "Tell her your age," I clarified.

"I'm eight," he said in a near whisper that belied his usually decibel-heavy voice.

She turned to Robin, whose body shaded hers like a beach umbrella. Robin's real name is Rolf. He was raised in Germany on bratwurst and beer, which is how he grew to be six foot four and 250 pounds. Robin didn't eat vegetables like the slim Vietnamese. He got his greens from grass-fed beef. Miss Ha shook his hand and giggled. "Ooooh, you so big!"

"Yeah, I get that a lot," he said with a mischievous grin. I slugged his arm.

Only a foot out of the air-conditioned terminal, we were slapped with a blast of moist heat. "My God, it's hot!" Robin bellowed. He took a deep breath. (Health warning: Don't do that.) "Ahhhhh, smell that? No other place smells like Vietnam." I loved it, too. The blend of exotic sun-warmed fruits, jasmine rice, sidewalk barbecues, fish sauce, cigarettes, and motorbike-exhaust fumes was bringing both of us happy memories of our last trip. Any previous concerns about moving here were immediately numbed by the familiar soothing highs of travel euphoria.

Beads of sweat formed on Robin's brow as he strained to maneuver a luggage cart with wayward wheels. The petite Miss Ha wasn't even moist. She gestured toward a tiny minivan that looked like it had veered off the track of a kiddie carnival ride. The driver's eyes widened when he saw how much luggage was hurtling toward him. With the back of the van open, he began strategizing how he'd fit it all in. Miss Ha attempted to help him by lifting a suitcase three times her size, but Robin grabbed it from her before the heavy piece crushed her itsy-bitsy bones. He put it in the back seat under Kai's legs. The driver tried pushing the door closed on the last piece of luggage, splitting the seam of a duffel bag.

"Teachers don't bring so much," Miss Ha said in an apologetic tone. "We never get whole family here."

"Don't worry about it," I said. "I can sew it."

By overlapping our legs, the three of us managed to fit in the back seat while the communion-wafer-thin Miss Ha sat in the spacious front seat next to the driver. It didn't occur to her to pull her seat up. Strangely, it didn't occur to us to ask her to, either. She turned around, smiled at us again, and explained that the typical English teacher was usually a new college graduate funding his or her trip around the world before settling down with a real job. That person normally carried a backpack and planned to stay only three to six months.

I thought about all the personal belongings we had sold to fund our trip here. At that moment I wished we had downsized even more, because what was packed in our cartons—clothes, Kai's toys, Robin's Mac and my laptop, bottles of bug spray, tubes of anti-itch cream, and antidiarrheals—was perched precariously behind our heads. One slam on the brakes and hundreds of pounds of life's so-called necessities could crush us to death.

Robin's stuff filled most of the boxes. He formed deep emotional attachments to everything his fingers touched. It wasn't until after I married him in 1998 that I learned he was one *New York*

Times short of being a hoarder. That side of him had been hidden in a warehouse his parents owned outside of Stuttgart. Not that I hadn't noticed his desk was always covered with stacks of unopened mail, expired oil-change coupons, Burger King receipts, and empty soda bottles. If I'd start to clean up, he'd warn: "Don't touch my stuff. You are messing with my system." I tempered my frustration with the certainty that one day he'd reveal his true inner German and display the tidy organizational prowess and efficiency of his countrymen. "*Vee al-vays* put *zings* in order!" (Heel click.)

His mother had wasted no time after our wedding before announcing she was sending the rest of his worldly possessions to us. "A few boxes," she said, were already headed our way on a container ship. Two months later, a semi with a forklift mounted on the back pulled up next to the driveway of the rental we lived in before buying our house in Burbank. The forklift operator unloaded four plastic-wrapped pallets, five-by-five-by-four feet each. Robin couldn't thank him enough, and he shook the man's hand far longer than would be considered culturally appropriate. Only the Publisher's Clearing House Prize Patrol could have garnered more enthusiasm.

After the truck left, Robin was nearly breathless as he ripped into the thick plastic with a box cutter and opened the first cardboard carton. "Schlumpi!" he cried, pulling out a mangy stuffed animal. "Oh, man, I loved this dog—carried it everywhere." As he lovingly turned it over and over, he stopped and gasped. "Oh, no, look! His tail is nearly torn off. Can you sew it?"

"Sure," I said, tenderly taking the beloved creature out of his hands. But when Robin turned around, I dashed over to the porch, dropped the toy, and breathed through my nose to hold down my breakfast. Schlumpi smelled like puke.

With a giddy grin, Robin ripped open more boxes and started to carry them into the living room, completely oblivious to the fact that our rental house was only slightly larger than the crates themselves. By the third box, I stopped him and pointed to the garage.

"The garage?" He looked stricken, as if I'd suggested he store his grandmother's ashes in a Folgers coffee can. "You can't keep these boxes in a dirty garage! These are my things!"

Right. I don't like "things." I like uncluttered, open spaces and clean lines that give the mind and body some peace. Why hadn't his parents told me he was a hoarder before the wedding?

Before our move to Vietnam, I'd had to be the bad guy and make him face reality: "Robin, we can't afford to store it and we can't take it with us." I'm sure Robin suffered great sorrow letting so much go, but he bravely donated or sold collectible figurines of Darth Vader; cassettes; LPs; and books numbering in the thousands—Karl Mai Westerns, science-fiction series, Indiana Jones paperbacks, school textbooks, and tomes on filmmaking and film scores—all in German. Strange, I thought, because it suddenly dawned on me that I'd never seen him read a book.

A few I'll-die-without-them cartons—mostly photos and, of course, Schlumpi—fit into a friend's garage. His greatest sacrifice, for which I was grateful, had been the $4,000 worth of rare, signed CDs he'd sold, which paid for our plane fares.

Miss Ha cocked her head and looked quizzically at the luggage stuffed to the ceiling of the van. "I guess you stay long time, yes?" I nodded. She said that keeping teachers in the city longer than a few months wasn't easy. Hence the incentive, according to the school's brochure, of an extra $700 toward moving costs if you stayed in your job twelve months. Of course, we'd signed up for a year.

The driver stopped to pay a twenty-five-cent airport fee, and then turned onto the main street without braking or looking for oncoming traffic. An unrelenting barrage of motorbikes, which comprise ninety percent of the traffic in Ho Chi Minh City, swarmed and encircled our taxi like ants attacking a dying beetle. I winced as our van swerved and nearly grazed the knees of a family of five on a Honda 80cc—preschooler in front, Dad driving, school kid in uniform, and Mom holding baby in the crook of her arm. No one heeded stop signs, red lights, or one-way streets.

It felt like we'd been sucked into the maelstrom of a video game, dodging obstacles at every turn, but scoring no points.

"How is it that they aren't all crashing into each other?" Robin asked, more amused than horrified, as he watched streams of motorbike drivers skirting the congestion by riding up on sidewalks, narrowly missing shoppers as they walked out of stores.

Miss Ha giggled. But then she saw my worried expression and grew more serious. As if to reassure us that, although accidents were commonplace, they were rarely deadly, she pulled up the sleeve of her silk top and showed us the underside of her left forearm. A nasty, purplish-green scab ran from wrist to elbow.

"I fell off Honda last week," she said, giggling again when Kai covered his eyes at the sight. I squeezed my eyes shut, too. Morbid thoughts were beginning to prey on my poor, jet-lagged imagination, and I pictured Kai getting knocked off a motorbike. At least in my nightmare he had a helmet on, which I noticed very few children wearing. The only element missing was road rage. No shaking fists, no finger salutes, and—here was a comforting thought—no guns, which were quite illegal.

CHAPTER 4

A New Home on Đoàn Văn Bơ Street

*"If you don't enter the tiger's cave,
how will you capture the cub?"*
(VIETNAMESE PROVERB)

FIFTY MINUTES LATER we were in District 1 and pulled up to the Happy Inn, a small hotel in the "backpacker" section, so-named for its block after block of inexpensive hostels, guesthouses, restaurants, and bars catering to the ninety-nine percent of us who don't tote Tumi or Valextra luggage. The city was divided into districts, like the *arrondissements* in Paris, which greatly helped *zee stoo-peed* French colonial occupiers find their way around the labyrinth of Vietnam's largest city. The French had made themselves at home here for nearly one hundred years when, one day, the Vietnamese asked for their country back. *Non et non! Impossible!* gasped the French, flinging their berets on the ground and stomping off to the nearest café for a baguette and coffee. Thus began the Anti-French Resistance War in 1945, which lasted until 1954. Fortunately, the Vietnamese kept the French-bread recipe and a smattering of elegant colonial buildings (now quite tattered), built along wide boulevards shaded with great canopies of kapok trees. The city had once been dubbed the Pearl of the Far East, and looking around one could imagine its once glamorous façade.

The young woman at the front desk kindly let us store our many boxes in the hotel's utility closet before unlocking our room for us. Two double beds, as soft and giving as cutting boards (better for your back, the Vietnamese believe), had just the tiniest slice of space between them. One fluorescent bulb gave the room its only light because the room's single window was covered with brown wrapping paper, a cheap alternative to curtains, apparently.

The room had a large shower; a television that worked if you pounded the top; and blessedly cool air-conditioning, which was our only real requirement. At eighteen dollars per night for the three of us, we were satisfied. Nevertheless, after showers and a short nap, it was urgent that we begin the search for a house or an apartment, because even at Vietnam's low prices, the room bill and restaurant meals would add up fast. Besides, in three days Robin was set to begin his monthlong teacher-training course to earn a CELTA (Certificate in English Language Teaching to Adults), and I didn't want to house hunt alone.

Before Miss Ha left us at the hotel, she handed Robin the business card of an establishment called Nice House, Real Estate Service for Foreigner [sic]. Teachers had "good lucky" with the owner, she said. We called him from the lobby.

"Sure, come my office now," said the man who answered. "I find you good place." He said his office was only a ten-minute walk. Thirty minutes later in ninety-five-degree heat and equally high humidity, we stood in front of a laundry business displaying the same address as on the business card.

"Let's just go home," Kai moaned, pulling on my arm with sweaty hands.

"You want to go back to the hotel already?" I asked.

"No, I want to go back *home*," he declared. He kicked at a small chunk of concrete from the fractured sidewalk and watched it fall into a gutter.

"Kai, look around you. We are in a whole new world. The kids in your school don't get to see this." To prove my point, I gestured toward two women wearing conical straw hats and shouldering baskets of dried fish on a pole balanced between them as they walked. Kai looked unimpressed. I couldn't blame him. Jet lag was making me dizzy, and all I could think right then was how much happier I would be chained to an air conditioner.

Robin frowned and sweated profusely as he glared at a foldout map from a 2001 Vietnam guidebook he'd found in the lobby of our guesthouse. All 800 square miles of Ho Chi Minh City lay in his hands with not one "You are here" dot.

Three Westerners scratching their heads over an address were prime pickings for two bicycle-rickshaw drivers who spotted us from across the street. They pedaled their "cyclos" over to where we stood.

"You like cyclo ride?" asked the first driver, a pencil-thin man whose lean, leathered arms had seen too much sun. "*Fy dolla.* One *ow-wah.* See city. Okay?" He tipped his baseball cap to greet us, and his smiling compatriot motioned for us to hop in. Pencil Man handed me a folder with laminated photos of sites included in the cycle tour: colorful pagodas, the War Remnants Museum, Independence Palace, and the neoclassical Post Office that was designed and constructed by architect Gustave Eiffel of Eiffel Tower and Statue of Liberty fame.

Kai climbed up into the seat. "I want a ride!" The skinny man smiled and gestured that I, too, could fit in the same seat. Robin could sit in the other one.

"Sorry, sweetie," I said to Kai. "We will take a cyclo ride some other time." As I pulled Kai off, the driver frowned. He took off his baseball cap and, in full tantrum mode, slapped it against the handlebars as he and his partner rode back to the other side of the street. I felt bad for them. Waiting around in the hot sun to pedal double-cheeseburger-eating Westerners twice his size couldn't be an easy way to make a living.

Just as Robin was ready to claw the map to shreds, a young man walked toward us, offering his help with directions. He was neatly dressed in a stiffly pressed white dress shirt, black pants, and flip-flops. Robin showed him the address on the business card. The man grinned, shook our hands, and introduced himself. It was Mr. Nice House himself.

He led us around the corner to a tiny office wedged between the laundry business and a noisy restaurant. Inside, the stifling room had chipped linoleum floors and unadorned walls, except for the ubiquitous photo calendar of sleek, long-haired girls wearing colorful *áo dàis* and sitting beside bubbly streams or in fields of wildflowers. Mr. Nice House pulled up three red plastic stools around his wood-veneer desk and turned on a floor fan next to us, which we hovered around like homeless people crowding around a trash-can fire on a winter night.

Robin began. "We need a furnished two-bedroom apartment or house in District 1 where I will be working."

"Okay, no problem," the smiling Mr. Nice House said as he fished around for something in the top drawer of his desk. There was absolutely nothing on top of his desk—not a pencil, pen, computer, or piece of mail. He pulled out a list of rentals, the first sign that this was a rental office.

"How much you pay?" he asked, not looking up from the list.

We had some idea what apartments went for because we'd done some online searches for housing before leaving California. The ads had shown several nice-looking two-bedroom apartments that could be rented for three hundred to four hundred dollars per month, although the ads neglected to mention location. Based on Robin's proposed teaching income and what I anticipated I could earn from a smattering of private students and freelance writing, we wanted to keep our rent under four hundred dollars a month, and Robin told him so.

"Impossible!" Mr. Nice House said, now nearly glaring at us. But in a more apologetic tone he continued, "In last year, all *pri-ah* [prices] go up in District 1. But no worry 'bout it. I know furnished *how-wah* [house] in District 4. *Ee-ah* [is] four hundred." Like nearly all Vietnamese, he inexplicably left the "s" sound off of English words ending with that apparently difficult consonant. "Foreigner don't know *thi-ah* [this] district," he went on. "It only ten minute over bridge."

Mr. Nice House sat back and smiled at us. We looked at him and smiled back. The fan continued to whir. Kai hopped on and off his stool. Our agent put his list back in the drawer, folded his hands, and waited. Robin and I looked at each other and then back at him.

"So that's it? Just one place to look at?" I asked.

"Yeah, everything else seven hundred *dolla* and more," he said. "I'm sorry, my city so expensive now. Come tomorrow, eleven in morning, and we go see *how-wah*."

He stood up. He was a busy man. Perhaps the postman would put mail on his desk. A real estate agent, after all, needed to be ready.

District 4 was a triangular island surrounded by stinking black-water canals on two sides and the muddy Saigon River on the other. As we crossed the bridge, I saw no parks, no grass, no flowers, and very few trees. Concrete crushed and asphyxiated every blade of grass and every inch of soil. In each block stood tall, impossibly narrow houses, some divided in half vertically to create two houses, each only four feet wide. Most needed repainting and appeared to droop tiredly under the weight of large families. Shacks cobbled together with corrugated metal sheets and scrap wood abutted four-story cinder-block houses. As we had seen on our travels here before, Ho Chi Minh City was a hodgepodge of poor and rich living side by side. Unlike District 1, which had the city's lush Tao Dan

Park with more than one thousand trees, there was absolutely nothing beautiful about District 4.

"Look, this apartment building open next year," Mr. Nice House said, pointing to a shiny, modern glass building. "And on that street another bridge soon open. It connect District 1. *Thi-ah* make you commute faster."

We must have looked dubious, because he seemed to be working awfully hard to sell us on the idea of living in District 4. Later, my neighbors would tell me that this district had been gangster territory fifteen years earlier. Unless you called it home, no one dared cross the bridge, not even the police. Even today, when you mention District 4, people cringe and say, "You live *where?*" Back then, if you owed somebody money and couldn't pay, the bad guys would cut off a finger or sometimes your whole hand. Still no money? They'd settle for a forearm. I did see more than a few people missing appendages, but it wasn't until later that I learned the other sad cause.

Our prospective neighborhood was no longer gang territory because in 1994, just after President Clinton lifted the trade embargo, the city leaders had taken notice of District 4's valuable real estate in close proximity to the city center. Police raided the island and jailed (or, more likely, executed) all the mob bosses and sent their families and cronies to a swampland far, far away.

Our taxi turned onto Đoàn Văn Bơ, a street so narrow I feared we'd sideswipe a house and knock its many occupants out. We could go only as fast as the man walking in front of us who pushed a wide wooden cart heaped with roasted peanuts. Peanut Man looked around at us, nodded, and smiled sheepishly, but he had nowhere to pull off out of our way because the sidewalks were cluttered with goods spilling out of each shop. Sidewalks were prime real estate for food vendors selling noodle soup, hot soy milk, French-bread sub sandwiches, and iced coffee.

Every hundred feet, along both sides of the street, narrow alleys branched off, accessible only to motorbikes and pedestrians. As we passed, I peered down each long alleyway. People lived cheek by jowl in two- to five-story houses with balconies only a couple of arms' length apart. How did they tolerate such closeness? Obviously, privacy wasn't the cultural imperative it was for Americans. Indeed, the architectural style spoke volumes about the Vietnamese culture and lifestyle. Every house's ground floor opened completely in the front, like an American garage, except the metal doors and gates pushed open to the sides instead of up. They were closed and locked at night, naturally, but in the daytime, one's family life in the living room was splayed out for all to see. *Yeah, I won't be keeping my entire front wall open.* As we inched along, my thoughts were interrupted by a kid walking alongside our taxi who knocked on my window and waved. "Heh-lo, Madam!" I waved back and he whooped excitedly.

When the taxi stopped several alleys down, people began to gather around us as we climbed out. Motorbike drivers threw double takes and slowed down; kids on bicycles pulled over and stopped to stare and giggle. A grandma holding an infant came out of her rice shop, pointing us out to the baby who looked first befuddled and then terrified at the three blond-haired, blue-eyed Westerners.

"Heh-lo, heh-lo," the grandma said, shaking the crying baby's wrist to wave at us.

"Hah! They never see foreigner in neighborhood," exclaimed Mr. Nice House, clearly enjoying the celebrity-like attention. We followed him through the alley, which was nicely shaded by everyone's overhanging second-floor balconies. A woman who squatted on a three-inch-high stool chopping up pig hooves held her heavy hatchet in mid-swing and stared at us, her mouth agape, as we passed. I had a momentary fright that she would hurl the hatchet at me. *Take that, you dirty capitalist!*

I quickened my pace and walked closer to Mr. Nice House. I couldn't help peering into each house as we passed. The main floor was more often than not where each family ran a business. One household cut rubber for making sandals. Another group sat in a circle, baskets of garlic between them. With swift, stained hands they peeled cloves and tossed them freshly naked into a bucket of water to be sold at restaurants or markets. Several women were seamstresses working on large workhorse sewing machines. As I gawked at them, they smiled back. One man washed a rooster in a bucket of sudsy water. Mr. Nice House noticed my bewilderment. "They must be clean for cockfight."

"Whoa, this is too cool!" Robin said. "This alley is exactly what I imagined a real Vietnamese neighborhood to be like."

I wasn't so sure it was "cool." I wanted an authentic foreign experience, but maybe I wasn't as adventurous as I thought I was. In my daydream, I hadn't pictured myself living in an alley where people chopped up pig parts and meticulously bathed roosters only to see them bloodied a few hours later.

Halfway down the alley, Mr. Nice House stopped at a four-story house so narrow it looked more like a long hallway with a front door.

"Here *how-wah*. Landlord got permission from *pol-ee* to rent to foreigner."

Robin and I looked at each other: *Really? The police are in on this?*

He unlocked a ludicrously large padlock on a sliding metal gate and opened the double doors. "You first foreigner to live in *thi-ah* neighborhood," he said, as if we'd already agreed to rent it.

Windows in the front door let in some light, but with no side or back windows, the house got progressively darker as we went in deeper. Kai pushed past us when he saw the stairs in the back and bolted up quickly. As we inspected the ground floor, we could hear his squeals and hollers echo through bare rooms as he checked out each floor.

"I thought you said this was furnished," Robin said to Mr. Nice House.

"Landlord bring furniture later."

I looked around at the hollow living room with its white tile floor and plaster walls. The small kitchen had a chest-high avocado refrigerator and a two-burner propane stovetop. Around the corner and tucked under the stairs was a toilet separated from the living area by a flimsy polyester shower curtain printed with fading turquoise fish. Weird, but handy.

We followed Mr. Nice House up the staircase, which was no more than eighteen inches wide. As we started up, I turned and looked down. Robin wasn't following us. "What's wrong?" I asked him. Robin shook his head. "Look at me!" he answered in disbelief. "I can't get up the stairs unless I twist sideways! Amazing!" His shoulders brushed against the sides as he climbed up. Each floor had one room. The second-level bedroom included a tiny, all-in-one, RV-size wet bathroom with a mini-sink, toilet, and shower nozzle in the wall. Multitaskers could pee, shower, and brush their teeth at the same time. The next floor was an exact duplicate. The fourth-floor room was half-size, with a washing machine and a door out to a balcony. The outdoor space had a clothesline and yet another set of steep stairs to access the spacious roof terrace, which rewarded one with marvelous views of the city skyline—a fitting replacement for the yard we'd left behind in California.

As I stood on the balcony looking down, I watched an elderly man in blue cotton pajamas deftly shovel noodles into his little grandson's mouth with chopsticks. I saw a woman running a length of fabric through her black '50s-era sewing machine. Farther down the alley a monk in a brown robe carried a begging bowl and sang Buddhist chants. I was overtaken with a sense of certainty that this was exactly where we should be, not in some modern high-rise full of expatriates. George Bernard Shaw once said: "I dislike feeling at home when I am abroad," and I concurred. Although the house was the first and only one we saw, Robin and I agreed we should rent it. I walked over to Mr. Nice House, who had stepped back inside to stay out of the sun.

"We'll take it," I said. "How soon can we move in?"

CHAPTER 5

Moving Day

"Trade distant relatives for close neighbors."
(VIETNAMESE PROVERB)

FOUR DAYS LATER the house was ours, but because Robin had already started his CELTA course and was knee-deep in phonology charts and cognitive language modalities, the move that morning was all mine to manage.

I pantomimed to my taxi driver to help Kai and me carry our belongings into the house, which he did eagerly when I tipped him five dollars. In the house, my new landlord Vinh and his wife, Duyen, were waiting for us.

Balancing on a high stool at the front door window, Duyen stretched the last panel of floral curtains over a flimsy metal rod and turned to see my reaction. The curtains were algae green and hung against freshly painted Pepto-Bismol-pink walls, a color combination garish enough to make a hairless cat cough up a hairball. I smiled at my next thought: *The recession won't be able to find me here.* Sure that I was smiling at her, Duyen looked pleased and said a few words to me in Vietnamese. In response to my blank expression, she looked over to Vinh, whose English was passable.

"She say we bring kitchen table tomorrow afternoon," he said. It was the only household basic that was missing. The living room already had a chrome love seat with thin seat pads, an aluminum lawn chair, and a seventeen-inch TV set on a wobbly metal stand.

I nodded my thanks, touched by her eagerness to make us comfortable.

"My wife like to decorate. She very good, yes?" Vinh asked with a proud grin as he stopped shuffling through the rental agreement papers and looked up at the new curtains.

"She is," I replied, hoping my smile looked genuine. He handed me a copy of the one-year lease we had signed a few days before. I looked around the room. Indeed, for only four hundred dollars a month, I was liking it more and more. It seemed like a bargain for a house with two bedrooms, each with its own A/C wall unit, and two bathrooms (not including that funny little toilet under the stairs). This newish 800-square-foot house was huge by Vietnamese standards, at least for only three occupants. It didn't cross our minds to negotiate the price. A few months later a neighbor would tell me that the previous tenants had paid two hundred dollars a month. *Dang.* No doubt the price difference had something to do with the fact that we were foreigners—rich, mollycoddled foreigners.

Vinh looked over to see Kai and me struggle to carry a heavy box up the skinny staircase. He motioned for me to wait and leaned out the front door to call over the next-door neighbor. In stepped a short, muscular man whose wiry hair looked like he'd just been in a fight with a lawnmower, and who smelled like cigarettes and motor oil. His dragon-tattooed chest—an unusual sight in a culture that resolutely frowns on tattoos—glistened with sweat in the muggy ninety-seven-degree heat. To the Vietnamese, tattoos labeled you as a "bad guy."

I doubted my landlord would put me in danger, but the tough little man didn't make eye contact, nor did he smile when I said hello in my friendliest voice. Perhaps he'd read how America's bank failures were causing economic catastrophe around the world, and now here I was, an evil capitalist interloper taking advantage of the cheaper prices in his country. Dragon Man slipped out of his sandals, gestured toward the boxes, and muttered something in Vietnamese that sounded suspiciously like "friggin' foreigner." I let out a nervous giggle.

"He help you take box up. Show him where to put," Vinh directed me.

Dragon Man grabbed a box, and I climbed the staircase ahead of him. The second floor, which we had designated as Robin's and my bedroom, had the same green curtains, pink walls, and white tile floors as the ground floor. It had a door that opened onto a skinny front balcony, which I assumed was the only way they could have hoisted furniture up to the higher levels. The room was furnished with a double bed. Period. The next floor, Kai's room, also had a double bed. We would need to buy dressers, night tables, lamps, maybe a chair or two. I hadn't anticipated the extra expenses, the prospect of which irritated me and angered my wallet.

Sweat poured off Dragon Man as he carried the boxes up, twisting his body at each juncture to squeeze the cartons and himself upward. I managed to stay out of his way on his many trips up, but Kai didn't. He pushed past Dragon Man without so much as an "excuse me" (not that Dragon Man would have understood him). Kai was wild with excitement and my admonitions of "Shh" and "Slow down" and "You'll disturb the neighbors" didn't have any effect. He raced up and down the stairs and into each room, pausing to yell "Hello" out of the windows to mystified neighbors who smiled, returned his waves, and even blew kisses at him.

Back downstairs and thoroughly drenched, Dragon Man had saved the worst for last—the heaviest box, Robin's desktop computer. He strained to pick the box up, and as he tried to right himself, it slipped in his wet hand. For a moment I pictured Robin's beloved Macintosh smashing before my eyes, but before my nightmare could get any traction, Dragon Man tilted the box against his thick chest, balanced it, and began to move upward again. Once at the top, he set the computer box on the floor, and with a renewed burst of energy, careened back down the stairs.

"Wait, wait, sir," I called out, once again forgetting that he didn't know what I was saying. He didn't stop. I intended to pay him right away, but I couldn't pull the money out of my pockets quickly enough. My cotton pants had grafted onto my skin from sweat, making the bills in my pocket too moist to budge. By the time I reached the bottom floor, Dragon Man had already escaped into his own house. Vinh and Duyen were packing up, getting ready to leave.

"Vinh, please, can you call him back? I wanted to pay him for his help," I said as I looked out into the alley to see if he was still outside.

"Good neighbors help each other; they do not ask for money," Vinh said sweetly. But, he added, in a tone of practicality, should I want to pay him "because he very poor," a typical moving fee would be forty thousand Vietnamese *dồng*. Dragon Man was standing just inside his doorway. Trying not to fixate on the horrible dragon inked on his chest, I walked up to the entrance where he stood. His wife and three children peeked around a half-wall behind him. I pulled out the US equivalent of two dollars. Dragon Man stared at me, took the money and—for a split second—smiled.

Vinh and Duyen went outside and mounted their motorbike. "You need question, you call me. I come back you house tomorrow," Vinh said, but before he could turn on the engine, a dozen or so curious neighbors, none of whom spoke English, came out of their houses and began to gather around him to ask questions. Vinh translated the questions as fast as they came, leaving little time for me to reply:

" 'Where you from?' 'How many people live in house?' 'How much you pay rent?' 'How old you?' 'One son? Only *one* son? What a pity!' " Though it felt a little like a news conference, the neighbors smiled as I returned answers for each question. I answered them openly, even though the age and money questions felt too personal. Nevertheless, now that they'd asked, I realized I wanted to know the same about them. This was no time to be anything but forthright.

Vinh finally waved them aside and recommended I lock the door right away. His comment suddenly unnerved me. *Lock the door immediately?* Would someone steal what few items we had? He threw me a "good luck" wink and drove off.

But my new neighbors didn't leave. In fact, as soon as Vinh roared off on his motorbike, they moved right up to my doorstep, a handshake away from where I stood. In the many books I'd perused on Asian culture, I'd not read anything about this penchant for unrestrained gawking, nor how to deal with it. I felt like the new panda on loan from China. I wanted to close the doors, but I didn't want to insult them. *Good foreigner, nice foreigner. See? So friendly.* I smiled as widely as I could stretch my mouth, and pretended I was perfectly at ease being watched while I pawed through a couple of boxes.

A squat woman, as wrinkled and sun-browned as a burnished raisin, stopped to see what everyone was looking at. She sold lottery tickets, and when she saw me, she stepped up to the doorway, leaned into the living room, and held the tickets in front of me. I shook my head. She brazenly stepped into the room and shoved them closer, this time flapping them vigorously right under my nose.

"*Không, cám ơn,*" I said. No, thank you.

My little attempt at speaking Vietnamese pleased my audience. Two grandmas giggled and applauded. But the lottery seller was undeterred. She didn't budge and locked eyes with me, her face defiant. A neighbor man spoke sharply to her, probably something along the lines of, "Leave her alone. What does a foreigner need with a lottery ticket, anyway?" She stared at me frowning for a few more seconds, gave up, and left.

But no one else moved. Cultural faux pas or not, I waved goodbye, and although I know bowing is a Japanese custom, I bowed low as I closed the double doors as unobtrusively as possible. And to prove what a sweet person I was, I refrained from locking the doors with the ludicrously large padlock or closing the curtains. I backed out of the room still bowing and then turned and began walking toward the stairs faster and faster. Twenty-four eyeballs seared my back like hot coals as I ascended out of their sight. Upstairs, I peeked down from behind the bedroom curtains and watched my neighbors, each slowly returning to his or her front-step perch.

With Kai happily playing in his new room and with the onlookers gone, I went back down to inspect the kitchen cupboard and take inventory: two plain white porcelain plates, one chipped rice bowl, a few pairs of wooden chopsticks, one bent carving knife, a neon-green plastic strainer, a red plastic mixing bowl, and two dusty teacups. This was going to be minimalist living at best. But wasn't living more simply my new mantra? No? Well, it should have been. Time to accept what was and deal with it. I had a flicker of cognizance that this moment just might be the first faint break with consumerism's seductive pull. In truth, I really did want to stop wanting things and live happily without so many material possessions and luxuries. Honestly, I did. I stepped over to the faucet to rinse out the teacups and looked into the sink. *What the hell? This kitchen doesn't have a disposal?*

I sighed and then squatted down to find the on/off switch on the propane canister below the two-burner stovetop. When I wiggled the canister, five fat cockroaches the size of mice darted out from behind it and fled into a crevice in the corner of the cabinet. Startled, I jerked and fell backward onto my butt. These five, I was sure, were on a reconnaissance mission. Their armies would soon follow. From my position on the floor, my eye caught sight of something else: a long, undulating black ribbon along the edge of the countertop. I looked closer and saw...*them*. Millions and billions of ants. They were the tiniest ants I'd ever seen. Kind of cute, actually, had there been only one. But this looked like the makings of a B horror flick. I quickly realized I was completely unarmed—no paper towels, no rags, no can of Raid. I took a deep breath to calm down and then reminded myself that, yes, I had knowingly and willfully moved away from my tidy American suburb. I had only myself to blame.

A tapping noise at the front door disrupted my minor panic attack. I saw Kai flash past me as he ran toward the door.

"Mom, kids! Lots and lots of kids!" he cried.

I stood and looked over at the door. Children were pressing their noses up against the glass, giggling, waving at us, and rattling the doorknob trying to open it. As Kai stood transfixed at this sudden mother lode of potential playmates, the door handle came unlatched and three of the smallest kids, who had been leaning against the door, fell into the living room. They squealed and playfully slapped at each other, kicking off their flip-flops and heading for the sofa as if I'd invited them over for lemonade and cookies. That emboldened six more children to step out of their sandals, pile them on the front doorstep, and enter.

I thought about all the times in California that I had ached for Kai when my efforts to secure play dates for him had failed. In so many urban and suburban neighborhoods across America, even the Pied Piper would be hard-pressed to round up ten kids in a five-mile radius who were at home after school or on weekends. Finding even one friend to come over to play meant bouts of phone tag with busy parents. Then the seemingly inevitable phone message: "We have to cancel today. Jeremy's got a cold." I'd feel so desperate, I'd call back and say, "That's okay, bring him anyway. Kai doesn't mind colds."

But now we had just scored nine chattering, smiling children in the living room, ranging in age from about four to twelve. We would have no shortage of neighbor children for Kai to play with on this alley. The children made a circle around Kai. One little girl handed him a piece of hard candy. Kai thanked her and looked at me.

"Go ahead," I said to him. "You can eat it."

The kids were delighted. I was enchanted. I wanted to grab them in my arms, squeeze them, and say thank you for being so ridiculously cute. I attempted my few memorized lines of Vietnamese: "Hello, how are you? What is your name?" But before I could spit out the words, a young man with short-cropped hair walked up to the doorway and spoke brusquely to the children. They were suddenly quiet, though still smiling. Whatever he said, they responded by waving goodbye and filing out. They talked noisily as each tried to locate his or her flip-flops jumbled on the steps. I didn't want the kids to go so soon. I could tell by Kai's face that he didn't either.

"Sorry," the twenty-something man said. "This is first time we see foreigner in neighborhood." He was short but had a muscular chest, broad shoulders, and sturdy legs. He held out his hand and introduced himself. "Welcome. I'm Hung" (pronounced *home*, thank God). "I work at Sheraton Hotel, so I have much contact with foreigner." He flashed an infectious smile.

"I live that house," he said pointing directly across the alley.

I was so relieved to find out that we had been blessed with a neighbor who could speak English, I nearly hugged him. I'd been stressing all morning about being alone, unable to communicate with my neighbors. What if there was an emergency? Who would I call? What was the Vietnamese equivalent of 911 and the word for "hospital"?

I motioned for Hung (whom I will henceforth call Homie, because that's what he became to me) to come in and sit down. Seeing that his shirt had blotches of sweat on it, I moved the floor fan closer to him.

"You must lock you door," he admonished. "Vietnamese people very friendly. They want meet you. They want walk in you house. Maybe you can't get them back out!"

I laughed. "I'm afraid to offend the neighbors. I don't want them to hate me on the first day."

"Who care! Let them talk," he said with a wave of his hand. "Soon they get tired and shut up."

"Okay, I'll lock the door. But really, the kids are always welcome. My son Kai could use some friends."

He looked over at Kai, who was standing by the front door watching the children play outside. I suggested to Kai that he join them, but he shook his head.

Homie smiled. "He very re-luc-tant."

"You know the word 'reluctant'? Your English is so good."

"No, I don't think so," he said, giving what I would come to recognize as a typically Vietnamese self-deprecating response to a compliment.

I had so many questions. Where could I find hangers, buckets, dishes, lightbulbs, lamps, linens—and bug killer? More pressing, what was the phone number for pizza delivery? My stomach was growling. But I didn't want to rudely trouble him with logistical issues so soon. I don't know why I thought that just because he spoke English, he would know about setting up a household. From what I'd observed in my few short forays into the market near our guesthouse, Vietnamese men, as a rule, weren't the ones out buying toilet brushes and laundry soap.

I smiled at Homie. *Maybe he'll go to the market with me.* But before I could ask, he stood up and politely excused himself to go to work.

"Wait," I said. "Where can I find a market? We have no food."

He pointed in the direction of the neighborhood's "very important market," gave me some confusing directions, and then stepped outside to strap on his helmet, straddle his motorbike, and drive off.

It was 1 p.m. and I was at once hungry and nauseated from all the anxiety of the last few hours. Somewhere in one of my bags were the last two granola bars, but I knew they wouldn't hold Kai all day. Big, brave, strong Robin wouldn't be home for five more hours. I realized at that moment that the only foreign country I'd ever traveled to alone was Canada. I'd always considered myself an intrepid traveler. I'd eaten goat stew on a mountaintop with descendants of the Crimean Tatars in Ukraine, gone hiking in a Borneo jungle, and helped a farmer herd sheep in driving rain and boot-sucking mud in New Zealand. That qualified me as intrepid, didn't it? Perhaps not, because I'd done all those things with Robin. To my chagrin, I realized I was more dependent on him than I'd thought, more than I felt comfortable being. In exotic countries, he was the one to hail the taxis, order food at restaurants, ask for directions, and calculate the currency exchange rate. I'd just stood and smiled for photos.

If Kai hadn't been with me, I would have chosen to go hungry to avoid leaving the house. But just as the primal need to hunt for the survival of my offspring had begun to override my fear, another scene outside the door made me hesitate. As we got ready to leave, I wondered if it was safe to venture into the alley at that moment.

CHAPTER 6

In Search of Food

*"He eats alone but calls the whole village
to help launch his boat."*
(VIETNAMESE PROVERB)

ACROSS THE ALLEY and one house over sat Hatchet Lady, the squatting vendor who had been chopping up pig hooves on our first visit. She was screaming and waving her meat cleaver at three customers perched around her. The housewives were picking up various cuts of pork from her cutting board with their bare hands, inspecting each sinew and ribbon of fat, and then throwing the pieces back down in overt gestures of righteous disgust.

Listening to the screechy inflections of the Vietnamese language, I could only imagine what they were saying. *You call this fresh? My great-uncle is fresher than this!* Hatchet Lady yelled back, driving her point home with several strikes of the cleaver through a ham hock. I flinched at every *whack*. The housewives weren't a bit intimidated. They continued to snort and squeal until they got Hatchet Lady to drop her price. Money, pork, and scowls were exchanged. Next customer?

If Kai and I moved fast enough, I thought, we could get past her without an errant cleaver sinking into our skulls. I wished I could slip out unnoticed, but it seemed like everyone was home. *Doesn't anyone have a job to go to?* Women peeled vegetables on their doorsteps, small kids played Chinese jump rope, and elderly men with smelly hand-rolled cigarettes and glasses of black iced coffee sat in folding chairs finding amusement in whatever darted past their eyeballs.

Kai and I stepped outside. I hooked the fist-size Ludicrously Large Padlock to the double doors, uncomfortably aware that the lock was so big, I might as well have held up a bullhorn and announced, "As you can see, I don't trust you people." I turned around and smiled sheepishly, hoping to convey that the Ludicrously Large Padlock wasn't my idea. *It came with the house. Honest.* Nevertheless, the neighbors were smiling warmly at me.

I grabbed Kai's hand and we walked toward the main street, only to find we were quickly becoming the source of a traffic jam when drivers rubbernecked. Tiny grandmothers in conical hats, black pantaloons, and silk tunics reached over from their sidewalk stools to touch Kai, stroke his blond hair, or pinch his cheeks. He didn't understand that they didn't speak English, so he was startled when they responded to his "What's your name?" with squeals of delight and bone-crushing hugs. I quickly sympathized with celebrities who couldn't leave their houses unnoticed. I was relishing this attention as much as I liked running naked in the street being chased by dogs.

It seemed odd, all of this attention. The Communist government had opened Vietnam to foreign businesses in 1987, and in 1990 allowed the first tourist visas, so it wasn't as if these people had never seen Westerners. Far away from the tourist areas in this corner of District 4, however, we did seem to be a novelty. Yet, although everyone we passed stared at us, no one seemed unhappy with our presence. In fact, I already had the distinct sense we were welcome.

We jostled for space on Đoàn Văn Bơ and stepped carefully

over broken, jutting slabs of concrete. School kids were arriving home for lunch on bicycles. They followed us, stopping when we stopped, continuing when we did, giggling, and coaxing each other to try out his or her English.

"Madam, where you go?" asked one boy.

"I'm going to the market," I replied.

He looked confused and rode on. When I heard the same question a few more times and received similar reactions to my response, I deciphered what they were really asking was "Where are you from?" So I answered, "America," and the kids broke into smiles, held their thumbs up, and said, "America, number one!"

Maybe they'd all learned English from the same textbook, the very book I had read about just a couple of days before in the English-language newspaper, *Viet Nam News*. A tiny article on a side column reported that a man from Hanoi was being prosecuted for publishing a textbook without a license. Its title: "*To Learn Well English.*"

"Madam, how *owed* you?" asked another child who shyly walked up to me. For no other reason than vanity, I really hate that question. In America, it would have been impertinent. But in Vietnam the opposite is true. Your age is usually asked first, because it determines how the person will address you. Was I an "elder sister," an "auntie," or—God forbid—a "grandmother"? Such honorifics might only be separated by a scant few years, so people truly needed to know. Nevertheless, when I answered the girl, I lied and took ten years off my age.

Out on the main street, and once I'd found my bearings, Kai and I headed for a crosswalk, waited for an opening in the traffic, joined hands, and ran across. On the other side was an outdoor fruit market, which seemed too small to be the "very important market" Homie had told me about. Good enough, I decided. I was already too far from my alley for comfort. The little fruit stands would have to do. Otherworldly tropical fruits—hairy rambutans, malodorous durian, custard apples, spiky jackfruit—were arranged in neat rows. Eager vendors waved us over to buy. One offered little tastes of the fruit and found it knee-slappingly funny when Kai bit into a piece of jackfruit, scrunched up his little face, and promptly spit it onto the ground.

Thirty minutes later, we were laden with mangoes, a bunch of finger bananas, water bottles, tea bags, and a package of crackers imported from Thailand. That would have to suffice for the rest of the afternoon.

Back at the crosswalk, it seemed traffic had gotten significantly heavier. Because I couldn't trust Kai to control his impulses, I held him back by his upper arm so he wouldn't dart out into the street. We stepped off the curb and tried to move forward into a mass of motorbikes, diesel-belching green buses, and pedestrian-be-damned taxis. Nobody slowed down. Nobody. Nor were there any gaps in the traffic for as far as I could see. I pulled Kai back up onto the curb, perplexed as to why the city would waste paint on crosswalks when no one ever yielded the right of way to pedestrians.

Three more minutes passed with no letup. I wasn't sure what I was going to do until I felt some tiny, powerful fingers grasp my elbow and give it a tug. An elderly woman, slightly stooped and half my size, kept a firm grip on my elbow as she stepped boldly into the traffic, the two of us in tow. She lifted up her knobby arm and waved at the vehicles, running interference between us and what looked like half of the city's 7.3 million motorbikes. This tiny Moses parted the Red Sea of motorbike drivers, who didn't stop, but simply drove around us. Once on the opposite sidewalk, I looked back at the traffic we'd just squeezed through and let out the breath I'd been holding.

"Thank you so, so much," I gushed in Vietnamese, hoping I'd said it with the proper phrasing and inflections. I put my palms together and dropped my head in an old-school gesture of respect. She nodded and smiled widely, revealing stubby teeth reddish-black from many years of chewing slightly narcotic betel nuts.

She put her palms together in return and then adroitly crossed back over to her side. As I watched her cross, I realized the mistake I'd made in those three anxious minutes. One must step out boldly and keep walking. Hesitation will kill you.

If that old lady had lived this long crossing these streets, maybe we could survive, too.

CHAPTER 7

First Night

*"One piece of food while hungry equals
a big box of food while full."*
(VIETNAMESE PROVERB)

WHEN ROBIN RETURNED HOME at six that evening, we fairly
pounced on him with hunger.

"I'm craving authentic Vietnamese food," I said, tongue-in-
cheek.

"Well, you are in the right place for it. Except here they just
call it food."

We walked up to Đoàn Văn Bơ in search of *phở,* the delicious,
fragrant noodle soup for which the Vietnamese are famous, and
found a stand only two alleys away. When I learned that *phở* is
actually pronounced "fuh," like "duh," I reflected on the several
California restaurants named Pho King and wondered whether
kids had pranked their unsuspecting immigrant parents.

Even though the evening was barely cooler than it had been
that afternoon, I hoped the steamy soup and Robin's protective
presence would help soothe my nerve endings, which were frayed
after a long day of being stared at. The whole day I'd been afraid

I'd make a fool of myself in front of these strangers. It occurred to me that one reason I liked travel was that I could be around people whose impressions of me didn't matter the way people's opinions mattered at home. I could totally relax. This time, however, I was going to be living in close proximity to people with entirely different customs—so what they thought of me *did* matter. Robin had no such egocentric trepidations. He thrived on being himself, a characteristic that was both emotionally healthy (for him) and embarrassing (for me).

At one noodle stall, short tables with stools the size of nursery school chairs sat under a plastic tarp. The soup smelled wonderful so we headed for a seat. Soup Lady ran ahead of us with what looked like a car mechanic's oil rag to wipe off one of the short tables and foot-high resin stools. She smiled broadly and motioned for us to take a seat. It might as well have been parents' night at nursery school. Robin's knees reached his shoulders. I couldn't get my legs under the table and had to sit sidesaddle. Only Kai was comfortable. The implausible scene made several passersby stop. Most of them waved or said hello and continued on their way. But a handful stayed to watch the absurdly large foreigners eat dinner. (This is a good place to mention that I'm not large at five foot six and 115 pounds, but sitting with Robin, who fills out most viewfinders, we looked like Jack-and-the-beanstalk giants.)

I pointed to Robin's nose, where a droplet of perspiration was getting ready to leap into his lap. He reached for the plastic napkin dispenser and gave the paper a tug. Out came a long strip of stiff toilet paper. He wiped, but the wad shredded into bits of sawdust across his face. As he brushed it off, he began to tilt ever so slowly to the right. At first, I thought he was trying to get a laugh out of Kai.

"Look, Kai, Papa is melting," I said.

Kai smiled. But Robin wasn't playing. His red stool began to curl outward on one side and, as if he were disconnected from his body and couldn't use his legs to catch himself, he toppled and hit the ground. Soup Lady leaped to his side and gave him two stacked stools for more support. Bystanders giggled—a common reaction in Asia, I had heard, when anything is embarrassing.

A cooling wind kicked up, signaling that rain would start soon. The plastic tarp above us billowed with each gust, flapping noisily. Moments later, a torrent of rain collected into the middle of the tarp like a heavy udder above our heads. I was so sweaty that I almost wished the tarp would give way and drench us.

I watched the vendor pull sticky, tepid clumps of cooked rice noodles from a colander with her bare hands and then ladle the steaming broth on top. As long as were going to live here, I thought, I would have to overlook the fact that food is not wrapped, packaged, and kept at forty degrees Fahrenheit. In a country where chickens, pigs, and rabbits (not to mention cats, dogs, and rats) are skinned and hung up at outdoor markets subject to heat, flies, and dirt from passing traffic, well, it was better not to think about it.

After a meal thankfully free of further excitement, we headed home to visit the ants, who were still marching two-by-two, hurrah, hurrah. Robin wet a T-shirt and walloped them until the floor was speckled with ant carcasses. (Note: No other animals were harmed in the making of this book. Well, except for cockroaches. Oh, yes, and one baby gecko in a dark corner that I mistook for a cockroach and slammed with my sandal. My heart broke. I picked him up and tenderly held him in the palm of my hand. "I'm so sorry, little guy." I had bashed him so hard that his tiny, shiny black eyeballs had popped out of their sockets.)

The three of us spent the first night in our new home in one double bed. At 11 p.m. we were exhausted. Kai was scared to sleep in his own room the first night, and bribes of new made-in-China toys wouldn't change his mind; he insisted on sleeping between us. The heat from his little body made me sweat all the more. The bed was damp. I hugged the edge of the bed so I wouldn't roll off, and tried to sleep. Outside, the alley was as raucous and loud as it had been in the daytime, perhaps more so. Shouting kids ran back and forth between houses, babies cried, music and karaoke singing blasted out of several houses and reverberated off the walls. Teens revved up motorcycles to show off for each other. *When do these people sleep?* I wondered. Was it going to be like this every night? In an American city, the police would have been called in for that much noise. Kai fell asleep right away. Robin did, too, and his snoring added to the cacophony. I lay in the dark, bone weary, and feeling as desperate as a surfacing scuba diver in the Great Barrier Reef who just discovered the dive boat had left. *Please, please, let it be quiet. Give me some rest and strength for Day Two.* Still, I marveled at the tolerance people had for each other. By the sound of the happy voices outside, the noise—which didn't abate until midnight—wasn't upsetting anyone except me. My last look at the alarm clock was at 1 a.m. The alley was finally, mercifully, quiet. But five hours later, we were awakened by entirely different sounds.

CHAPTER 8

Late to Bed, Early to Rise

"Let's all steadfastly love on one another."
(SEEN ON A PINK T-SHIRT WORN BY A MAN)

"EARTHQUAKE!" KAI SCREAMED. It was six in the morning, and he bolted upright in bed when he heard a *thwack, thwack* that, since it only rattled the left side of the house, I knew was something other than an earthquake.

Robin rolled over and grumbled mightily. I woke unrested, my eyes burning from so few hours of sleep. But Kai ran downstairs to look outside for the source of the disturbance, and I was right behind him. Dragon Man, it turned out, was using a hammer and an ice pick to chop up a large block of ice that sat in an iron pot against his front entrance. Because we shared a wall, we shared the rattle. His wife, Mrs. Dragon, a chubby woman with strands of hair falling out of a ponytail, was setting up collapsible chairs and paint-chipped metal TV trays in front of their door to sell iced coffee. She had the deep, gravelly voice of someone who'd been smoking all her life. A few minutes later a man with a basket and a booming voice walked down the alley calling *"bánh mì đây"* ("bread here"). As if waiting for its turn to be heard, a rooster crowed from the house next door. Hatchet Lady, too, was already setting up her cutting boards, and her chopping would soon assault my nerves.

Kai turned on the TV to *Shaun the Sheep* cartoons, so I went upstairs and got back into bed. Stealthily. Quietly. Sleep was Robin's happy place, and I didn't want to interrupt his dreams, his favorite form of entertainment. He was already awake, though. "Damn!" he said, flopping onto his other side, "I was in the middle of dreaming I wɛ the fourth Muske⁺eer." He closed his eyes again, hoping to jump back into his swashbuckling alternate universe, but the alarm he'd set went off fifteen minutes later. We didn't know it yet, but it was the last time we'd ever need to set the alarm. The whole 'hood was awake, alive, and open for business by 6 a.m. And, as I discovered later, neither our neighbors nor the damn rooster took a day off. Ever.

Robin's teaching certificate course was going well, but his homework load was substantial. He had exams and had to prepare lesson plans for all age groups. His CELTA course was like trying to jam three years of teaching skills into one month. He left for class that morning at seven. By eight, the morning was already sweltering, a fact that helped explain why, when I opened the curtain, I spotted Homie standing in front of his house wearing only a thin pair of light blue boxer shorts, his hair still unruly from sleep. He smiled and waved. As I unbolted the door, he fairly flew onto my front steps and walked in.

"Have you eaten?" he asked, with a wonderful, radiant smile. I wasn't sure if he needed food, was inviting me to breakfast, or was simply curious. But yes, we had just finished eating.

"I warmed up leftover *phở* from last night," I said.

"What means 'leftover'?"

He wrinkled his nose when I explained the concept.

"Vietnamese not eat leftovers. Make you sick."

Many Vietnamese still didn't trust refrigerators, appliances that were relatively recent additions to most households. In fact, Homie told me it was the advent of the refrigerator that had put his father out of business in the mid-1990s. He'd been an ice-delivery man.

"What does he do now?" I asked.

"You can see what he do," he said, pointing out of the window at his father sitting on a lawn chair in their living room. His father saw us looking at him and waved. We waved back.

"He do nothing. He sit in chair all day. Make my mother crazy," he said.

I wanted to ask more about his family because I'd noticed so many people walking in and out of the house and I didn't know who actually lived there, but Homie sat down and changed the topic.

"You from California, yes?" he asked, as he pressed down on the love seat's half-inch-thin cushion, apparently noticing, as we had, just how uncomfortable it was. "And you husband will become teacher of English, yes?"

"Yes, how did you know?" I said, trying to avert my eyes from his rather tight boxer shorts and hairless chest and legs.

"My mother talk with you landlord. Vietnamese very talkative!"

I took that to mean gossipy. I told him I might eventually teach, too, but first I wanted to get a handle on learning Vietnamese so I could function in the neighborhood.

"Do you know someone who can teach me? I need a tutor to come to my house, because I have Kai here with me."

"Maybe I teach you Vietnamese, and you help me speak English. No need to pay."

Bartering. I wished the practice were more common in America. It would save everyone so much money, I mused, as I went into the kitchen to pour two glasses of iced tea. I looked over at Homie, who seemed remarkably relaxed—not to mention under-dressed—for someone who had just met me the day before. He had swung his legs up and over one arm of the sofa, and was lying back trying to adjust the throw pillows under his neck for comfort. He might have been one of my daughters, so quickly, thoroughly, and instinctively had he made himself at home. For a second this felt wrong, but the truth was I loved the elimination of preliminary social niceties. We were neighbors; why not cut to the chase?

I handed him a glass of iced tea, but he jumped up suddenly, as if he'd forgotten to do something (perhaps put his pants on?). He thanked me anyway for the tea and announced he was going home to take a shower. Afterward, he said he'd show me around the market. I was immensely grateful, because I faced yet another day with little food in the house.

If Kai and I had walked one block farther the day before, it turned out, we would have found the "very important" market Homie had referenced. The mammoth two-story concrete structure encompassed an entire city block and appeared to have been painted green at one time. As Homie, Kai, and I got closer, though, I realized the patches of green were not paint, but algae growing where water leaked from slimy, broken gutters onto the gray walls.

Inside, the light was dim, the temperature sultry, and the air redolent with the blended odors of fish, raw meat, sugarcane, spices, and trash bins of rotting fruits and vegetables. Barefoot vendors squatted atop wooden platforms built above their produce bins. At several stalls, hammocks were hung in which babies and old people napped above colorful arrays of produce, some bulbous and extraterrestrial-looking, with names Homie couldn't translate for me. Except for some green beans, carrots, and scallions, I didn't recognize anything, nor did I have a clue how to cook it, let alone discern which part of the plant was edible and which part could be digested only by a goat. Particularly strange was a five-foot-long, two-inch-diameter plant that looked like a branch someone had ripped off a tree. "It for tea when stomach hurt," Homie told me.

For a few cents more the vendor would chop, shred, or peel the produce of your choice into more manageable pieces. That, at least, helped me to address the question of which parts of the plant could be eaten—not how to cook it.

We climbed to the second floor, which was insanely jammed with shops full of goods stacked to the ceiling. The air was even more stifling, though most sellers had electric fans pointed at themselves. The floor housed fabric stalls; ready-made clothes shops; and vendors selling made-in-China clocks, rice cookers, floor fans, and cheap plastic toys.

"See?" Homie said, stretching out his arms as if he were an actor in a cosmic grocery-store commercial. "Everything you need."

"Cocoa Puffs?" Kai asked.

Homie dropped his arms and bent down closer to Kai. "Co—what?"

I expounded: It's a crunchy, chocolatey little ball made of processed grains, corn syrup, glycerin, cocoa processed with alkali, red dye No. 40, yellow 5 and 6, blue 1, tricalcium phosphate, trisodium phosphate (which also makes a mighty fine cleaning agent), artificial flavor, sucralose, sulfiting agents, and BHT. And then you pour cold cow's milk on it. Or you can tilt your head back and shake them directly from the box into your mouth. Actually, I stopped at "chocolatey little ball."

"You American eat bad breakfast," he said. "You need soup. Better for stomach. It warm stomach in morning." I'm sure he had watched plenty of US tourists at the Sheraton's breakfast buffet who passed up the lovely soup pots as they headed straight for the acrylic cornflakes and Froot Loops dispensers.

Back downstairs, we passed the seafood section, stepping cautiously across slippery floors where live eels, squid, catfish, and snapper swam in water-filled metal tubs. I watched as a customer chose a fat, gray, eighteen-inch-long carp. The seller set Mr. Fishy on a board and bashed him on the head over and over with a wooden stick until he stopped his frantic, futile flopping.

"Aaack, that's just horrifying," I said to Homie as I moved in front of Kai, trying to shield him from one of life's awful realities. In a high-pitched voice mimicking the fish, Homie teased, "Oh, please stop! I have four children at home. What will become of them? Let me go!"

Kai looked stricken. "Those poor fishes. That's so mean," he said. Homie shook his head. "Vietnamese like fresh food. If already dead, they won't buy."

From that day on, Kai was a vegetarian. He refused any more meat or fish.

Sellers and shoppers alike looked shocked to see foreigners buying food in District 4's main market. At each stall they asked Homie who I was, how he knew me, was I French *(Mon Dieu, non!)*, and, as always, how old I was. I understood one vegetable seller who asked me how old Kai was. I was pretty fluent with numbers up to ten, so I answered *tám tuổi* (eight years). She hooted and then yelled out *tám tuổi* to the next vendor, who nodded and turned to tell the next vendor. Just like the children's game of telephone, it got repeated all across the floor. I wondered how old Kai had become by the time the message reached the far corners of the market.

Homie helped me find rice, vegetables, cooking oil, herbs, bowls, plates, cups, cookware, and utensils, all of which only added up to twenty dollars. The last item on my essentials list was more of the exquisite mangoes I had eaten the day before. As the fruit seller set four mangoes onto the scale, I noticed he was three fingers short of a full hand. Only his pinkie and thumb remained on his right hand. Having heard that District 4 was once Vietnamese mafia territory, I asked Homie after we'd left the stand if the man had been one of those victims who had neglected to repay his loans.

"No, he cut them off himself," Homie said matter-of-factly. "He no want to fight in American War, so he chop them off," he continued, pantomiming a hatchet falling like a guillotine across his fingers. "Then he could no shoot a gun. He very courageous."

Courageous? In America, some vets might have given him a

very different label. In America, draft dodgers just needed to hop the fence to Canada. They got to keep all their fingers.

As we reached my door, three neighbor women rushed over to peer into my bags. They were smiling—the neighbors were always smiling—and very, very curious. Always anxious to be accepted, I opened my bags wide and let them look.

"What is she cooking for dinner tonight?" one asked Homie. He translated the question for me but didn't bother to answer her. He apologized for the nosy housewives.

"Vietnamese want to know everything about everybody, especially foreigner."

I told him their curiosity didn't bother me a bit and that, indeed, I thought it rather endearing. Which was true, up to a point. I thanked Homie, waved goodbye to the smiling women, closed the door—and locked it.

As I was unpacking our purchases, our landlord Vinh arrived, carrying the kitchen table as he'd promised us the day before. Somehow, he'd managed to tie the thing onto his motorbike and ferry it to our house. It would never cease to amaze me how much stuff the Vietnamese were able to load onto a tiny two-wheeler: furniture, doors, five-foot refrigerators, and many other items for which Americans would have required a semitrailer.

Vinh carried the ice-cream-parlor-size table into the living room, plunked it down, and from his back pocket, produced a flimsy oilcloth table cover printed with lurid orange roses. "From my wife," he said shyly. "Protect table."

Before leaving, he proceeded to run through the list of bill collectors (cash only) who would come to the door monthly: phone (two dollars), trash pickup (sixty cents), cable TV (four dollars), and electricity (about twenty dollars). Together, these totaled less than a tenth of our monthly utility bills back home. Vinh warned us though: Use of the upstairs air conditioners would push the electric bill up to an exorbitant sixty dollars per month. I gasped in horror for his benefit.

But one thing I knew already: The cheek-by-jowl living, make-yourself-at-home neighborliness, and low cost of Vietnamese living were already making me feel safer and more secure than I had in a long time.

CHAPTER 9

The Alley–Unplugged

"No sweet without sweat."
(VIETNAMESE PROVERB)

THE NEXT MORNING, I'd just sat down to do some paperwork when the effervescent Homie called "Ms. Karin!" through a crack in the door. He cupped his hands against the door's window and when he spotted me, he waved. Our house had a doorbell, an oddity because it was unnecessary when the front of every house was wide open all day. The neighbors probably thought it freakish behavior that I shut my door, but Homie kept insisting I do so because "thieves" assumed all foreigners were swimming in cash, and might run into the house and steal something. Our doorbell was only ever used, later, by children to tease Kai as they played Ding-Dong Ditch.

"Have you eaten?" he asked, as I opened the door. There was that odd question again. Why did he want to know if I had eaten? I asked him about it and he told me it was the equivalent of "How are you?" I remembered reading Pearl S. Buck's *The Good Earth*, in which the Chinese peasants believed that a sick person wouldn't die if he or she had eaten something. If you are too sick to eat, then you must be really, really sick.

Homie said that the Vietnamese greet each other with "Have you eaten?" because if you have, then it means you are fine and happy with a full stomach. In other words, you are not sick. It finally helped to explain why when one neighbor woman saw me each morning, she'd mime eating with an invisible spoon and bowl. And here I'd thought she just had food on the brain.

Homie, twenty-six, said he wanted to introduce me to his "younger brother." That's when I met my soon-to-be tutor, Tin, who was taller and thinner than the short, sturdy Homie. Tin smiled and formally, but warmly, shook my hand. "So happiness to meet you," he said.

I was immediately smitten with his sophisticated charm and chiseled good looks. He wore impeccably neat clothes and had the modern, choppy haircut of someone who followed the latest fashion trends. Tin and Homie didn't look like brothers at all, and their personalities were as disparate as their bodies.

Tin gave me a slight nod and said he had to get to his job at the Franco-Vietnamese (FV) Hospital, where he worked the emergency room admitting desk. But Homie seemed to have some time on his hands. "Ms. Karin," he asked, "you come meet my mother?"

"Absolutely! Who all lives in your house? I see people go in and out all the time," I asked, as I reached back to close my front door and follow him.

"They customer. My mother make cloth-ee," Homie replied. He gave me a quick rundown on who lived in the three-room house: his mom and dad; his sixteen-year-old sister; and an unemployed thirty-five-year-old brother with his manicurist wife, and their five-year-old son, Kiet. Brother No. 2 had died several years before and Brother No. 3 lived elsewhere with his wife and son. I assumed that Tin lived there, too, and thought it odd Homie didn't mention him.

Mama Hang was working on a black 1950s-era Singer sewing machine, just like the one I remembered my own grammie had. Homie's mother stood up and shook my hand. She looked tired, but had the same wonderful smile Homie did. Her hair had streaks of gray, and like most women in the neighborhood, she wore it long and tied back. Figuring she was in her mid-sixties, I greeted her in Vietnamese using the polite *chị* or "elder sister."

"Did I say that correctly, Homie? Do I call her *chị* or *bà?*" Mama Hang giggled when she heard *bà,* an honorific, Homie revealed, reserved only for elderly grandmas. My cheeks reddened when Homie said she was fifty—a year younger than me.

"My mother make all these *cloth-ee,*" Homie said, looking admiringly at his mother's four-dollar top-and-pants sets hanging at the front entrance. The floral or patterned polyester-knit outfits that look like pajamas are ubiquitous in southern Vietnam and worn by seemingly every woman over thirty. Mama Hang sat back down on a hard metal stool, which, except for her husband's aluminum lawn chair, was the only other piece of furniture in the room. No need for a dining table; up and down the alley I'd noticed everyone ate their meals on the floor. At Homie's, two long tables flanked each wall, covered with large spools of thread, bobbins, scissors, and partially completed clothes. Beneath these tables were barrel-size plastic bags full of brightly colored fabric, which I would later discover made really comfortable beanbag-style seats on karaoke nights. Homie told me his mother sewed from 9 a.m. to 9 p.m. seven days a week. For her efforts she earned about $200 a month.

"She work so hard," Homie said, shaking his head. "Make me so sad. My father not work. He injured. Rock go in one of he eye. Now he only see from one of he eye."

It seemed to me that with one good eye he still ought to be able to get a job to help out his overworked wife, but I didn't say anything. Homie continued: "My mother work to buy food and pay school fee for my sister."

"School isn't free here?" I asked incredulously. I'd always assumed education was free in a Communist country. Wasn't that the whole socialist point? Take most of everyone's hard-earned income and then give it back as free education, free healthcare, and pensions?

"School is one million *đồng* (fifty dollars) every month," he said. "But I help my mother."

Homie earned $270 per month as a full-time waiter at the Sheraton, a coveted job he had scored by diligently studying English and Japanese over many years. His language skills made him valuable even though he hadn't gone to college. Learning another language, particularly English, could mean a ticket out of the country or, at least, a way out of poverty by working for a foreign company in Vietnam.

Suddenly the whir of Mama Hang's machine was silenced, the fluorescent light overhead went dark, and—most alarming of all— the floor fans stopped. I looked outside and noticed the electricity was off at other houses, too. How odd. It wasn't stormy or windy. I glanced across the alley. Kai peeked out of our front door looking nervous, but I waved and yelled over to him that the power would come back on soon.

"No, no, not soon," Homie corrected. "If electric go off, it off for whole day."

"Why?"

"City make repair," he said, not appearing the least bit annoyed.

I'd heard that electricity in the city could be spotty, but not about daylong outages. I groaned thinking how the ruse of "repair" was a clever way to explain rolling blackouts to the masses.

"Don't worry, power come back at five," he reassured me.

At *five*? How could they? I had plans! Well, not really. I couldn't shake off the feeling of urgency that I needed to be somewhere or be doing something, an insidious trait of Americans, especially Type-As like me. Of one thing I was certain: Whatever it was that I was supposed to be doing, it involved the use of electricity.

Homie's voice betrayed nary a hint of frustration with the blackout. In fact, he sounded rather relieved. He watched as his mother's shoulders relaxed and she set her sewing aside. The outage meant she could rest.

Without an electric fan blowing directly on me, my skin was already tacky with sweat. The boxy cinder-block houses, ubiquitous in Vietnam, had no insulation. It was as if someone had rolled up the windows, turned off the A/C, and left us sitting in a car on a sweltering day. The heat instantly became unbearable.

"If the district planned this outage, why don't they warn people first?" I asked, thinking about the precious ice cubes that would soon be melting in my freezer.

"Do they warn you in America when they take electric down?"

"No. But...." I didn't want to brag that America's electricity was plentiful and rarely, if ever, purposely shut off.

I watched as families began to gather at their front entrances, bamboo fans in hand, to sit and visit with their neighbors. Women took off their conical hats to scoop up the still air in great whooshes to cool off their babies.

"Homie," I said with a whimper, "how will I stay cool? Americans would drop dead in heat like this. The president would have to declare a state of emergency." I thought about the heatwave in France in 2003 that caused the deaths of more than 14,000 people, most of them elderly. How was this any different? Maybe I wouldn't survive. I pictured myself frothing on the floor like a slug sprinkled with salt.

"Keep you hair wet and lie down on floor and go sleep," Homie suggested. "The tile very cool. You will see."

For someone who simultaneously uses the toilet and applies makeup, who does biceps curls with cantaloupes while grocery shopping, and who strokes a cat with her foot while typing, squandering time was one of the Seven Deadly Sins. What would happen to the trajectory of my goals if I were forced to give in to a slower tempo of life? Already I saw things were going to go very differently here. Nevertheless, what choice did I have? I felt faint and desperate to get back in the house, take a cool shower, and try out the tile-floor survival method.

Kai had locked the door and stood at the window. "You can't come in this way," he said resolutely. I looked through the window. He had spread his train tracks across the living-room floor in an elaborate configuration that crept all the way up to the door. Evidently, the heat wasn't slowing him down.

"Kai, come on, open up," I pleaded. "There's no other way to get into the house."

"I can't get the lock open."

"Come on, you can do it with your eyes closed."

"No, I can't see that way."

He fumbled a second with the Ludicrously Large Padlock and said, "Got it." But he still wouldn't let me in. "What's the password?" Kai had a fondness for passwords. It didn't matter what the answer was, as long as it was inane.

"Chicken butt," I responded. He seemed satisfied and opened the door.

Right away, I folded back the door panels, leaving the living room wide open like my neighbors' to catch any breezes and bring in more light. Thieves be damned. After my shower, I got a wet cloth for my brow and lay down on the living room floor next to Kai. Homie was right; the tiles were wonderfully cool. I began to relax my body, letting it sink and flatten into the floor, which cooled each limb and every inch of skin. Every ten to fifteen minutes I scooted to a cooler patch of floor. Though the floor made the heat tolerable, time passed with excruciating slowness. I felt impatient. My obsessive drive to stay occupied every minute of the day was evaporating faster than a droplet of water on a hot frying pan. Even holding up a book or pushing a pencil was too exhausting. *How can anyone get any work done in this country?*

I resigned myself to stop fighting the heat, stop complaining, and I passed the time listening to my neighbors, who chatted nonstop with each other from their stoops and balconies. They laughed often and easily. What was so funny? What could possibly be funny in this heat?

On each porch, women cooked on single-burner propane stoves or painted each other's nails. Men fell asleep easily, not one worry infiltrating their drafty little heads (proof that men are the same the world over). At eleven-thirty schoolchildren began to arrive home for their three-hour (!) lunch break. One boy and three girls spotted Kai and his trains, dropped their backpacks at their homes, and ran right over. The kids were polite but not a bit bashful as they wiggled out of their sandals and left them heaped on the stairs. They gathered around Kai. In spite of the language barrier, he immediately started talking to them about his project. He told them about the different train cars and how the switch tracks worked. Excited and interested, they asked him questions. He listened, nodded, and then answered, and in the space of a few minutes all five kids disproved the widely held theory that people need to speak the same language to understand each other. I was delighted. Living on this alley would trump any supervised play therapy Kai had had at home.

As I lay, I languidly watched vendors push their carts through the alley, hawking plastic buckets and baskets, vegetables, fruits, and leathery squid jerky. A woman who carried a tray heaped with pastries stopped at my door and pulled off a piece of clear plastic from the tray to show me her perfect little French confections: small croissants, cream puffs, and tiny cakes wrapped in waxed paper. I sat up.

"Bao nhiêu?" I asked.

Five cents each, she replied, giggling that I knew some Vietnamese. I stood and pulled the equivalent of fifty cents out of my pocket to buy ten. With so many choices, I hesitated. An elderly man who noticed my indecision walked up and stood next to the tray. He pointed to a flaky little roll, nudging me with his eyes to take it. I thanked him. More passersby began to gather. One pointed to the cream puffs, another to the croissants. A girl shyly pointed to a little square cake that was filled with shredded coconut. I took two of them. Even though I felt awkward with all the attention (junk food being very personal), I felt bathed in the warmth and helpfulness of these strangers.

When the vendor left, I noticed the neighbors were staring at me. They looked at the plastic bag full of pastries I was clutching and then back at me. I could read it on their faces: *That foreigner is gonna get fat.*

I conspicuously put the sweets on a plate and handed them to the kids, who said, "Zank you, Mom." Kai's new friends called me "Mom," not because they knew what the word meant, but because when Kai said it, I answered.

For reasons I wouldn't fully comprehend until many months later, these power-outage days were to become some of my all-time favorite days in Vietnam.

CHAPTER 10

A Call from Home

"A bad compromise is better than a good lawsuit."
(VIETNAMESE PROVERB)

BY THE END OF OUR FIRST MONTH in Vietnam, Robin had nearly completed his CELTA course. Now all he had to do was pass the final exam and find a job. Language schools in the city typically paid native English speakers fifteen to twenty dollars per hour. Would they accept a German native? Prerequisites for the certificate were a college degree and no visible tattoos. Robin had no tattoos. Finally! Here was a job outside of the entertainment industry for which he was qualified. I knew this because he'd once been my German teacher—that was how we met—so he could truthfully write on his résumé that he had teaching experience.

While waiting for him to get a job, I obsessively calculated all of our bills and remaining funds. Fear of lack had always been my issue—well, except for my little travel addiction. Financially, we were cutting it close. Our savings had been fizzling faster than Mentos in Diet Coke. It didn't matter that most food and household items in Vietnam were cheap. With no income, living expenses were adding up dangerously fast. With a jaunty grin, I thought to myself, *Thank goodness we have tenants in our California house to pay the mortgage.*

And then one evening around six, the phone rang.

"Mom?" I heard.

My eldest, Marisa, was calling from California. It was three in the morning her time, which meant this was not a "Hey, I just wanted to hear your voice" kind of call. So I panicked.

"What's wrong? Are you okay? Is Talia okay?" My voice quickly shifted into shriek mode as I braced myself for certain doom, clutching the receiver as if it were my last handhold on a sinking ship. (Let the record reflect that such behavior only happens when my children call. Otherwise, I'm quite normal.)

"Calm down, Mom, I'm fine. I couldn't sleep. Your property manager called yesterday and said nobody is living in your house."

I felt my face drain and pinpricks of cold sweat stung my neck. *I knew it! I knew it!* This whole move across the ocean had gone *too* smoothly. Life just doesn't work that way. Why couldn't I get that through my head? I should have known better. I reflected back on my gut instincts about the strange renters who had shown up at our door only a week before our departure. My massive marketing campaign in the *PennySaver* had failed. At that point, we'd hired a property manager to help us look for tenants. While the recession raged, houses in our neighborhood sat unrented and unsold. The manager informed us we should anticipate a five-month lag time to find viable tenants. "Even if we drop the price?"

"Even then. At least you're not trying to sell," she'd said with a giggle. "You'd be waiting a year."

We had only had enough money to pay three more months on the mortgage. I'd begun to picture a bright red foreclosure sign in our front yard, posted with instructions to contact Washington Mutual (which would be bought out by JPMorgan Chase two weeks after we moved).

Then, five days before our flight to Vietnam, a real estate agent and his two clients had come to the door of our now-empty house and said they were looking for a place just like ours. His finder's fee would be five percent of the rent up front, for a one-year lease. "But what if they skip out and don't pay their rent?" I asked after pulling the agent aside. "Do we get back some of your fee?" "No," he said. "Your security deposit will cover that." If the clients liked the house, he would guarantee the rent would cover our mortgage and then some.

Robin hadn't cared who rented our house. But I'd hoped that whoever was going to live in our home would appreciate the charming details: dormers, pansies in the window boxes, and a wood-burning fireplace. My dream tenants would joyfully gurgle, "Oh, look at these adorable window seats. I can see myself sitting here reading a book."

"Yes," I would respond breathlessly. "And they double as storage bins for your grandma's home-sewn quilts!"

The prospective renters were two rootin'-tootin' cowboys from Texas, complete with ten-gallon hats and "real" 'gator boots. As they took a gander at the house, Robin and I hopped around alternately pointing out the great closet space, the antique light fixtures, and the new double-glazed windows. They stomped across the newly polished hardwood floors and gave the most cursory glances into each room. My heart sank. However, at the sight of the backyard they finally perked up.

"Why lookee thar! A swimmin' hole." (I'm not kidding, they really did talk like the characters on *Duck Dynasty*.) Cowboy No. 1 bent down to feel the warm, sparkling turquoise water, then snickered and said, "Ah hope the neighbors don't mand if ah swim nekked."

He stood back up and laughed out loud at his own pluck. Pantomiming a freestyle stroke, he said, "Ah just luhve swimmin' nekked!"

Robin glanced over at me and mouthed "OH. MY. GOD." Cowboy No. 2 was preoccupied with his shiny boots and turned his foot from side to side, apparently looking for grass stains or just admiring the boot's exacting seam work. Cowboy No. 1 didn't bother to consult No. 2. He held out his hand to Robin and declared, "Okay, we'll tek it."

Robin happily shook his hand. My intuition began to shriek, *"What the...are you stupid?!"* I ignored the feeling that maybe these cowboys were shysters. Finding these tenants just days before we were to leave the country proved that this move was meant to be. Besides, this was no time to be picky. Their money was green, and we knew we were lucky to have renters at all.

Now, my fear hung in the air. "My God! Marisa," I gasped, "what happened to the cowboys?"

"The Texans left a note on the doorstep," she said. "Your manager scanned it for me. Be forewarned. It's a four-letter-word nightmare."

She read it to me. By way of frequent foul adjectives, the note indicated that the cowboys had found a patch of black mold in the garage. They were demanding their first and last month's rent back, as well as reimbursement for moving expenses and electric, gas, cable, and phone start-up fees. "'If you don't return our money in one week, we will sue you because you didn't disclose the mold issue,'" Marisa read to me.

Mold issue? What mold issue? We'd left the house spotless: repaired, recaulked, resanded, repainted, and relandscaped with trimmed trees, green grass, and fresh flowers in the window boxes. The house couldn't have looked cleaner or more beautiful. In fact, once we were finished, I had almost changed my mind about leaving.

When Robin got home from class I gave him the news. To add to the stress, the fifteen-hour time difference meant we couldn't even call California right away to try to sort things out. Waking someone at four in the morning probably wouldn't have helped our cause. We just had to wait.

I was shaking now, my blood turning cold. Suddenly, ninety-five degrees with ninety-nine percent humidity didn't feel so hot. While we had been swathed in a warm cradle of care and friendship in Vietnam, potentially devastating trouble had been brewing in California. I'd been yanked back to the cruel reality that trouble can follow you anywhere on the globe. My yin and yang had never felt so polarized, as if stretched to almost tearing. As the hours crawled by, I paced the floor and manically chewed gum. My heart pounded in my ears. Good God, mold removal—if indeed a mold problem existed—would cost thousands. Even more costly: our mortgage, with no tenants in sight.

Robin and I stayed awake until midnight, which was 9 a.m. in California, then began making calls.

Some of my many questions were answered in the ensuing hours. Why had the property manager taken so long to let us know? (She was trying to solve the problem herself; didn't want to bother us.) Would the broker return our two-thousand-plus fee, given that the cowboys had never moved in? (Nope. "Not my problem.") Most important, why hadn't the cowboys just asked us to send someone out to clean up the supposed mold? I couldn't help feeling like we'd been scammed.

"We found a #@%&* patch of mold in your #@%&* garage behind the #@%&* shelves," said Cowboy No. 1 when Robin finally got him on the phone. "Mold gets into the #@%&* air ducts. Your whole house is #@%&* infested! You #@%&* knew it was there. You #@%&* lied to us."

"There is a brick wall between the garage and the house, for God's sake!" Robin retorted. "There *are* no air ducts connected to the house. There isn't even a door that connects the house and garage." My knees were shaking as I listened in, able to hear both sides of the conversation. Their cussin' was so raw it could pucker a hog's butt. I was just happy Robin was dealing with them. Had I been the one on the phone, I would have been standing in a puddle of pee by then.

They'd found mold *behind the shelves?* The garage shelves hadn't been moved in years. Paint cans with leftover paint (placed there in case the renters wanted to touch up the walls) sat alongside boxes of paint supplies and some gardening tools. The cowboys didn't explain why they had been dismantling the shelves in the first place.

"The lease says you can't get your deposit back when you walk out of the deal," Robin continued. "You didn't even give us a chance to fix the problem."

"Y'all will be #@%&* hearin' from our lawyer."

I called our homeowners insurance company next. "I think I have mold in my garage, and I need you to assess the damage and tell me how much is covered for mold removal."

"Mold?" the representative said. "Oh, that's not covered in California."

Of course not. How silly of me to ask. Isn't it an insurance company's core value to benefit disadvantaged shareholders everywhere by wriggling out of paying on claims? "Okay, what about water damage," I inquired. "I'm guessing there's mold because water must have seeped in, no?"

"If there is water damage," he explained, "we only cover it if it happened in the last twelve months. If there is mold, the water damage would have been much, much older. And if it was from a rainstorm, insurance only covers the damage until the raindrops hit the ground." (I'm not making this up.) "Once the water is on the ground, it's considered flooding."

"And is that covered?"

"No. Flooding is not covered."

Then, exemplifying his company's selfless service, he offered: "I can come over in half an hour if you would like me to see the damage."

"We live in Vietnam. We can't exactly meet you in thirty minutes."

"Oh, well, then let me just say straight up that our company wouldn't cover it anyway."

A few days later, the mold inspector reported that he'd found only a two-inch-diameter patch and it wasn't the toxic black sort.

Seeing that the garage was a tad leaky, however, he did recommend we have all the drywall removed and the wood treated so no one else would get scared off. The cost: $1,800. Thank goodness for Visa, the only company that has never said "no" to me.

The cowboys must have known the work was being done, because a few days later they called us. "Okay," dickered Cowboy No. 1, "we'll make y'all a deal. If you fax us the report that the mold has been removed, we'll move in. But we expect you to cover our moving expenses, plus $4,000 for last month's temporary housing costs. So, let's see here…'cause I know you folks don't have no cash, and that's why y'all moved to 'Nam, we'll just take it off our rent. Okay, now…."

There was an interminable pause with the clickity-clack of a calculator in the background. "Looks like our first rent check to you will be in six months. I'll send you an agreement and you just fax it right on back, okay?"

"Uh, I don't think so," I said—politely, because I like confrontation as much as I like stepping in doggy doo. "If you would be so kind, please put the keys under the doormat. I think it's better if we all start fresh and find new tenants."

"Well, we'll be #@%&* seein' ya in court to get our #@%&* deposit back."

"Fine," I said.

"Fine," he said.

We hired a new property manager, who said we would have to drop our rental price several hundred dollars because finding tenants was getting increasingly difficult. The problem, she suspected, had something to do with the recession (ya think?). It might be a long wait, she warned.

Surrounded by the helpfulness of Homie, a landlord who ferried over a kitchen table on his own bike, Kai's flock of new friends, and the availability of freshly cut pig hocks at 6 a.m., I'd actually, stupidly, begun to breathe again. I'd thought there might be hope we were clawing our way out of our hole. Now I didn't know which financial bubble was going to burst next in my shaken, not-stirred, life.

CHAPTER 11

New Friend on the Block

"Chewing, one eats.
Reflecting, one speaks."
(VIETNAMESE PROVERB)

ALL WE COULD DO NOW was wait for new tenants and hope Robin would get hired soon. Some of Robin's fellow classmates had already secured jobs at elite international schools ($40,000 annually, with health insurance and one paid trip home per year). But such positions weren't the norm. Only those who had been credentialed teachers in their home countries got those jobs.

Robin flashed his CELTA certificate under the noses of language-school directors. With his blond hair, blue eyes, and immaculate American accent, what Vietnamese school director wouldn't hand him a pen and say, "Sign right here, Mr. Visigoth"?

In the meantime, I kept myself occupied conjuring up financial doom-and-gloom scenarios. I forecasted the number of weeks it would take before we'd be living along the Saigon River in a cardboard box. One afternoon, as I was obsessively jabbing figures on my calculator, Robin leaned over my shoulder and punched in a few errant numbers. "Ro-binnnn, quit it!" I yelled. In the past, his playfulness usually helped calm me, but now it only served to make me feel alone in my anxiety. Nothing worried him. His unflappable conviction that the world would always right itself was a constant foil to my credo that no one should ever, *ever* get silly around calculators. "Oh, I give up!" I said to Robin, feeling my knickers start to twist. "If you aren't going to take this situation seriously…." He smiled and patted my overheated head, telling me not to worry because he was *this close* to landing a job.

I needed to get my mind off of the visions of disaster and a perfect diversion was a new neighbor I'd met just the evening before. She had stood in her doorway to greet me when a motorbike taxi driver had mistakenly dropped Kai and me off in front of her shop instead of at our own door. "Hello, Madam, I talk little bit English. You come my house, talk to me?"

"I'd love to," I'd told her. "I'll come by tomorrow morning."

Now it was about 10 a.m., so I put down my calculator and walked across Đoàn Văn Bơ to the pharmacy. I waited for her to finish up with a customer whose eyes bugged out when I went up to the counter. "Moment," she said, holding one finger up. The tiny woman wore a white medical coat and when the customer left, her face radiated with excitement to meet me.

"My name is Bích," she said, extending her hand. "It mean 'jade.' " (Though not pronounced the same as a female dog, the name appears so in print, so I'll call her Jade.)

Her shop, on the ground floor of her two-story house, could have fit into a garden shed, which meant that the second-floor living quarters wouldn't be any bigger. On the street side sat a plexiglass display case that held sun-bleached boxes of overpriced French sundries—La Roche-Posay sunscreen, Sanoflore deodorant, and Oscillococcinum tablets—all under lock and key as if they were valuable jewelry.

Jade was essentially half my size, a fact I wouldn't fully realize until months later when we stood side by side for a photo.

From the start, her large personality and exuberance disguised her stature. She was a graying sixty-year-old Tinker Bell who flitted around the pharmacy and fanned her baby granddaughter, who lay asleep in a hammock.

"You American?" she asked, and without waiting for an answer, said, "I have brother in California. He in San Flan-kis-ko." She bade me sit on one of two plastic stools across from the counter and then disappeared behind a flimsy rayon curtain to fetch a bottle of cold water and two glasses. The curtain was open just enough for me to peek in and see a closet-size kitchen with a pink wall-mounted bathroom sink. Most of my neighbors' kitchens consisted of little more than a garden hose and bucket next to a floor drain. At least Jade had the luxury of standing up to do the dishes.

She came back out, set down our water on the sales counter, and scooted her stool directly in front of mine, so close that our knees touched. She leaned in, her head firmly ensconced in my personal space. Whispering, she said, "I were nurse for American soldiers in war." She paused, searching my face as if she'd been waiting to unload the information on someone for the past thirty-odd years.

Why the whisper? Was the fact that she'd nursed Americans a secret? I didn't know what kind of response she wanted from me, but I figured I should be equally stealthy. I mouthed a "Wow!" And I meant it. Sitting in front of me was an eyewitness to history in a country that had closed itself off to the world for a dozen years after the war, and I wanted to know everything. My inner journalist was itching to pull out a notebook and debrief her. Had she been on the battlefield? Had she ever been injured? Had she been sent to one of the infamous "re-education through labor" camps after the war for being a counterrevolutionary?

But I held myself back. It occurred to me that her saying too much might be dangerous for her. Visiting Homie recently, I'd gently tried to question his dad about life after the war. "It was good," he'd sidestepped, abruptly leaving the room.

The Vietnamese seemed so open and honest that it was hard to remember this was still a Communist country, and open discussion of the war, politics, or human rights was never a good idea. It was no surprise, either, to discover that Vietnamese Big Brother had been checking us out. Shortly after arriving, we'd noticed clicking noises on our phone. (The clicks would stop after six months, when the government spies apparently decided they just weren't that into us.) The week before, our landlord, Vinh, had come over, and after a quick how-are-you chat, asked about my upcoming trip to America. My head flinched backward. What trip? "I'm not going anywhere."

"Oh, sorry, my police friend say you go soon."

Then I remembered: I had been pricing airfares back to Los Angeles on the internet in case some emergency came up. Vinh seemed embarrassed and left.

Another evening, Robin and I had been sitting in the living room watching a documentary on the BBC. The show mentioned the Vietnam War, and suddenly the picture and sound turned off. When I got up to see what was wrong with the TV, Robin said, "Don't bother. It's called censorship."

So the hushed way Jade spoke made the situation all the more intriguing. Even without my prompting, she continued. "I had chance go to America after war. I tell American doctor I want come America with him. But he tell me I only be cleaning woman in United States. I listen his advice. I stay. But I think he very wrong. My life could [have been] better," she said, shaking her head dolefully. Then, poking her forefinger into my leg, she added, "Even cleaning womans in America have life better than me. My brother say so. America very rich. It true, yes?"

She poured water into the two glasses as quickly as she had poured out her anguish. She'd missed an opportunity for a better life and wanted me to know it and acknowledge that fact. I chanted some shallow cliché about how life was difficult in America, too, but quickly realized how insensitive that sounded. I couldn't know the fear and deprivation she and her family, or anyone else in the country, had experienced during and after the war. Nevertheless, I tried to explain.

"Not everyone in America is rich. Some people are very poor, like here, like everywhere in the world. Plus, Americans don't have the strong family bonds that the Vietnamese have. Here, it's as if the whole neighborhood is one big family. I admire that. Americans are more isolated, with six-foot fences and the curtains drawn. It can be lonely."

I watched her expression. She wasn't buying it. My next paltry effort, filled with good intentions, fell even more flat: "And the food in America is not as delicious as it is here." She only managed a little smile.

Jade continued. After the war she'd met her husband, who owned the pharmacy. Since their marriage in 1979, she had lived and worked in this two-story house seven days a week without ever taking a day off except for the three days when she'd given birth. She had two sons and one daughter, all of whom were now grown and out of the house. Jade's husband, a white-haired sixty-five-year-old whom I'd seen once before in the shop, had recently declared himself retired, she told me, leaving her to take care of the business—and the cooking and the babysitting—alone.

And here I thought my life was hard. (That sentiment would repeat itself over and over while living in Vietnam.) Suddenly I had a greater appreciation for Robin, who, even though he was often jobless, would cook and do all the shopping. And he was a great dad to Kai, who truly benefitted from having an at-home parent.

Jade's granddaughter woke up. I finished my water and promised I'd stop by the next day. But first, I bought some Imodium because my stomach had been churning. One can't have too much Imodium in a tropical country. I also wanted to give Jade a little business. She hadn't had any customers since I'd walked in an hour before.

CHAPTER 12

Lose a Toe, Find Five Friends

"Smile, breathe, go slowly."
(THÍCH NHẤT HẠNH, BUDDHIST MONK)

THE NEXT MORNING Homie came to my door. "Hello, Ms. Karin. My mother say you have diarrhea. She hear it from pharmacist."

"Why, yes, Homie," said I, burying my red face in my hands. Wait, isn't a nurse-patient relationship supposed to be confidential?

"My mother say stop eating street food. Cook you own food. She come tomorrow. She teach you."

I loved street food. Why heat up the kitchen when crunchy spring rolls or rice pancakes cooked with onions, bean sprouts, and a sweet sauce were so delicious, so cheap, and so available right in the alley? But I wasn't going to turn down free cooking lessons. I wanted to be able to go home and amaze all my friends and relatives with an authentic Vietnamese meal.

"Fantastic, Homie!" I enthused. "How about if she comes over at ten?"

But the next morning, the cooking lesson had to be canceled.

As I was rushing to stop the bread man to buy hot rolls, I opened the metal sliding door that cages up the front door too quickly, and one of its heavy metal bars came loose and fell with a ghastly clank onto my bare toe. I screamed in pain. When I extricated my foot, the nail on the second toe of my left foot was mangled and nowhere near where it was supposed to be. The metal had also cut a deep gash below the nail; blood and toe stuffing were all over the living room floor, creating a scene reminiscent of *Night of the Living Dead.*

"Robin, quick," I shrieked. "Go get Jade!"

He glanced at the blood, said "Eeew," and ran out. In less than a minute I saw Jade run down the alley clutching a black medical bag, her grandbaby bobbing up and down on her hip. Robin was close behind. Once inside our house, she handed him the baby and quickly got to work bathing my toe in clear liquid solutions that bubbled up and smelled properly medicinal. Then she unwrapped sterile gauze and bandages and wound them carefully around my toe to stanch the bleeding.

By this time, several neighbors had run over and joined in, partly to help, partly to get a closer look inside a foreigner's house. One woman found my mop and washed the floor. Another took Jade's granddaughter from Robin, because the Teutonic giant was terrifying her. Mrs. Dragon came over with a shoebox full of her own homemade medicine stash, green and brown liquids stored in soft-drink bottles and food jars, which were then sealed with a piece of cloth and a rubber band—potions, in other words, that would likely put me in the hospital. Not too gently, Jade waved off Mrs. Dragon and her shoebox. Jade was the neighborhood nurse, after all. Mrs. Dragon looked disappointed, but did have one item Jade didn't bring with her: a roll of toilet paper. Mrs. Dragon dropped it into my lap with a smile, but I protested, knowing it cost her twenty cents. She insisted I keep it.

Children saw the open doors as an invitation to run up the stairs and play with Kai, who wouldn't leave his room because blood freaked him out. Five housewives settled themselves in a circle on the floor of our living room and talked all at once. Jade interpreted their staccato advice for me, some of which sounded like guidance from sixteenth-century Lê Dynasty physicians.

"Don't eat anything yellow," cautioned Mrs. Dragon.

I looked at Jade. "What's wrong with yellow food?"

Jade didn't have a chance to answer because another woman piped in with more food no-nos.

No shellfish or peanuts. And no sticky rice.

"But why? What will happen?"

"Your toe won't heal if you eat those things," Jade said.

That didn't answer my "why" question, so, much later, after everyone had cleared out, I emailed my Chinese-American friend Brenda in Los Angeles with a list of questions. I ended by writing, "Aren't these old wives' tales just adorable?"

She answered, "They are not 'adorable,' they are valid. Asian medicines and regimens have been tested for thousands of years. Don't reject their suggestions."

She went on to explain that yellow is the color of infection, and sticky rice might clog my digestive system, hampering the food's journey down to the toe. She wasn't sure what the deal was with the prohibition against shellfish and peanuts. For good measure, she added, "In case you injure your head, eat soup with cow's or sheep's brain. The soup is doubly advantageous. It will also make you more intelligent." (Hadn't anyone noticed that cows and sheep aren't particularly smart?)

I put my wounded foot up on a chair in front of the TV, prepared to sit as long as was necessary for the bleeding to stop. I really hoped it would. Without health insurance, I didn't want the expense of a hospital visit.

The news that the foreigner had sustained an injury spread quickly down the alley, and a steady stream of neighbors began stopping to look in the doorway, point at my foot, and shake their heads. Around noon, several whose names I didn't know came in, sat down, and started watching TV with me. We could barely put two words together in each other's language, but it was obvious they loved what I was watching: *Ai Là Triệu Phú?* or *Who Wants to Be a Millionaire?* The top prize: about $7,000. Despite the ubiquitous rhetoric that money doesn't bring happiness, I found out that *Who Wants to Be a Millionaire?* is one of Vietnam's most-watched shows.

The mother of one of Kai's friends brought me a lunch of hot soup (delivered in a plastic bag) and a package of giant, pizza-size rice crackers with black sesame seeds. Kai loved the crackers. Despite the incredible love, soup, companionship, and helpful advice to not eat deadly yellow foods, by nighttime my toe showed no signs of healing.

The next morning it looked considerably worse, so I hobbled to a taxi and went to the emergency room at a District 1 Australian clinic. Three stitches and one less toenail later, I was home with a Western-size doctor receipt in my hand for $300.

My masterful plan to live cheaply suddenly had the trots. Did I actually think I could escape one of the most universally acknowledged laws of finance? We all know it. The moment you've paid off your bills and finally have some extra money to play with, your freezer spontaneously defrosts and dies. Next month, you tell yourself, you can finally buy those titanium Google glasses with Optical Head-Mounted Display. But a few weeks later, your Little Leaguer slides into second and breaks his bony little arm. That's when you find out your health insurance policy specifically stipulates that injuries suffered in ballparks on Saturday afternoons are under the extreme-sports clause and, thus, not covered. So, here is a question for the cosmos: Is it ever possible to get ahead? Legally, I mean.

If Vietnam wasn't going to be the sanctuary of cheap living I'd envisioned, then no place would be. I would need to rethink my relationship to money. It was time to play the lottery.

CHAPTER 13

The Ladies Who Lunch

"Elephant knows elephant,
horse knows horse."
(VIETNAMESE PROVERB)

BEFORE I'D GIMPED OUT of the clinic that day, the doctor and I had been talking about adjusting to life in Vietnam. He'd been in the country eighteen months and said his kids loved their international school and his wife liked all the opportunities for shopping. He'd suggested that I connect with an expatriates' club called the International Ladies of Vietnam, a gaggy, anachronistic moniker.

"The ladies are a good resource for foreigners," he said. "They can help you find the best lacquerware furniture, antiques, tailors for your husband's suits, and European-trained hairdressers."

I nodded and smiled. *Why yes,* I thought. *That's what's missing in my life: thickly shellacked furniture and expensive suits.*

Nonetheless, when I returned to Đoàn Văn Bơ Street, I lost no time in looking up their website. The doctor had mentioned that, through friendships within the group, I might find an English-speaking playmate for Kai. That alone would be worth making contact.

The ladies' Thursday-morning coffee gatherings, the website said, were held at the five-star Rex Hotel in District 1. So the following Thursday, I conscripted Robin into taking Kai to the zoo, while I waved a dollar (fifty cents more than the going rate) in front of Dragon Man to take me to the Rex on his motorbike.

The French-colonial Rex had been built in 1927 as a Citroën auto showroom and garage, converted to a hotel in 1959, and renovated in 2008 with dark woods, lush Oriental carpets, and shiny white-marble staircases. The hotel was palatial, and gloriously air-conditioned. Beautiful young women with long black hair wearing traditional *áo dàis* of red or cobalt blue stood smiling by doors and staircases throughout the hotel, their sole purpose apparently being to enhance the décor like pieces of expensive furniture.

I followed signs to the Tea Garden room for the ILV meeting. Slightly windblown, helmet in hand, I quickly picked particulate matter out of my teeth before I reached the sign-in table.

"Hi, this is my first time here," I said, standing in front of a woman who had a notebook of names and countries.

"Well, good on ya then!" she said in a thick Aussie accent that made every sentence sound like a question, if you know what I mean? Her name tag read: "Shirley/Australia." "*Eeeeff ya* wish to join," she continued, "*meeembership eees tweeenty* US dollars *pah yeeeeah*? And each weekly meeting *eees* five dollars? That covers the costs of *refreeeshments?*"

Refreeeshments? I'd just eaten breakfast. But I pulled out 500,000 Vietnamese *đồng*, made myself a name tag, and walked into a noisy roomful of women. Most of them were wearing flouncy dresses, high heels, and enough heavy jewelry to put them at risk of throwing out their backs. Clearly they hadn't arrived here perched precariously on the back of a motorbike. I looked down at my plain white blouse and rice-paddy pants, a gauzy black pair that my sister Loriann had sewn for me just before we'd moved to Vietnam. The lightweight fabric had been on sale for a dollar a yard, and she had guaranteed the pants wouldn't stick to my thighs no matter how oppressive the humidity. The pants were terrifically comfortable. As for jewelry, Homie had warned me not to wear any. Westerners were targets for drive-by motorbike thieves, who had been known to rip a necklace or wristwatch off of a tourist, knocking her or him down in the process.

I looked around the pretty room with its honey-colored wood paneling, bright upholstery, and Asian wall art. Tables of four and eight were arranged in half circles facing a screen for a PowerPoint presentation titled, "Stages of Cultural Adaptation."

I claimed a seat by setting my helmet on a chair at one of the larger tables. A couple of friendly women from Canada on the end of my table greeted me, and then I joined the line at the buffet tables. Oh goody, I thought as I picked up a small plate and shiny fork. Not one gummy cassava patty or bowl of sweet green-bean soup anywhere. Though I enjoyed Vietnamese desserts, I hadn't realized how much I'd been craving decadent Western sweets.

In glorious, gluttonous splendor lay dainty cakes, cookies dipped in chocolate, tiny ramekins of *crème brûlée,* sliced fruits, and hot tea on two flower-bedecked tables. My food hoarding instinct kicked in (probably a latent reaction to my job loss, but let's not waste time getting analytical here). I wasn't terribly hungry, but for five bucks I was determined to choke down at least two of everything, and then wrap up some cookies in a napkin and stuff them in my bag for Kai.

"*Leeesen* up, girls?" another Aussie woman announced. She paused to wait for the chatter to settle. "Don't *forgeet* to order your *tee-keets* for the Christmas dinner-dance? *Thees yee-ah* it will be held the fifth of *Deceembah* at the Intercontinental Hotel? The cost is one hundred *feevty* dollars per couple? Last year, you may *remeember*, we sold out fast? So be sure to see Doreen to buy your *tee-keets* before you leave today?" Doreen, a large woman in a floral chiffon tunic, long skirt, and a bulbous Wilma Flintstone necklace, stood up, yoo-hooed, and waved tickets in the air. Several women ran up and stood in line for *tee-keets.*

I popped a pastry into my mouth, stacked several more atop my plate, and headed back to my table, which was now fully occupied. I pretended not to notice that the Canadian women were staring wide-eyed at my ridiculously full plate. Astrid from Germany, who was to my right, looked up as I introduced myself. She had been in Vietnam for two years with her husband, an executive with Bosch, she informed me. To my left was Ingrid from Switzerland, well-coiffed with thick makeup and a bracelet chockablock with silver charms. The dangling pieces nearly knocked over my teacup when she reached across to shake my hand. Her husband was an engineer for an oil company.

The room was too loud to converse with anyone else at the table. I tried to fit in by showing off my mostly fluent German, which duly impressed Astrid and Ingrid, but after a few niceties they seemed to want to talk with each other and both perched over my plate to do so. Politely, I leaned back in my chair so they wouldn't have to strain their necks around my bulging, cookie-stuffed cheeks. As they discussed flying two hours to Bangkok for a weekend shopping trip, I managed to reach my plate with my fork and stab bites of cake out from under their chins.

Feeling slighted, I finished my plate and excused myself to wander around the room and eavesdrop on other conversations. As I walked away, I looked back just as Ingrid slid over into my chair and moved my belongings onto her seat.

I read countries on name tags: Singapore, New Zealand, Ireland, Canada. Strangely, the USA was underrepresented. When I finally spotted a compatriot, I went up to her and introduced myself. Kricket seemed enthralled with her foreign tablemates and was not nearly as excited to meet a fellow American as I was to meet her. It quickly became apparent that Kricket had the personality of a lawn dart. Still, I managed to get a little information out of her. She was a recent transplant to Vietnam, too. Her husband had been sent here by Nike on a four-year contract. *Cool*, I thought. *Maybe we'll become best buddies and I can get a great discount on running shoes.* But despite my oozing charm, our friendship was not to be. *Her loss,* I thought to myself. As I wound my way around tables back to my seat, the chairwoman of ILV stood at the podium to introduce the guest speaker, a psychologist from England.

"Good morning, ladies," the shrink began. "I'm sure you've all experienced some emotional ambivalence about leaving your home countries. Today I want to talk about the adaptive stages an expat goes through. We'll talk about each stage, and then I'll take questions."

Hotel staffers dimmed the lights, and up came the first slide. Listed on the screen were:

1) Culture shock
2) Loneliness
3) Homesickness
4) Acceptance

All that was missing was "denial," à la Elisabeth Kübler-Ross's stages of grief. From what I had gathered by eavesdropping over the previous hour, most of the other women were here because their husbands had been sent to Vietnam by large corporations that gave housing allowances of $3,000 to $6,000 a month in wealthy District 2, which lay outside the city center and across the Saigon River. Conversations had circled around their lives within gated compounds with green lawns, swimming pools, international schools for the kids, personal drivers, and daily maid service. They talked about silent auctions for spa treatments and resort vacations with minimum bids equal to my last year's income. They planned charity dinners, tennis matches, and bridge tournaments.

So with each adaptive stage the psychologist discussed, I grew more cynical. How hard could it be to adapt to riding around in one of the leather-seated, air-conditioned Land Rovers that I'd seen lining the curb as I'd entered the hotel? This was obviously the wrong social group for me. How could I ever relate to these women? Our life experiences were polar opposites.

The speaker finished her slides. Up came the lights.

"Okay, what are some of the issues you have to deal with daily that you don't have in your home countries?" asked the psychologist.

Someone's hand shot up. She yelled out, "The language barrier!"

"Good example," the psychologist said in a syrupy I-hear-you voice. "It's stressful, isn't it, ladies, when you want hot milk for your tea and the waiter brings cold because he didn't understand you?"

I looked around the room for a brick wall I could bang my head on. While the Q&A session continued, I got up and walked over to the chairwoman, who sat against the wall by the door to welcome any latecomers (and to keep out the riffraff). I quietly asked if she knew of any schools that took special-ed kids.

She looked perplexed. "Oh, my," she said, putting her hand to her heart. "I don't think *any* do."

"You mean, of the some 50,000 expats in Ho Chi Minh City, not one of them has a kid with developmental issues?"

"Maybe they just leave them in their home countries."

I don't think she heard how insensitive her comment sounded, because she waved her hand toward a table, and said, "Brochures for all of the international schools are over there. You can call and ask them."

I tiptoed back to my table to get my helmet, waved goodbye to my tablemates, grabbed a few more cookies, and slipped out into the muggy, yellow air and the noisy streets clutching brochures that showed rapturously happy, uniformed kids walking arm-in-arm across campuses that featured swimming pools and tennis courts. Out on the street, a woman with lottery tickets walked by. I bought one and then hailed a motorbike taxi driver.

As I rode back home, I wondered what it would be like to be pampered and cared for by a large corporation. How would it feel to let go of money worries? How many good-karma points would it take to secure a corporate expense account? I wasn't asking for much. Just a power generator for blackout days. When the city shut off District 2's electricity, the women I'd just met had only to flip a switch to keep the A/C on. Not one drop of sweat was spilled.

Back in the alley, Homie and Mrs. Dragon were sitting in chairs in her TV-Tray Café drinking iced coffee. Mrs. Dragon was holding her four-month-old grandson, Hoa. I paid the driver and plopped down in a chair next to Homie.

"Ms. Karin, you look so beautiful!" he said. "You dress up," he said with a wink. "Where you go?"

"To this stupid social club for foreign women."

"You meet new foreigner friend?" Homie asked.

"God knows I tried," I answered with a long, low sigh.

Mrs. Dragon set Baby Hoa in my lap while she went inside to stir up an iced tea for me. The baby flashed a toothless grin, which lifted my mood a few notches. I uncurled his tiny fingers and put my forefingers into his fists to feel that wonderful reflexive grip babies have just before they pull your finger to their mouths to gnaw on you. Today he was docile. Several days earlier when he had been particularly fussy, I had taken turns with other neighbor women, walking him up and down the alley until he fell asleep. In the absence of strollers and lulling car rides, the arms of neighbor women were superior baby-soothers.

Homie sensed my mood. "Why you sad, Ms. Karin?" he asked, laying his newspaper down on the tray and setting his watery iced-coffee glass on it. "Meeting foreigner women not fun?"

"It was supposed to be a support group for expats," I explained. "But they were all *rich* expats. Their lives are so easy. It makes me mad when they complain about their stupid little problems."

"Oh, so sorry for you, Ms. Karin," he said consolingly. "In America, money so important, is it true? People work many hour for to get more money, is it true?"

I nodded and shifted Baby Hoa to the opposite knee to bounce him gently.

"In Vietnam," Homie continued, "what important most is not how rich you is. What important most is if you a good neighbor. Good neighbor help you, take you doctor, watch you children, pick up for you food at market, let you borrow money."

"That is a much healthier attitude," I said. "But don't you feel jealous when you see a rich person?"

Homie tossed his head back and laughed. "You rich! See? I not jealous of you!"

I smiled. Perhaps I was afraid of my own envy and what it would do to my sense of well-being.

"Ms. Karin, money not make people happy. Happy to me is good friend I share my heart with. Like you!"

I took his hand and gave it a squeeze. "Thank you. You are my good friend, too."

We sat silently for a moment. I exhaled and said, "Listen, it's not like I hate rich people. Some of my best friends are rich. I just don't like how clueless they are about how those without money live. They act so daft."

Homie pulled out the pocket-size Vietnamese-English dictionary he always carried.

"Daft," I said, before he could look up the definition, "means stupid or silly." I usually tried not to speak quickly or use more advanced vocabulary with Homie and Tin, but "daft" was oh-so-appropriate.

Mrs. Dragon handed me a glass of iced tea, took Baby Hoa out of my arms, and began to pace with him in front of her house to get him to sleep.

As I sat sipping tea and perspiring in the heat, it occurred to me that as far removed as I was from the Kardashian lifestyles of the corporate housewives I'd met that morning, I was still more fortunate than most, if not all, of my District 4 neighbors. In their eyes, I was the rich foreigner who could afford to fly on a jet across the ocean, rent a newish four-level house to accommodate only three people, and have a clothes washer and my own laptop computer. I considered with shame how I must sound to people who struggled daily with a completely different level of poverty. Did Homie secretly shake his head and call me a spoiled bitch when I turned my back? I doubted it. I hadn't ever sensed jealousy or contempt coming from him. Nor did I get the feeling that I was just a novelty he could show off to his friends. (Well, he did a little of that, but I didn't mind.) He got a kick out of me because he considered me his foreign friend—not because I was "rich."

Homie and I sipped the last of our drinks and watched the perpetual motion in the alley: noisy motorbikes, squealing kids, chatty neighbors, and vendors who hollered to get people to buy this or that. None of it disturbed Baby Hoa, who now napped like, well, a baby in Mrs. Dragon's arms. I laid my head back over the lip of the chair and let the alley's vibe fill my senses. I felt as if I was being hugged by life here. I discerned a momentary but pleasant flicker of what it felt like to be happy—or at least not so whiny. I handed Homie the lottery ticket. "A gift for you."

Could it be that in the short five weeks since our move, I was already letting go of my belief that a 3,000-square-foot house, a master bath with a double vanity, and a kitchen with marble countertops was the only path to satisfaction? Maybe not. I wasn't going to be able to let go of the materialistic side of the American Dream that fast. But, aside from that morning's little ILV-induced fit of jealousy, I was noticing blips on my radar indicating that slowing down and living with less might be liberating. This happy state of mind would prove to be maddeningly difficult to sustain—my fears and hopes for the remainder of my stay would fluctuate wildly. However, feeling optimistic came easily when an earth-shattering event occurred mere days later: Robin landed a job.

CHAPTER 14

Bagging a Bargain

*"I love to go and see all the things
I am happy without."*
(SOCRATES)

THE FOLLOWING WEEK, Robin came home from a job interview and announced he had been hired at ILA, a large District 1 language school. I experienced a wildly transcendental moment. Birds tweeted over my head; butterflies alighted on my fingertips; choirs of angels sang; and kittens, lots and lots of tiny, meep-meeping kittens, leaped into my arms. *Drop-kick me, Jesus, through the goalposts of heaven. My husband has a job!*

One must understand how monumental a moment Robin's announcement was for me. He hadn't had a real job for eight years. He had worked only a short time at a Hollywood record label as a production assistant before the company caved in from a lack of sales and closed its doors, as had many other labels since the advent of iTunes, internet piracy, file-sharing, and MP3 technology. Robin, concerned that nature abhors a vacuum, rushed in to open his own record label.

Now, with this new job news, I suddenly felt woozy and

light-headed and grabbed onto Robin's arm to steady myself. He grinned. My world was where it was supposed to be, where I'd always wanted it to be: a world in which men work twelve-hour days and women go shopping.

The first few mornings, Robin waved down a motorbike taxi to get to work, but when Landlord Vinh heard Robin had a job (and no, we didn't tell him), he offered Robin his wife's motorbike to rent for forty-five dollars a month. So now we had a Honda Dream, the 100cc model that is practically ubiquitous in Vietnam. Mrs. Dragon sweetly suggested Robin park it in their living room for nine dollars a month. Motorbike theft in Vietnam is an absolute certainty unless the bike is locked up inside the house at night. Without insurance, which most people don't have, a stolen bike could mean the loss of half a year's income. So, up and down each alley, muddy motorbikes morph into indoor chaise lounges for watching evening TV.

We were happy the Dragons were willing to share their space with us. Unlike our above-ground-level house, the Dragons' house was level with the alley, so Robin wouldn't have to heave a 350-pound machine up a plywood ramp. Nine dollars must have meant a lot to Dragon Man's six-member family because Robin received no disgruntled looks from the Dragon children when he wheeled it into a living space the size of most master bedroom closets in a Boca Raton subdivision. Dragon Man's wife, two sons, and daughter (mother of Baby Hoa) could barely stretch out their legs when everyone was at home at the same time, let alone allow a motorbike inside. The upstairs wasn't much bigger. To reach another hundred square feet of bedroom space, they climbed a wooden ladder nailed to the wall to access a loft area where the family slept on mats laid side by side. Dragon Man smiled at me more easily now that we were a new source of cash. And clever Mrs. Dragon would soon find more ways for us to share our money with them.

Robin's monthly take-home pay would be about $1,800—plenty for our new low-cost lifestyle. By adding some private students and my freelance-writing income to the piggy bank, we could accomplish our goal of saving at least $10,000 within a year. Still smacking me upside the head, however, was the worry that our California house continued to sit empty two months after the scalawag cowboys skedaddled. The good news, at least, was that they had dropped their lawsuit and ridden off into the sunset. That was because I capitulated (I shouldn't have, but, like I said, I hate confrontation) and gave most of their security deposit back. Anyway, no new tenants were crawling out from under the recession's rock, even when the property manager dropped the price by $500.

Setting the stage for simple living, I played the part of a tightwad and would second-guess every item in my shopping basket. I followed my neighbors' example. If they didn't have a microwave, I didn't need a microwave. If they didn't have a toaster or a blender, well, I could live without them, too. I could make do with one paring knife and one mixing spoon; one set of sheets for each bed. Kai's chocolate-stained T-shirts became kitchen towels. I marveled at how much stuff I *didn't* need to make a relatively comfortable home. I was starting to see how easy it was to be so used to luxuries that you think they're necessities.

Our only indulgence was running our bedroom wall air conditioner in an effort to cool off the ground floor in the daytime and to keep us from sleeping in sweat-soaked bedding at night. Even with Vinh's earlier warning about the cost of electricity, I couldn't tolerate the heat and refused to turn it off. Plus, I figured utilities would certainly be cheaper than they were in the States. When the meter-reader came by one day and saw the meter's mini-Frisbee-size disc rotating so fast that a dog nearly chased after it, he cupped his hands over his mouth and, with frantic miming and a firm *không* (no), told us to turn off the A/C. My reaction: *Noooo, I'm an American. If I'm forced to step outside of my comfort zone, I'll have to be hospitalized.* A few days later, the meter man handed me the electric bill: $100. I told no one. Naturally, the electric man ratted on us because that same day, one horrified housewife after another came to our door shaking her head and pointing wildly at our meter as if a skull and crossbones were stamped on it. We kept the A/C mostly off the next month and bought more floor fans to set on both sides of the bed. I still bemoaned the heat, but I did cool off slightly when our next electric bill arrived: seventeen dollars.

The Vietnamese are masters at stretching their money, recycling, reusing, or just plain living without. My neighbors figured we needed to know how to live this way, too, and scolded me for throwing out this or that, including rotting, blackened bananas. I set my nightly trash bag out one evening, and Homie's mother spotted the bananas.

Homie translated for his mother: "She say you can eat. They still very good."

I made a face. Mama Hang laughed, slipped into her flip-flops and scurried across the alley to get them. Neighbors dug through my trash bags every evening looking for anything they could reuse or sell. It was embarrassing to have our state secrets splayed out for all to see. I solved the problem by putting all cans, bottles, boxes, and newspapers out on my stairs, free for the taking. Within seconds, the recyclables were gone. Mama Hang asked if I would set the newspapers aside for her. She needed them to make patterns for new clothes.

I was always surprised that my neighbors cared how we spent our money or whether we could squeeze three or four lives out of whatever we bought. Rather than exploiting us for profit, which would have been easy, they were protective. The neighbors knew that roving vendors or shop owners might try to charge me too much because I was a foreigner. Occasionally, Tin or Homie would tell me to hide around the corner while one of them went into a shop and purchased items for me. When the deal was done, I'd show up to pay, infuriating the shop owner, who could have otherwise scored a windfall from a supposedly well-heeled foreigner. My neighbors tried to teach me the art of bargaining at the market, which required overt acts of sulking and righteous disgust. I refused to practice it, however. How much profit could be made on one kilo of water spinach that cost me twenty-four cents? Was it moral for me to negotiate it down to eighteen cents? I couldn't do it.

One day, Jade stepped out of the pharmacy when she saw me on her side of Đoàn Văn Bơ buying four mangoes from a vendor whose basket of fruit was tied to the back of her bicycle. I handed the seller my money and turned to cross the street with my bag. Jade motioned for me to wait there, as she quickly wiggled her way through the traffic. She looked into my bag and then back at me, narrowing her eyes and frowning. "How much you pay for them?"

I hesitated to answer. I could tell she was gearing up for an argument, but I wasn't sure if I would get a tongue lashing for being so gullible, or the vendor would for cheating me. "Um, well, I think about one dollar a kilo."

"*Ối trời ơi!* (OMG!) Give me the bag!"

Jade stomped up to the mango vendor, a dark-skinned, sun-wrinkled woman wearing a mismatched pajama outfit of floral pants and a geometrically patterned top. Her hands bore the scars of someone who had planted rice or picked mangoes all her life. Honestly, I was happy to pay her more than the locals did. I backed away from the two women in case either started throwing punches. Jade spoke sharply to the vendor, then opened the bag and showed her the lousy-looking mangoes I'd just been given. I thought they looked fine, and the price was far better than in America. I felt uncomfortable about Jade making a scene on my behalf, and I became downright mortified when both of them pointed at me during the argument. The vendor raised her voice and refused to refund any money. I leapt back over to Jade's side and whispered, "It's okay. Never mind." I wanted desperately for both of them to quiet down. A crowd was gathering to watch us. Jade ignored me.

She picked up and inspected four bigger mangoes and, when the woman turned her head, grabbed a fifth and stuffed it into the bag. Jade turned to lock arms with me in solidarity and yanked me back to the alley. The vendor shook her fist at us.

Jade sniffed, "That woman is a thief!"

Red-faced, I carried my five jumbo mangoes back home. Homie was sitting at Mrs. Dragons' TV-Tray Café. To my relief, he said nothing about the mango event, though I was certain he had heard the yelling.

"Ms. Karin, look, I buy for you," he said with a sly smile. On the tray were two glasses of iced coffee. He knew I detested coffee; I'd told him many times. Why do people keep bugging you to try something that you are certain is vile? Wearied from one battle, I was reluctant to ready myself for another. But Homie wouldn't listen to me. Vietnamese rarely tolerate the whims of personal tastes. The General Line of the Party states you will drink what the masses drink (whip cracks). Seeing my nose wrinkle, Homie admonished, "You must to try!"

My lips tightened. If I didn't like it, he said, he'd give it to his mother. I looked over at her. She had dropped her sewing and was now watching me intently from across the alley. I had to be polite. In Asia, it's considered rude not to accept a gift, even if it only costs thirty cents. Mrs. Dragon stood over me, smoking a cigarette. She, too, was waiting to see my reaction. I squeezed my eyes shut to steel myself against the bitter taste that I knew would instantly trip my gag reflex. I sipped. I swallowed. I breathed. My face must have registered pleasure because Homie's parents began to cheer.

People say it is the first line of cocaine that hooks you. That's how it was with *cà phê sữa đá,* an elixir of such magical powers that residents of Vietnam's sultry south set glasses of it on home altars as a gift to the gods. Mrs. Dragon made it from thick-as-mud espresso sweetened with condensed milk. Then she added lots and lots of crushed ice and stirred until every piece of ice was coated. It was a liquid drug, and I was instantly addicted. I had no idea caffeine could make one feel so happy. No wonder early buyers of Starbucks stock had become rich. I took back every evil thought I had had about Dragon Man's early morning ice-hammering practice. Tin joined us a few minutes later and taught me to sip *cà phê sữa đá* from a spoon—ever...so...slowly. The beverage was much too rich to gulp down, he said. Several days before, he'd watched in horror as Robin, who hails from the land of autobahns and beer bellies, drank it down like he was on spring break in Fort Lauderdale. Later, Tin and I often had contests to see who could make our coffee last the longest. Tin always won. I hadn't yet learned to quell my American-bred compulsion toward instant gratification. I started ordering *cà phê sữa đá* wherever I went in the city, but none was ever as delicious as Mrs. Dragon's. She must have known her coffee had strange powers over me because within days she exploited my helpless addiction as bait to "borrow" money.

Here's how it happened. A few evenings later, Homie and I were sitting in front of the Dragons' house. Mrs. Dragon popped out, wiped off some dried condensation rings from the TV tray next to us, and set down two glasses of iced coffee. No charge, she said with a quick smile, before going back in her house. Homie's eyes widened. "She never give *me* free," he said, lowering his voice as if she could understand English. A few minutes later she came back out, pulled up a plastic stool, and, leaning toward Homie, whispered her request: Could she have two months' pay in advance for keeping our motorbike in her living room? Only 300,000 *đồng*, or eighteen dollars.

Homie hardly needed to translate. I got the gist. Absolutely, I said, with a generous smile. She shook my hand. I went inside to get the money and handed it to her as discreetly as she had asked for it.

The next morning when Tin came over, he said, "It probably not good idea to give she money. I think her gamble."

"First of all, how did you know?" I asked, before realizing what an inane question it was. The shelf life of secrets on the alley was about 3.4 seconds.

"And secondly, it wasn't a handout," I said dismissively. "I just won't pay her for two months for parking the bike."

But two mornings later, Mrs. Dragon was back. This time she came directly to my doorstep with a glass of iced coffee in her hand. No need for a pesky translator. "My gift to you," she said with her eyes. Oh, and by the way, could I have another *hai tháng* (two months') rent up-front? I've always been a soft touch and nothing brought out that trait more than the smiling Vietnamese, with or without a free glass of coffee in their hands. I consistently tipped waiters too generously, put big bills into the conical straw hats of beggars, and overpaid motorbike taxi drivers. It was the least I could do after my country turned Vietnam to rubble ever so many years ago.

I stood and took the cold glass, pleased that I understood several of Mrs. Dragon's words. Naturally, I gave her the money; her family needed it. I doubted Mrs. Dragon could earn much from her coffee business. Nearly every alley had its own coffee vendor, which meant only immediate neighbors were customers. Dragon Man earned money with his old, rusty cyclo delivering quarter-inch-thick slabs of rubber to sandal-makers, or bricks or bags of concrete to construction sites. He didn't get work every day, though, and when he did, it was only a couple of dollars per delivery. According to Homie, the family also received six dollars per month from the government because they kept their oldest son, who had cerebral palsy, at home rather than send him to an institution. The seventeen-year-old couldn't walk and spent every day scooting around the floor or sitting on a folding chair outside with the customers. His speech was impaired and he had to be spoon-fed. Neighbors said he was born that way because he and his parents had done something bad in their past lives.

Other non-earners in the Dragon household were a chubby ten-year-old boy with whom Kai played occasionally and Baby

Hoa's mother, the Dragons' nineteen-year-old daughter. Though she was married, it was tradition that she live in her parents' home for the first year of the baby's life so they could help her care for the baby. I also think she wasn't too wild about her mother-in-law, but I'm just surmising based on the fact that daughters-in-law in Vietnam are virtual slaves to their husband's mother. And the girl wasn't overly ambitious; she adored TV.

As soon as Mrs. Dragon got her cash, she slipped out quickly, and I joined Homie on his steps. He was reading a newspaper and looked up at me.

"More free coffee, Ms. Karin?" he said with a wink. "How much you give her?"

"Another two months' rent."

Homie shook his head. "She uneducated!"

In a country where education is next to godliness, it was just about the worst insult one could give. Homie taught me an equally inflammatory saying: "I see you live near the market but far from the school." The statement is so contentious that if you say that to someone's face you are likely to disappear in the night—sans flip-flops.

"In America, bad parents put children in washing machine and kill them—or leave them out in the cold," Homie said.

"What?! Where in the world did you hear that?"

"Here," he said, rattling the paper. "I read it in newspaper *Viet Nam*. It true," he stated with a look that said, how dare you question newspaper content. "You hear 'bout that?"

I sipped another spoonful of coffee. "No, that is not true. Well, okay, maybe one or two kids a year get laundered, but generally, no."

"Well, American preh-ah (press) prolly don't tell you."

"Homie, don't forget to pronounce the 's.' The word is 'pressssss.'" It really stumped me why ending a word with an "s" sound was so difficult for most Vietnamese. They could say "s" in the middle of a word just fine.

"Okay," I said, "say 'nice...sss.' "

"Nigh...sss."

"Please...sss."

"Plea...sss."

Homie pointed to his butt and said "Ass...sss."

Silly boy. I looked at my watch and jumped up. I was late for my next daily task, one that I was already getting nervous about: home-schooling Kai. I gave Homie a pat on his head and headed inside.

CHAPTER 15

Homeschooling Kai

"For Extremely Difficult Children"
(ON A CHARITY DONATION BOX AT THE AIRPORT)

HOMESCHOOL WAS SUPPOSED TO START at 9 a.m. every day so Kai would learn the discipline of adhering to a schedule. We worked on assignments in increments of forty-five minutes on task, then fifteen minutes off task, until noon. Then lunch and playtime with his little neighbor mates followed by one more hour of dedicated academics. However, with Kai's penchant for nonstop chatter, we weren't getting very far in his workbooks.

When some US friends and relatives worried aloud about what kind of education Kai was getting in Vietnam, I defensively painted a glorious picture of his instruction outside the confining walls of a classroom, using such terms as "expansive worldview," "intimate cultural knowledge," and "real-life" learning. I understood their concern, though. Taking a special-needs kid out of school for a year did appear dunderheaded, if not illegal. I hadn't signed up for any official, government-approved homeschooling program. It made me glad we were in Vietnam so nobody could call the Department of Children's Services and turn us in on truancy charges.

After many weeks of trying to homeschool Kai, I realized his learning issues were a bigger challenge than I had anticipated. I don't know what made me think that by moving to Vietnam I'd miraculously turn into a homeschooling supermom who could keep Kai's attention rapt. During the few times I'd sat with him to do his homework in the US, my anger and impatience shocked me because he just…wouldn't…pay…attention (fist slams table). I blamed this frustration on my being tired after a long day in the office. But now I had plenty of time, yet my irritability was just as raw.

Via email, Kai's schoolteacher gave me tips for working with him, but after many weeks, he wasn't learning anything from me. Day after day, I could no more channel his scattered thoughts than I could spoon dark-matter particles into a Tupperware container. Kai's method of getting from Point A to Point B was via C, D, E, and F. Nor could I quiet his motor-mouth: He talked all…day…long. The constant chatter was causing me to grind my teeth down to little white nubs.

"I know why people die," he said one morning while I was reading him a book about forest animals.

"Why?"

"They need a break."

I moved the book closer to him.

"Okay, Kai, pay attention." I read aloud, "The grizzly bear hibernates in the wint—"

He'd already stopped looking at the book. A mouse-size cockroach under the TV stand distracted him. The Kafkaesque creature was belly up, struggling to right itself.

"Why didn't God make a leg on the back of a cockroach so when it gets stuck on its back it can use the extra leg to flip over?"

"The cockroach is probably lying there wondering the same thing. Kai, are you going to listen to this book or not?"

"I wish cockroaches weren't afraid of people. I wish they would just hold still so I can smash them."

I nodded and then started again, this time louder. "The bear's heavy coat of fur keeps it wa—"

"What do you like better, bears or dogs?"

"Bears," I answered. "Dogs bark too much."

"If I were a dog and I barked too much, would you take me to the dog pound?"

I looked up at the ceiling and heaved a heavy sigh. *The dog pound. Hmmm.*

"Okay, break time," I announced. Though his chatter was occasionally insightful, and sometimes hilarious, it was also exhausting. I felt depleted, desperate. Even if it meant spending money already earmarked for such frivolities as food and rent, I needed help. I rationalized that getting a tutor was in Kai's best interest. After all, wouldn't that be a whole lot nicer than me tossing him over the balcony? I ran upstairs to my computer to look at an expat services website. One classified ad offered English-speaking university students for part-time babysitting or house cleaning at five dollars per hour. Pretty expensive for Vietnam, but like I said, I was desperate. Tutoring a special-ed kid wasn't on their list of services, but I figured I could ask them to at least *try*. At least it would give me three hours a day to do some freelance writing or study Vietnamese. I called and asked for someone to start right away.

Two days later, a senior sociology major from Ho Chi Minh University arrived right on time at 2 p.m. Her name was Lan.

"Did the agency tell you I have an eight-year-old son who is hyperactive and developmentally delayed?" She hadn't even stepped into the house when I hurled this question at her. I was pretty sure no one had warned her because she was insanely overdressed for the job. From head to toe, she was combed, curled, belted, and pressed into a white taffeta blouse with a frilly front, a tight black pencil skirt with a black patent leather cinch, a fake pearl necklace and matching dangly earrings, and toothpick-thin black stilettos. No way would she be able to sit on the floor and play with Kai in a skirt that looked shrink-wrapped to her body. Her shoulder-length hair was neatly curled with long bangs she swept off to the side but which kept falling back down into her eye. She looked at me with one eye. I had to fight off the urge to grab a barrette or pull out a pair of scissors.

"Yes, my boss told me about your son," she said with a nervous squeak in her voice. She cleared her throat and took off her shoes, which lowered her height to below my chin. "I love to work with children. I have many nieces and nephews. They also don't like doing their homework."

"Well, it's a little more complicated than 'not liking' homework," I clarified.

I'd read that ADHD and Autism Spectrum Disorder weren't terms in anyone's vocabulary in Vietnam. Children like Kai simply didn't go to school. I needed a way to discuss his learning issues in simpler English. I told Lan that Kai's birth mother was addicted to vodka when she was pregnant and because of that and severe malnutrition during his first eighteen months of life, his brain didn't work normally. I explained to her that sitting still was nearly impossible for him and that she would need to give him a lot of exercise breaks between math problems and reading workbooks.

Lan seemed unfazed. Good, I thought. She's probably dealt with this before. But a bit later in the conversation it became clear to me that "unfazed" was actually "didn't understand." Her speaking skills, as it turned out, were far superior to her comprehension of English. We had the following conversation:

"How would you like me to pay you?"

"Yes."

"I mean, do you want it weekly or once a month?"

"Yes."

"Well, which would you prefer?"

"Yes."

Kai hopped and jumped noisily down the stairs to meet her. She went to him and bent down on one knee to make eye contact with him. Impressive. She didn't topple over in her tight skirt. Lan then stood up and put her arm around his shoulder as they walked to the staircase. She stroked his head and talked soothingly to him. Lan wasn't unique in her immediate touchy-feely manner. Strangers reached out to touch our hands and arms and Kai's hair frequently. Vietnamese women often hold hands or lock arms while walking down the street. Men, especially young boys and teens, walk with their arms draped around each other's shoulders. Men even sometimes hold hands with one another. I think this human touching is one of Vietnam's most endearing social mores. But a public display of affection between two people of the opposite sex? No. Here, romantic love is steered hands-free.

After showing Lan the workbooks and lesson plans, Kai's math tools, and writing supplies, I left them alone and went down to my room to read, where I promptly fell…not exactly asleep—I'd say more like into a coma. When I came to about twenty minutes later, I realized I couldn't hear any sounds coming from Kai's room. Normally he liked to test the mettle of all new teachers by defiant behavior, but I wasn't hearing his usual jumping, shouting, and throwing.

After ten more minutes, I couldn't stand it anymore. Something was wrong. Something was very wrong. Had he been kidnapped?

No.

It's my contention that anyone who kidnapped Kai would return him soon after with a big sign: *"Puh-leeze, take him back. He won't shut up!"* I cracked the door open and peeked in. Kai was bent over his writing table. Lan was telling him in hushed tones to copy the math problems. He looked up and saw me.

"Hi, Mom!"

Not wanting to break their focus, I waved at them without speaking and tiptoed back out. Whether she knew it or not, Lan's instinct for teaching him was that of a child-whisperer. For most people, including Robin and me, to elicit eye contact or keep Kai's attention, the natural tendency is to want to sound an air horn or bang pots and pans together. But each time I peeked in, Lan was guiding him through his tasks without raising her voice. Even the physical exercises she did with him looked more like some slow-motion celestial dance than the American-style boot-camp calisthenics he was used to. The result was that within a few days, Kai was finally getting through some of his workbooks. Plus, he adored her and couldn't wait for her to come in the afternoon. It was a huge relief that he was getting some academic basics, and I was getting some quiet time.

One afternoon, as Lan worked with Kai upstairs and I sat before my computer, a thought crossed my mind: *I wonder if she'd agree to move in?*

CHAPTER 16

The Bliss of Silence

"You catch fish with two hands."
(VIETNAMESE PROVERB: MAKE UP YOUR MIND)

ONCE LAN WAS KEEPING KAI OCCUPIED for three hours a day, four afternoons a week, I decided to dedicate the first hour of my free time to studying Vietnamese and the second two hours to fulfilling my dream of writing a bestselling novel. Never having had any uninterrupted moments since college—beyond prolonged bathroom breaks—I wondered what this newfound me-time would feel like. I imagined it was akin to walking hand in hand with Johnny Depp on a secluded Caribbean beach (he's in pirate costume, of course) with a large jar of Nutella and two spoons.

I was determined to use this windfall of time productively. I would become a focused, disciplined writing warrior, my words spilling forth unimpeded, saturating every page. I sat down one afternoon at the computer, took a deep cleansing breath and typed "Chapter 1." *Man, how heady is this? I'm going to write a novel. I'm really going to do this!*

An hour and a half later, I'd picked the calluses off the bottoms of both big toes, written three emails to my mom, run downstairs to the bathroom twice, refilled my water glass three times, and stopped once to peek in at Lan and Kai hunched over a book. The only progress I'd made on the book was changing "Chapter 1" to "CHAPTER 1" after I decided capital letters would enhance the excitement and pull in more readers.

To me, writing is as easy and as natural as gouging out my eyeballs with a melon baller. It takes an interminable amount of time to settle myself and get started. I'm like a dog readying itself for a nap, circling, pawing the blankets, rolling and twisting and grunting. It wasn't until two years later that I discovered that if I started reading random pages in books by some of my favorite authors— Rosemary Mahoney, Bill Bryson, Elizabeth Gilbert, Heather King, and J. Maarten Troost—then the cramps in my head would soften and I could get some words out. Then, if no one interrupted me further, I'd finally quiet myself long enough to write. But if intruded upon, the process would have to start all over again.

In a Vietnamese neighborhood, there are no long stretches of uninterrupted time—even for the locals. I frequently wondered if it would be kosher to just hire someone in place of me to sit and chat with my neighbors. On one of my forays to the ground floor to get more water, it didn't surprise me when a stranger showed up. I noticed a thin-haired sixtyish-year-old man standing in front of our house. Attached to his hip was a little girl, about two years old. From my kitchen, I accidentally made eye contact with him, and before I could pretend I hadn't seen him, he raised his hand and gestured for me to come out. I'd never seen him before, but we were getting used to random neighbors rapping on our window just to wave or families shoving their nervous children up to the front door, coaxing them to say something to us in English.

Though it was a muggy ninety-five degrees outside, he was wearing a sweater, a zippered hoodie, and baggy long pants. Add a shopping cart to that picture and he'd be a homeless man in Phoenix.

"I speak French," he said—in English. "Do you speak French?"

I told him no but that my husband was fluent. "He'll be back tonight at seven."

He took a seat on our stairs as if he planned to wait. It was 4 p.m. I felt obliged, at least, to ask his name (which I've since forgotten) and chit chat a bit. He set the little girl down to play on the steps and began telling me his story. He was an army officer for South Vietnam and had learned some English from the American soldiers. But his French was more fluent because school was conducted in French when they were under occupation. Anyway, after the American War, his status of "enemy of the people" didn't further his career goals. In fact, he couldn't get a job; no one was allowed to hire him. So he became the neighborhood babysitter for the next thirty-three years, and the tot who now moved on and off his lap was one of his current charges.

"So that's not your granddaughter? I just assumed…."

"No, I have no children. My wife had to work. No time for children. No money for children."

He was gentle with the little girl, occasionally brushing an errant hair away from her face. He watched her six days a week from 7 a.m. to 7 p.m. while her parents worked. They paid him about thirty dollars per month.

"Do you like the Communists?" he asked as casually as if he were asking, "Should I buy pink or blue towels for my bathroom?"

"Well, I…" I hesitated because of the slight risk that this was a trick question. If he were a government informant, the wrong answer could ruin all chances of getting my visa extended beyond three months. Robin's visa was good for a year because he was a teacher, but I was on a tourist's visa, which had to be renewed. So I answered, "Um, I guess I wouldn't vote for them."

He shook his head and looked down at his hands, which hung heavily with bitterness. This unassuming man looked too sad to be a spy. I'm sure he felt emasculated in this male-centric country, his wife being the breadwinner and all. I felt sorry for him, but after thirty more minutes of small talk, I was restless and feeling anxious that my quiet time was being consumed. One more hour and my fluffy-headed blond boy would be released from his studies and would glom onto me once again like a tick. I excused myself politely and invited Mr. French to come back at seven. To my relief, he stood up, picked up the toddler, and left.

I'd barely reached the top floor when I heard Homie calling me from the alley. I looked over the balcony and saw him smiling up at me. Tin was with him, too. "Come down, Ms. Karin. Time to learn cooking. My mother, she come now."

I guess I had no choice. There they were, noses pressed to the glass. Mama Hang had a basket of vegetables. Her sister Hanh, Tin's mom, stood next to her, smiling. I loved their love, their generosity, their pure joy at sharing their culture and talents. But it also baffled me that they assumed I had no other plans at that moment.

The four of them came in, went directly to the kitchen and plopped down on the floor in a circle. Homie and Tin set out chopping boards, sharp knives, and plastic baskets. Mama Hang and Hanh pulled out a fistful of cilantro to chop. I joined them on the floor, sitting cross-legged. Tin and I worked on the morning glory leaves. He showed me which part of the stems and leaves to keep and which to throw away. Tin methodically and oh-so-slowly picked the leaves with the devotion of a monk fingering his prayer beads. I was soon feeling hot, prickly, and a bit edgy. *At this pace, we're going to be here all night.*

"Can't we just chop off the stems and be done with it?" I asked.

Tin stopped, looked at me, and raised his eyebrows up to his hairline.

"Not *every* leaf is delicious!"

How often I'd watched housewives sitting on porches, picking, shelling, or snapping green beans, morning glory leaves, cilantro, mint, or Chinese broccoli. Preparing vegetables was a daily activity and it gave the women a chance to sit on their steps and chat with each other across the alley. None was in a hurry to finish the task.

It wasn't easy for me to slow down, nor did I see any value in doing so. Over the months I'd noticed that my neighbors either worked or they slept. No one took part in leisure activities other than karaoke. Kids didn't have after-school sports or music lessons. Nobody was painting or doing crafts. No one went to the theater, and few read books or magazines (though everyone read the newspaper). The reason was sadly obvious. Who had extra money for a guitar? Who could afford art supplies? Where was the money for a theatrical performance or to buy a racket and balls to play tennis? Playwright Moss Hart, who grew up very poor, wrote in his autobiography, *Act One*, that the worst aspect of poverty was boredom.

My neighbors didn't need to learn to slow down. However, because life was slow, people had time to focus on what was most important—family, community, and the perfect leaf to make the most delicious food.

I took a deep breath and willed myself to chill out. "What are we cooking this afternoon?"

"Spring rolls and water spinach with garlic," Homie said.

Kai finished his tutoring session with Lan and I heard them coming down the stairs. Lan was delighted to see I was learning how to prepare Vietnamese cuisine. Kai noticed a small black plastic bag on the counter moving—walking away, actually. He caught the bag before it took a leap onto the floor. I jumped up. "What is in that bag?"

Homie laughed. "Shrimp." He opened the bag and poured out six large shrimp, very much alive, their many legs trying to gain traction in the air and their antennae flailing wildly. If ever there was a country that could incentivize you to write out a very large check to PETA, this was it. Homie dropped them into a pot of boiling water and they instantly turned pink. "These are for the spring rolls. Very fresh."

In my tiny, one-person kitchen, the five of us put out the most amazing meal: rice; spring rolls with basil, shrimp, and noodles; peanut dipping sauce; and a garlic-infused bowl of gorgeous, emerald green water spinach. The cooking lesson was fun and sat-isfying, but two years later I would forget the recipes. What stuck with me was the sense of community, friendship, and warmth with no expectation of anything in return.

CHAPTER 17

How Do You Say...?

"Large Head, Stupid Anyway."
(VIETNAMESE PROVERB)

I was feeling more desperate to be conversant with my neighbors, first to assuage my growing feelings of isolation (despite all the attention laid on me as the neighborhood curiosity) and second to get beyond the absurdly simple conversations we were having. How would I get richer, deeper friendships on a vocabulary of fifty words? More pertinent, I wanted to eavesdrop on their gossip (and no one is better at gossip than the Vietnamese) because I have a primal need to know everything about everybody at every moment, particularly—*especially*—when it's none of my business. Come to think of it, it *is* my business. I didn't go into journalism to leave people's private lives private. Besides, I had an incredible offer from Mrs. Dragon that piqued my resolve to study harder. She said she'd tell me all about her life once I became fluent. Her background was much too private, she said, to go through Homie's translations.

Until now, Tin and I had been meeting erratically for Vietnamese lessons, and Homie had only been teaching me cuss words or silly sentences ("I want to pee," "I want to poop," and "Get lost!"), which had the neighbors rolling when I haltingly repeated them. Tin and I agreed to meet Monday and Wednesday afternoons, and Saturday mornings after Robin left to teach his youngest students. Sweet, generous Tin wanted no money for teaching me, but after much coaxing he agreed to two dollars per lesson.

On that first Saturday morning, about ten minutes before Tin was due to arrive, Robin stood by the open door ready to leave for work. He shouted up to us, "Hey, you guys, hurry down, I'm late. Give me a kiss goodbye!" Kai ran and jumped up into his father's arms, giving him a tight hug and generous kiss on the cheek. I glanced out into the alley, where the neighbors stood giggling at this TV-commercial moment. When Kai hopped down, Robin grabbed me suddenly and leaned me over backward so far and so fast that I flailed and clawed at his neck for fear of slamming to the floor. To my chagrin, he gave me a long, drawn-out kiss. I squirmed and managed to suck in enough oxygen through the side of my mouth to say, "Robin, you're going to be late!" He pulled me back upright, and I felt the blood from my head pool rapidly into my cheeks.

Robin's eyes twinkled and he gave me a hug. "Oh, yeah, that was delicious!"

What bemused and/or horrified reaction this vaudevillian moment must have elicited from my neighbors, I don't know, because I wouldn't—couldn't—look over at them. I immediately shut the door.

Because privacy in Vietnam is hardly sacrosanct, and because our neighbors lived so close, Robin's effusive behavior meant I needed to be more vigilant about keeping the curtains closed. From now on, if one of us were going to be anywhere near the front windows, we needed to A) look busy, B) smile, and C) keep our hands off each other. Robin the Hun moved through life hurtling etiquette against the wall to make way for the real world, with all its burps, farts, temper tantrums, pops of silliness, and explosions of laughter. It didn't matter who was watching or where we were. A few years back, in the middle of a pin-drop-silent meditation class, Robin decided that it was a good time to stretch and twist his torso in an attempt to get his back to crack. He followed it by throwing his head back and vocalizing a yawn, thus interrupting everyone's effort to find his/her happy place. I'd glanced over at the always-blissful Guru Dev, our teacher, who was glaring at him and smoldering underneath her white turban. We never went back again. At home, safely behind closed doors, however, I could relax and enjoy Robin's antics and wacky humor. He always cheered me up. And I needed cheering up often.

Still feeling discombobulated after shutting the door, I grabbed the Ludicrously Large Padlock, threaded it through the hasp and staple (I had to look this up) from the inside, and inexplicably squeezed it into the locked position, a subliminal "Quick, hide!" reflex.

Tin arrived minutes later and plastered his face against the window, cupping his hands to see in. I headed for the door but suddenly realized I had no idea where the key for the Ludicrously Large Padlock was. Did Robin take the ring of keys with him? I looked hastily around the room before motioning for Tin to wait. He nodded and sat down on the doorstep. After a quick look under newspapers, on countertops, in baskets, and in the trash can, I hurried upward, taking the stairs two at a time to Kai's room to ask him. He usually knew where things were located because he was invariably the one who took them.

"Kai, where are the keys?"

"Keys?" he repeated, without looking up from his Legos.

"Yes, come on, hurry up. Tin is at the door."

"Tin? Who's Tin?"

"It doesn't matter, Kai, get up! I need the keys." The "H" in his diagnosis of ADHD, which stands for hyperactivity, had inexplicably shut down. He could hardly be motivated to wiggle a toe.

"GET. UP!"

Without lifting his head he said, "I don't have the keys."

Sweat was running down my forehead and into my eyes, blurring and stinging them. *Why, oh, why am I such a nimrod?* And then, a visual flash: I remembered seeing the keys on the floor on Robin's side of the bed.

Back at the door with the jumble of keys in hand, I wiggled them one by one into the Ludicrously Large Padlock. Why did Vinh give us more keys than we had locks or doors? By the sixth key, it crossed my mind that if there had been a fire, Kai and I would be pretty crispy right about then. Metal bars were welded onto every window. The only escape was the front door, which at this minute I couldn't get open. (Note to self: Label the keys.) The sixth key was the winner. Tin smiled as he entered, removed his flip-flops, and politely stood just inside. I motioned him over to the kitchen table.

"Sorry," I said.

"*Eee-ah* okay," Tin said, batting away my apology. We sat down and I opened up my notebook, ready for a regimen of drills. I was excited. This would be easy. With more frequent lessons and discipline, I'd be fluent in six months. After all, I had the benefit of simply stepping outside my door to practice with the natives anytime I wanted.

Vietnamese has a Latin alphabet, a fact that triggered a peculiar reflex whenever I picked up my textbook with the portrait of French Jesuit Alexandre de Rhodes on the cover: I genuflected. This brilliant missionary, who thought the Vietnamese language resembled the "singing of birds," helped develop the present Vietnamese alphabet and in 1651 wrote the first Portuguese-Latin-Vietnamese dictionary, titled *Fun with Diacritical Marks*. Then, when the French began to colonize Indochina in the nineteenth century, they passed a law making the ABCs the official script of Vietnam. No more cat-scratch Chinese characters, thousands of which hapless children in China must memorize in order to read the *Workers' Daily*. Another wondrous feature of Vietnamese is that the grammar is fairly simple—no tenses to alter the word, no funny plural forms, no adjective endings, no irregular verbs. If I could master German grammar with its infamously hellish syntax (one perk of being married to a descendant of the Hanseatic League has been all the free German lessons), Vietnamese grammar would be just about effortless.

We sat at the kitchen table and began with sentences so freakishly difficult to pronounce, I began to wonder if I had a brain-eating amoeba. Tin was methodical, patient, and kind, but after about twenty minutes, I began to see my efforts would have to become Herculean to succeed. When Tin took a bathroom break, I wearily dropped my chin into my hands and began to think about the first time I'd met Tin. I felt I'd known him all my life. But he also had a deep sadness about him that I wanted to fix, because God knows how much I love to fix people. When he returned to the table, I told him how fortunate I felt that he lived across from me.

"No, I not live there. She my aunt. My family live Cu Chi."

I was perplexed. "But Homie introduced you as his 'brother.' And you are always over there."

"No, he say it wrong," Tin corrected. "I am he cousin. I here every day because I rent small room near hospital. Four walls. No *ting* to do when I not work. I so bored. I come here."

Tin's hours at the emergency room admitting desk of the Franco-Vietnamese Hospital were often long and arduous, but he was proud to work there. FV is a modern facility used mainly by expats, the nouveau riche, and Communist Party muckety-mucks. Cu Chi, about an hour northwest of Ho Chi Minh City, was certainly too far for him to commute daily. (If the name Cu Chi sounds familiar, it's because the town is home to one of southern Vietnam's most visited tourist sites, the Cu Chi Tunnels. It's a blatantly unpleasant and propaganda-infused tour of the string-bean-size underground tunnels that provided hideouts and surreptitious weapon-supply routes for the skinny Viet Cong during the war. Nowadays, tourists pay good money to crawl through sections

of the tunnels—now greatly enlarged for big American butts—
to experience the same oxygen deprivation and hysteria-inducing
claustrophobia the soldiers faced while scooting like earthworms
through pitch-black holes. Thankfully, there is a light at the end
of the tunnel where a guide reaches down to help you out and
then cheerfully leads you to an exhibit of elaborate bamboo torture
apparatuses and an arcade for shooting guns, because, really, who
doesn't want to play war and shoot a real gun? So here is my warning: Small children and Quakers should avoid Cu Chi.)

Now that I'd steered Tin off topic, I told him I wanted to hear
about his childhood. He set his notebook down, happy to put me
out of my misery for the moment. This was Tin's story:

Each time Tin's mother, Hanh, had a baby, her husband,
Dung, would get thrown in jail. When Tin was born in 1985,
Dung celebrated his first son's birth at a bar. His drinking went
on too long. Someone said something to him he didn't find funny
at all. Drunk and angry, Dung threw the first punch. The brawl
ended with his arrest and a jail sentence of one week for bodily
injury and damages. When Baby Boy No. 2 was born twenty-four
months later, Dung was tossed in prison again for fighting, but
this time he was locked up for a year because the drunken brawl
ended in the untimely demise of the other guy. Hanh's third pregnancy was several years later, a beautiful baby girl, born in 1995.
By then her husband was living with his new girlfriend, and they
ran a brothel together. The two were caught and thrown in jail for
six months.

After Dung was freed, he was without a girlfriend, a home, a
job, or food. So he ran back to Tin's always-responsible mother,
who smartly refused to take him back. Soon after, she divorced
the slug. Now alone, she was left to raise their three children in a
four-by-eighteen-foot rental "house" with a hole for a toilet and a
water spigot for a kitchen. Her third-grade education didn't leave
her many career choices. She was determined, however, that her
children would finish high school, even if it meant she had to

work eighteen-hour days. On the street, she sold iced coffee and flip-flops made from old tires, but her livelihood was precarious because when the police caught her, they would confiscate all her goods for selling without a license. A simple bribe would have sufficed, but she didn't have enough money to bribe them. On the days when the police took her belongings, the boys helped by scavenging the city for metal to sell.

The hunger and poverty were grinding: She had too many mouths to feed. In desperation, Hanh called on her ex-in-laws to take the boys in. The grandparents agreed to feed (just barely, as it turned out), clothe, and shelter the boys, but Hanh would have to keep paying for school tuition. The grandfather hated Tin for reasons the ten-year-old never understood. The cruel man would allow him to eat only rotten food. But the grandmother loved Tin and would prepare fresh food for him and hide it around the corner or on another street and then tell him where to find it. If his grandfather found out, it would mean a beating for both of them.

After three years, the grandfather said the boys were no longer welcome in his house, and he threw them out. They went back to their mother, who could feed them or pay tuition, but not both. When skinny little Tin would show up at school without tuition in hand, his teacher would beat him with a stick and then make him kneel outside on the hot concrete the whole day.

Hardship continued to follow the family over the years, but Hanh managed to get an old motor scooter and was paying on it monthly. One morning between errands, Hanh parked her scooter in front of their house. She'd gone in for a drink of water—just for a moment. Hanh suddenly heard her scooter's engine, and when she ran out and saw a man riding off with it, she screamed. Tin rushed to her side just as the thief disappeared around the corner. Tin tried to chase him on foot but couldn't keep up. He went back home and held his mother's hand while they both cried. As if a beloved puppy had been ripped from her arms, she moaned, "Where is my bike, oh, where is my bike?" Tin continued to hold her hand as they walked through the neighborhood late into the night, hoping to spot the scooter or the man who took it.

For fourteen-year-old Tin, this was a new low. His mother was in debt for the scooter that was now gone for good. He decided he was a burden to his mother and could see no good in his future. It was time to kill himself. So, he walked to a store and bought two packets of rat poison. With his last few coins, he headed to a bakery down the road to buy a little cake. How fortuitous, he thought, that his favorite dessert was also the cheapest. The manioc-root cake was big enough to hold the two packets of poison, small enough to eat in one sitting, and sweet enough to mask the taste of the poison.

Tin sat down on the side of the road, pushed the pellets into the thick, gummy treat, and ate it in six bites. Back at home, he said goodnight to his younger brother, baby sister, and mother and went to bed. At about 5 a.m. he awoke with agonizing stomach cramps. Only one thought ran through his mind: "Damn, I'm not dead!"

He tiptoed past his sleeping family and went outside, where he started retching. In the twenty minutes it took to walk to the Saigon Bridge, from which he planned to jump, he stopped to vomit five times. Still writhing in pain, he leaned over the railing. The sunrise began to light the river below, making it easier to see the muddy water and the clumps of uprooted plant growth tangling, swirling, and bobbing on the waves. Only one thought ran through his mind: "Damn, I can't swim."

The memory made him snicker.

"My God, Tin. So what did you do?"

"What you mean? I still alive! I go hospital and doctor pump stomach. My mother, she shave her head. Vietnamese shave head when someone die."

"But, you didn't die."

He shook his head and looked out of the window. A shadow of melancholy crossed slowly over his face at the memory. "I make her so sad. She cut beautiful hair."

I didn't press him for more details. The little I'd heard about the acute deprivation nearly everyone experienced after the war would have made me to hurl myself into the Saigon River, too. If I were to pick any neighbor born after 1975 on my alley and listen to his or her childhood reminiscences, the tales would be fraught with similar hardships. These weren't carefree memories of family road trips, school dances, piano lessons, and Little League games. Yet, the telling of these stories was rarely cloaked in clouds of anger, resentment, or defeat. Tin was a sage with the wisdom of a hundred years. He had experienced far more in life than I had. And very little of it was good.

CHAPTER 18

Christmas in Buddha-Land

"It came without ribbons. It came without tags.
It came without packages, boxes, or bags!"

(FROM *HOW THE GRINCH STOLE CHRISTMAS!*)

BY EARLY DECEMBER, District 1 had transformed itself into a winter wonderland despite persistent ninety-plus-degree temperatures and cloying humidity. Twinkling lights were strung across major streets, and department stores frosted their windows and set up displays of plastic snow, snowmen, glittery stars, and fat inflatable Santas. Luxury hotels hoisted up mammoth artificial Christmas trees with giant red bows in their lobbies. And although nearly seventy-five percent of Vietnamese practice Buddhism or folk religions—a medley of Confucianism, Taoism, and ancestor worship—my neighbors seemed keen on helping to make our Christmas traditions as wondrous on Đoàn Văn Bơ Street as they were in the States, especially because my daughters would be arriving soon. Homie and Tin asked endless questions, and were eager to help us find colorful lights and buy a fake tree, locate Western foods for a sumptuous feast, and suggest local gifts to put under the tree.

But, I had no intention of doing any of it. I was sorry to disappoint them. I can barely tolerate the massive explosions of mirth, overindulgence, and conspicuous consumption that constitute Christmas. At home, a typical Christmas celebration included little more than a phony tabletop tree that goes right back into the box on December 26. In the past, Robin was always disheartened by my dismissive Yuletide sentiment. He had grown up taking annual treks to the charming Christmas markets in Nuremberg, and his family enjoyed monthlong festivities around Stuttgart drinking warm mulled wine and eating spiced Lebkuchen. In my defense, I never once forbade him to festoon our place. By all means, knock yourself out, I said. He didn't. Too much work. Kai and the girls were used to our spartan Christmases anyway.

Jade was particularly excited to show me around District 1 at night. She was Catholic, a religion introduced to Vietnam by Portuguese Dominican missionaries who sailed there in 1533. They got off the boat and attempted to convert the baffled natives. Then one day, a priest, who sat frantically fanning himself, said, "We really ought to rethink these heavy black woolen robes. Let's go home." And they did. About seventy years later, the Jesuits landed on the shores of Dai Viet (an old name for Vietnam). They hadn't gotten the message about what to wear and were last seen around 1616 running for the ship—naked, sweating, their scrawny white heinies dotted with fiery red mosquito bites.

That's a wee exaggeration, for which I apologize. Not all of them left. Many hardy missionaries stuck around and accepted that saving souls was worth the unrelenting heat, frequent torture, and occasional executions. When the French colonized the country in 1887, Catholicism gained even more converts. Nowadays, Catholics and other Christians, most of whom live in the south, make up about eight percent of the population.

"Ms. Karin," Jade said on the phone one afternoon, "can you

come my *how-ah* at seven tonight? I show you *Chrit-mah* light in
District 1. So beautiful. You will like. Bring you camera."

That evening we waved goodbye to our respective husbands,
and I climbed on the back of Jade's well-worn Honda Dream. Unlike most drivers on the road, Jade was sane and wended her way
carefully through knee-to-knee motorbike traffic. The locals had
come en masse to ride under the canopies of sparkling lights. Jade's
younger sister, a fifty-six-year-old schoolteacher, who was short in
stature and hair, had taken an hourlong bus ride from her home to
the city center. We met her in front of Saigon Center, an upscale
shopping mall on Lê Lợi Boulevard, which had a blow-up Santa
in a sleigh at its entrance. This was the sisters' annual Christmas
outing to walk around the one-half-square-mile of District 1 given
over to commercial dazzle to lure Western tourists into shops to
buy silk, jewelry, and lacquerware.

Jade's sister Lang (which means sweet potato) was the happiest
person I'd ever met who'd been named after a root vegetable. She
spoke no English, so when I introduced myself in Vietnamese and
said "How are you?" she patted my hand and laughed so hard I
feared she'd need an inhaler to catch her next breath. I had no idea
whether I'd said something inappropriate or if she simply found it
preposterous to hear Vietnamese coming out of a white person's
mouth. Jade said her sister had always been a giddy, joyful person,
even in the darkest days of the war and the postwar years.

The two tiny sisters got on either side of me, and the three of
us linked sweaty arms while we walked past ceramic Buddhas don-
ning red Santa hats and enjoyed baubles and bells in every window.
Or at least they enjoyed them. Lang never stopped smiling or giggling. Jade said she believed her sister's happiness was due to the
fact that she had never married. "She lucky. No man tell her what
to do." Lang had come close to marrying once. In her early twenties, she had fallen in love with a handsome young man, but he was
Buddhist and her Christian father wouldn't allow them to get married. Instead, she stayed at home to care for her aging parents until

they died, after which she became a fifth-grade teacher, where today she is earning sixty-five dollars a month. (I'll explain how teachers supplement their income later. Hint: blackmail.)

In front of every store display, Jade lifted up her pocket Instamatic, a camera I hadn't seen since the '70s. She went through two twenty-four-exposure cartridges of film in the span of three blocks. "Okay, Ms. Karin, now you stand front that *Chrit-mah* tree [click]. Now you take picture of me and sister [click]. Now, you and me take picture over here [click]. Now just me [click]." Sweat was rolling down my back, a palpable reminder that despite District 1's wintery decorations, this was still southern Vietnam.

A week later, Jade phoned me. "Come over," she gasped with a crackling in her throat that sounded as if she'd just swallowed a pouch of Pop Rocks. "I have gift for you." I ran quickly to the pharmacy. As soon as she saw me, she pulled out a stack of four-by-six-inch prints, all forty-eight of which looked exactly alike except for those where her finger covered half the lens. I gushed over each one, for her sake. On the backs of several photos she had written: "To Ms. Karin, Lucky Christmas Wishes 2008, your friend, Ms. Jade."

Aside from District 1's decorations, it wasn't Christmas anywhere else in the city. In fact, December 25 was a school day like any other. In an effort to help the Westerners feel less homesick, the director of Robin's language school decided to throw a party, except it had a decidedly non-Christmas motif: Come as your favorite movie character. For Robin, the theme was a dream-come-true opportunity. He spent the next several days planning his costume in secret.

The night of the party (to which spouses were not invited, thankfully) was his big reveal. I was on the top floor. I could hear him heaving himself up four flights of stairs, his breathing getting heavier with each step. He opened the door and panted, "Guess [huff] who [puff] I [huff] am."

I must have looked like the poor soul in Edvard Munch's *The Scream* because he quickly said, "It's okay, it's okay! It will grow back!"

"Please tell me you are wearing a latex bald cap."

"Nope. I shaved my head!" And then, with a satisfied smile, he chirped, "I'm Blofeld."

"Who is…?" I meant to finish my question, but I just couldn't take my eyes off his head. Who knew my husband had such a lumpy skull?

"You know who he is," he coaxed, "the evil mastermind in the James Bond film *You Only Live Twice*." I shook my head. "Dr. Evil from the Austin Powers movies!" he intoned. I nodded.

He bent his head down toward me. "Touch it! It feels weird."

"It looks weird. Get it away from me! My God, what will the neighbors think? A shaved head is a gesture of mourning. You'll worry them!"

He wasn't listening. He stood in front of a full-length mirror, exploding with pride. The rest of the costume, a gray Mao-style suit that a shirtless tailor on Đoàn Văn Bơ Street had made for him, actually looked pretty good and could be used for work. Other accessories included Blofeld's cat (Robin had ransacked Kai's toy box for a stuffed kitty) and a monocle (from a plastic bottle cap).

Outside in the alley, neighbors gawked as Robin's bare-naked head streaked by. Homie asked in all earnestness, "Did someone die?"

"Nobody died," I answered, as we stood watching him pull his bike out of the Dragons' house. "It's part of his costume for the Christmas party tonight."

Homie shook his head.

Straddling the bike, Robin stuffed the toy cat and monocle into his jacket pocket, wiggled his sweaty bald head into his helmet, and drove off.

CHAPTER 19

The Girls Arrive

"Rice and Crapmeat"
(MENU CHOICE AT A RESTAURANT)

MY DAUGHTERS WERE DUE TO ARRIVE the next day, the twentieth of December. That, for me, would be the true meaning of Christmas. Homie and Tin were already making plans to take them places and entertain them, for which I was grateful, because I hadn't planned much sightseeing. I'd already come to the opinion that Vietnam wasn't a country to which one journeys to see sites, as much as a place to sit and observe culture. Besides, they'd already been to Ho Chi Minh City, a metropolis of scant tourist attractions, in 2006. We'd already seen the depressing War Remnants Museum and the eerily empty '60s-era Independence (aka Reunification) Palace. The structure was built in 1966 and was the governmental center for the South Vietnamese. But it's most famous for its gate. The Associated Press ran a photo of a North Vietnamese tank ramming into the gate on April 30, 1975. The shot seen round the world signaled the end of the war—and the beginning of yet another era of struggle.

In my eagerness, I arrived at the sterile Tan Son Nhat

International Airport an hour before the girls were due to arrive, and waited outside the baggage claim area with some fifty other people, most of whom were part of one large extended family. Grandma reached into her picnic basket and passed out grilled shrimp paste on sugarcane sticks to her grandkids as they waited to welcome back a family member. Families whooped and cheered when their loved ones emerged from the doors.

To pass the time, I'd brought along my copy of the *Viet Nam News*. The daily subscription kept me apprised of important goings-on in Vietnam. Then-President Nguyen Minh Triet was highlighting plans for the country in the New Year. Sounding every bit as vague as an American politician running for office, Nguyen said: "The party and the state have already developed plans and programs in order to meet the country's full potential. It is necessary to focus on strengthening the national unity. Everyone should work diligently—it is necessary to focus on core issues."

Fully edified, I looked up from the paper just as my girls walked out of the terminal, and as I jumped and waved, the Vietnamese turned around to see my reaction and cheered for me. Marisa, my oldest, spotted me first, and pointed me out to Talia. My blue-eyed, blond-haired younger daughter suddenly burst into tears. I ran and wrapped my arms around her. "Baby, what's wrong? Were they mean to you? Did someone hurt you? Do you need me to beat someone up?"

"No, it's just that I realized how much I missed you," she said, trying to hide her face from the great gobs of nosy Vietnamese who now gathered around us to stare at her and giggle their embarrassment that she was crying in public. I gave Marisa a tight hug and helped both of them steer their luggage past the crowd toward the taxi stand.

"I guess I'd been holding it in all these months," Talia said, still sniffling as we climbed into a green and white Vinasun taxi. Marisa wrapped her thick brown hair into a bun, dug through her handbag, and handed Talia a tissue. I knew I could depend on

Marisa. If Talia had happened to need toenail clippers or purple bubble gum, I'm sure Marisa could have whipped those out of her bag, too. She was mature and dependable beyond her twenty-seven years. She was born that way—confident, disciplined, and best of all, compassionate. I have often mistakenly introduced her as my sister, which always startles the both of us. I don't know why I blurt it out, except she seems to be on the level of best friend/sister rather than daughter. Talia, on the other hand, was born three fertility specialists, one surgery, and seven years later. I still haven't stopped babying her.

That I had abandoned two of my beloved children to live in Vietnam was the antithesis of everything I am. Marisa and Talia are my neurotransmitters of happiness. I need to be near them and in constant communication with them for my emotional health. They are my addiction, my passion, my elixir of joy, my destroyers of pain. They are also the sole reason I have any semblance of maturity. No matter how many times life has caused me fear, grief, illness, injury, injustice, and scarcity, and no matter how many times I've wanted to react by wallowing in depression or throwing a tantrum (as my German mother-in-law has so often said to me, "Vee don't do zat in Churmany"), I have stayed strong for them. I am the mom, the protector, the adult in the scenario. Which is why I began to wonder why the loss of something as temporal as my material possessions and job had caused me to turn and run away so quickly. I hadn't even stopped to think about how my absence would affect them, and how I had been treating the move like an extended vacation. Without their dad or any relatives within one thousand miles of Los Angeles, I was their only family member, and now I might as well have been one bar short of cell-phone service on Denali.

I thought back to the last time we'd ever been truly apart. Summer 1995. One pain-filled week. They'd asked to go to a sleepaway camp for a week because some of their school friends were going. They'd only be two hours away in the San Bernardino Mountains, near Big Bear Lake. I had to suck it up and be selfless. How could I say no and deprive them of this requisite childhood rite? And anyway, whether they were two hours away or two blocks away, my fear of losing them was, and still is, equally intense. However, I couldn't diffuse my nightmarish fear that a week in the woods might end badly. It wasn't a commercial gimmick that persuaded the founding fathers of the town to name it Big Bear. Little campers in their skimpy white Keds were mighty good eatin' to a hungry bear. My spasms of anxiety abated, thankfully, when we drove up to the entrance of the summer camp. The perimeter was surrounded by a ten-foot-high fence. Even better, Sacred Heart Sisters ran the place. The camp was, in other words, a maximum-security prison. The only danger I could think of was the possibility of them choking on a roasted marshmallow while singing "Kumbaya My Lord" around the campfire.

Thankfully, my now-grown-up girls were safely with me again in Ho Chi Minh City, enjoying an air-conditioned taxi ride while happily counting how many people the Vietnamese could fit on the head of a motorbike. They were also duly impressed when I gave directions to the driver in Vietnamese. As we arrived at the alley entrance, excited neighbors leaped up from their steps and called out "Heh-lo, madams." The girls were touched, too, when Homie ran to the taxi, grabbed the luggage out of their hands and hauled it up our stairs.

The girls looked left and right, awed, like I was, by the skinny houses and the warm reception.

"Your house is so…so pink!" Marisa said, laughing as she stepped inside. "And so small."

Talia went wild for the ever-present geckos on our walls. "Oh, I want one!"

Homie came back down and shook the girls' hands again. "I take, you go, coffee, yes? You will enjoy?" He was eager to take them to a coffee bar by the Saigon River to sit and watch the boats, a pleasant spot where he'd taken me. The girls nodded.

Tin had been in our kitchen all morning cooking up a feast for my daughters. He was an adept, talented cook, as were many Vietnamese, thanks to a high school graduation requirement: a cooking class. Its prerequisite: How to Shoot a Gun—mandatory for both boys and girls.

The kitchen smells were aromatic. Before Kai took his sisters up to his room, where they would be staying, Tin stopped them, wiped his hands on a towel, and shook Marisa's and Talia's hands.

Tin was so polite, so genteel. He had the all characteristics I wanted in a boyfriend for my daughters. Hardworking, ambitious, selfless, well-kempt. Because Marisa already had a boyfriend who fit all of the above requirements, I mentally paired Tin with Talia, my tall, thin, quiet girl. It wasn't that I was eager to get her married off. She was much too young. It's just that I wanted Tin in my family and I was pretty positive his mother wouldn't let me adopt him. Marrying him to my daughter was the next best thing.

But Robin was certain Tin was gay. "Look at him," he'd said a few days before. "He cooks, irons his clothes."

I rolled my eyes.

"Come on, he's so gay, I think I hear a show tune coming on. Besides, he's never had a girlfriend."

"Just because he cooks and dresses nicely—how do you know he's never had a girlfriend?"

"I asked him."

"Really? He admitted he's never dated?"

"Well, no, he just said that girls take up too much time. He said, 'They want to go here, they want to go there….' He said he's too busy."

"Who's gay?" Kai asked, overhearing our conversation as he entered the room.

"No one you know, Kai. Do you even know what 'gay' means?"

"Yeah, I know," Kai said assuredly. "It means he's Mexican."

Robin and I looked at each other and stifled our laughter. We would need to have that conversation with Kai sooner than later.

Gays are tightly closeted in Vietnam, and we didn't want Kai's loose lips bandying the word about with anyone's name attached.

In the meantime, Talia's future husband—or not—had cooked his specialty, *thịt kho tộ,* or caramelized pork. I dipped a spoon into the salty-sweet brown sauce, blew on it, tasted it, and feigned writhing in ecstasy. Tin shook his head modestly, but I also saw a smile cross his face. On another plate was braised water spinach with garlic, one of my favorite dishes, and a pot of steamed jasmine rice. For dessert, Tin lifted the lid and showed me a pot of *chè,* a popular sweet soup of green mung beans, sugar, and coconut milk. He would serve it warm, although I'd also seen it served over ice cubes in a glass.

"Please, enjoy. I will go now," Tin said, turning to leave.

"No, don't go. Eat with us!" Tin loved to please, but he wasn't keen on receiving anything for himself. He usually backed out politely whenever we wanted to give him something, asked him to stay for lunch, or allowed me to fill up his motorbike with gas after he'd taken me on errands. But this time he meekly accepted. I think he wanted to see my daughters' reaction to his exquisite cooking. They agreed, it was the best Vietnamese food they'd ever eaten. And who knows? Maybe he wanted to get to know Talia better. A mom could only hope.

Just then our landlord Vinh rang us. "I heard you have house-guests." I wondered who in the neighborhood snitched on us?

"Yes, my two daughters are here for Christmas."

"I happy for you. Okay, and now I come over. Police want copies of their passports and visas."

I knew I would never get lost in Vietnam. Local government watchers always knew where I was and what I was doing.

The gawking activity on the alley had ratcheted up now that Marisa and Talia were in town. Not that the stares and double takes had slowed or stopped for me, Robin, and Kai. Indeed, they never would. But my daughters' presence had already caused one slack-jawed teenage boy to trip over a trash box as he passed our door.

The next morning, I kept the curtains closed for a while because I wanted undisturbed time alone with the girls to talk with them and see how they were faring. Once the doors were opened, I had warned them the night before, all hell would break loose—in a good way, of course—that is, as long as they didn't mind children screeching in the stairwell chasing Kai, old men chain-smoking on our front steps, and visits from any one of the 93 million Vietnamese who have learned to say, "Heh-lo, how-wa ah you?" One just needed to be mentally and physically ready for the onslaught of interruptions.

Despite jet lag, the girls were up early, victims of the alley noises that launched our dawns. After I got dressed, I went up to the third floor and knocked on their bedroom door. Talia was just coming out of the bathroom, a towel wrapped around her long, wet hair, balancing on the top of her head. "You know, Mom," she stated, as if in the middle of a thought, "this little bathroom…it's all you need."

I'd been writing shock-and-awe emails to the girls about how implausible it was that my neighbors appeared so much happier and contented than me, though they lived in two-room houses that in many cases housed eight to twelve family members. Talia mentioned an episode of HGTV's *House Hunters* we had watched together in which a family of four could no longer find happiness in a 2,500-square-foot house and wanted—no, *had to have*—3,500 square feet. We were exasperated when one kid said, "I don't like sharing a bathroom with my sister anymore. We get in each other's way." The camera rolled in to show them jabbing elbows while brushing their teeth.

Marisa was already dressed, hanging up her clothes and taking Christmas gifts out of her suitcase. She was happy to be free of the stress and long hours of her graphic design job. Talia was between semesters and seemed calmer than usual. The girls were excited to get out and explore the neighborhood, so I decided to wait until the end of the vacation for any deep discussions about what psychological damage I'd done to them by moving away. We had only a week and I wanted to start it off right—with Mrs. Dragon's iced coffee and the bread man's hot French rolls for breakfast.

CHAPTER 20

Homie and His Grandma's Ghost

"Pansy breakfast"
(SEEN ON A T-SHIRT)

WHEN ROBIN WAS AVAILABLE to stay home with Kai, Homie, Tin, my girls, and I ate our way through the city for the next several days, rode motorbikes, explored out-of-the-way temples, poked through souvenir shops, and chatted away the hours in trendy coffeehouses. The girls were now officially addicted to Vietnamese coffee, spring rolls, and *phở* for lunch. Alas, Talia and Tin weren't a match, though they certainly made a good-looking couple and they enjoyed each other's company. Our time together was all too splendid, and at the end of the week, I decided that discussing my guilt and sorrow for leaving them alone in the world would only muck up the memories of this delicious time together.

The nearly nine months left on Robin's contract would be harder to face than the three months we'd just gotten through living apart. My heart ached as the girls and I hopped in a taxi to the airport. They, too, were somber for most of the ride. I wanted to grab them and burst into tears and tell them that in all actuality, I had moved *for* them. I was protecting them from the discomfort of being asked, "What's your mom up to these days?" If I hadn't moved, their answer would be: "She's unemployed and her house is in foreclosure." Instead, good, selfless me got out of Dodge so they could say, "Why, how nice of you to ask! She went to Vietnam to do volunteer work teaching English to the poor."

Except, I hadn't moved for *them.* I had moved to avoid my own embarrassment. We acted swiftly to sell everything and leave town. Before anyone could see what losers we were, we were gone. Poof! It had been so easy to fall for the soothing, seductive travel siren singing in my head: *Go on. Leave it all behind. People will even think you are cool, daring, proactive. Dignity will be restored. When you return home, no one will be the wiser.*

I held back my tears and once again asked Marisa and Talia how they were faring. They hadn't said much up to now. But to my surprise, as they prepared to fly back to the States, they said it wasn't so much their loneliness without me that upset them, as it was concern for my safety and health. They'd lost their dad. They couldn't lose me, too. But now that they'd seen how my neighbors took such good care of us and how the Franco-Vietnamese Hospital was close enough to enable survival of a fall into a fish vendor's tank, they were less anxious about our separation this time. Their maturity and bravery surpassed mine. Here I'd wanted so desperately to plead my case, yet they hadn't been holding me guilty in the first place. Still, the bottom line for me as we pulled up to the airport was that I wouldn't see my babies for a very long time. I was miserable.

The next morning, I opened the doors early to get some cooler air into the living room. Homie was sitting on his doorstep in nothing but his boxer shorts, his hair alternately matted and sticking up from sleep, and, as always, his mood ebullient.

"Tin say he come over soon. We enjoy coffee, yes?"

I smiled and nodded. My two buddies knew my heart was hurting and were there for me, always ready to ply me with caffeine. But first I needed comfort food—oatmeal. It was a Christmas gift from Marisa. As I stirred up a pot, in walked four of my favorite little neighbor girls (phonetically spelled): Mayee, age ten, from two houses down; sisters Choop, nine, and Dee, seven, from across the alley and one house down; and squirmy little Yee, five, from six houses down, who loved opening every drawer, cupboard, and closet to inspect our belongings. After the girls' initial fascination with Kai and his toys, they were now following me around as often as they could sneak in while the front door was open. They liked to watch me work on the computer or help me with housework. They'd comb my hair, sit on my lap and count the polka dots on my blouse, or teach me Vietnamese words. When I sat to watch the BBC, they'd paint my toenails with glittery pink polish while chatting with each other. With nearly every visit they'd bring a gift for me: barrettes, strips of salty shrimp paste dried onto waxed paper, a piece of ribbon, a hard candy, or a glossy sticker.

Here was proof that all I had to do was stick my toe back into alley life, and my spirits would lift quickly. And they did. Mayee grabbed the spoon out of my hand to stir, so I set the table with five little bowls. I wanted them to try a staple of an American breakfast, which to my taste buds was far superior to congee, the slimy rice gruel many Asians eat for breakfast or when they are sick. I topped the bowls with a few banana slices and added a little milk. All four took tiny bites. All four made faces. All four dumped the oatmeal back in the pot. Kai came downstairs and happily polished off the pot, eating straight from it.

While the girls drew pictures on our white board, two six-year-old boys sat on our front steps playing with Kai's Game Boy. One boy was a bully in the making, complete with a dysfunctional family of twelve in a two-room house, a sullen dad, a drunk uncle, various cousins (two of whom slept on the balcony at night for lack of indoor floor space and were often rained on), a bored mother, and a foul-mouthed grandma. Bully Boy decided it was his turn for the Game Boy, so he gave Nice Boy a punch and yanked the toy away. Nice Boy's mom saw what happened and yelled at the bully. Bully Boy's mom, her hair up in fat, pink curlers, came out of her house and told Nice Boy's mom not to scold her son. Curler Lady and Nice Mom started screaming at each other. I pulled the girls away from the front, quickly shut the door and drew the curtains closed. I felt embarrassed for the women and wanted to pretend I hadn't noticed a thing. Fight? What fight?

Apparently, I was the only person running for cover. The screaming brought out all the neighbors, who gathered around to listen and even speak their piece. The girls wanted to watch and pulled the curtains back again, giggling at every high-pitched insult. Neighbors began to take sides, which intensified the argument. This continued for the next thirty minutes, always re-ignited by Curler Lady's desire for the last word. I supposed these infrequent outbursts were cathartic for a neighborhood in which I was sure it required superhero patience to keep the peace while living in such close proximity.

By the time the alley residents returned to their houses, Kai got his Game Boy back from Nice Mom and Tin had arrived. It was safe to come out again and we sat down at the TV-Tray Café. Right off, Homie and Tin began goading each other on, trading jabs: "Tin, I give you five thousand *đồng* (about twenty-five cents) to shut up" and "You are too fat for this chair." They were doing it to make me laugh, but I also began to detect a rivalry between the cousins. When the internet wasn't temporarily being blocked by the government, which seemed to happen a couple of times a month, they played their favorite game on Facebook, Restaurant City, a simulated restaurant business that required frequent updates to keep the virtual customers happy and the staff alive. In Homie's restaurant, the character who cleaned the toilets was named Tin. In Tin's restaurant, Homie was the janitor who always hovered near death because Tin fed him only water.

Tin, who was a year younger than Homie, often secretly boasted to me that he possessed better survival skills and was more mature than Homie, whose childhood was a lot less harrowing. Homie's family owned their house. Tin's didn't. Homie's parents were still married. Tin's weren't. Tin was clearly jealous.

As the three of us sipped coffee and watched passersby, I said to Homie, "It's amazing. You've lived on this alley for twenty-six years!"

"No, I not grow up here. I live with my 'auntie and uncle' across river."

It turned out, Mama Hang had three older boys and could barely feed them. Once weaned, Baby Homie went to live with an older, childless couple, friends of the family, but not blood relatives. They were more than happy to take Baby Homie and raise him even while knowing he would someday return to his biological parents. In a culture where children are expected to one day support their parents in their old age, the couple's sacrifice for him was out of pure love, not anticipation of an easy retirement. Homie still had contact with his foster family on Sundays.

I couldn't imagine handing my child over to someone else, but such an arrangement was quite common in Vietnam. Did Homie harbor any resentment that he was the one chosen to leave the family home? No. He knew his parents loved him. When a close friend of the family's helped build another story onto their house, Homie got to return, at age thirteen. By then, little sister Ngoc had been born. His parents continued to struggle to afford food *and* send their children to school. Worse, if they wanted their children to excel in school, they also had to pay the teacher under the table before exam time. Teachers purposely withheld information for the test, so students were obliged to go to the teacher's house and pay extra to get the rest of the material. Blackmail, pure and simple.

One day, the teacher told Homie he could not return to school because his parents were two months behind on tuition. That night he cried himself to sleep. He had a dream that his dead grandmother visited him. "Why are you crying?" she asked.

"We have no money to pay for school."

"Don't worry," she said, "I will tell your uncle in America. He will send your family the money."

The next day his uncle called his mother from San Francisco. He'd had a dream that his mother told him to send money to the family for the kids' school tuition for the rest of the year. Grandparents and parents are revered in Vietnam and few children would dare to cross them, even dead ones.

As Tin continued to explain the value of family, Homie pointed to a house four doors down. "Only two people live there," he said. "Very sad."

"Why is that sad?"

"Only two people," he repeated with an "isn't-it-obvious?" tone. "Three rooms in house. So sad. But I hear son move back soon with wife and daughter. Then everyone will [be] happy again."

I wondered if people felt the same about us—only three people in four rooms. Maybe that explained my neighbors dropping by so often. They figured we were lonely or bored. One morning, a man and his wife asked Homie why our parents didn't live with us. He shrugged and mumbled something along the lines of "That's America for you."

"But why?" they persisted.

Homie looked over and asked me. All I could come up with is that it was a cherished American tradition to live as far away from your in-laws as possible. He translated for the couple, and the two stared at me silently. My sarcasm didn't translate into knowing nods and guffaws as it would have in the United States.

In truth, I was jealous that nurturing family bonds and neighborliness played such big roles in Vietnamese culture, even if the closeness resulted in occasional neighborhood tiffs. Unlike

Americans, who move an average of eight times in their lives, most families on our alley had owned their houses for generations. The phenomenon left little chance to become lonely or forgotten. The neighbors drew us in more and more throughout our tenure, and we were grateful to become part of such a big family. In fact, we'd been invited by Homie's family to the biggest holiday of all: Tết (Lunar New Year).

CHAPTER 21

My Tết Offense

**"Be the first to arrive at a feast,
the second to cross a river."**
(VIETNAMESE PROVERB)

TẾT IS CHRISTMAS, New Year's Day, and your birthday all at once.
The holiday includes nonstop feasting, gambling, and giving
gifts of money to children in shiny red envelopes. Fireworks blast
throughout the city to scare away bad spirits, and everyone turns a
year older no matter what his or her actual birth date. The whole
month before, our neighbors were absolutely giddy with anticipation. Homie could hardly get a sentence out about the holiday
without bursting into a chorus of "You will enjoy!"

Though the holiday lands sometime between the end of January and early February, preparations start at the beginning of
January. Everything must be swept, scrubbed, repainted, and re-
furbished to shoo away the bad luck of the old year and ensure
good luck in the new. Up and down the alley, families were painting their houses inside and out, and those who couldn't afford
paint washed down every wall and window. In solidarity, I washed
the grime off of our front door, something I'd been neglecting for

the very reason that it was too damn hot to scrub anything. Fortunately for Homie's seamstress mother, Hang, the tradition at Tết is to wear new clothes. From January first and on, women filed in and out of her living room every day to get measured for new polyester-knit tops and pants. Hang was putting in long hours and sewing late into the night to fill all of her orders. Even her lazy husband helped by ironing reams of fabric. Still, she couldn't keep up and finally needed to hire a young seamstress to help her finish at least sixty new outfits. After paying for fabric, thread, and part-time help, she cleared about $300 in two weeks' time. It was a blessed windfall.

Everyone's conversation during this time concerned the Lunar New Year. Robin noticed his students could hardly concentrate on their workbooks. Many skipped classes or left town altogether to spend an extended holiday with relatives. No matter where you lived in the country, the tradition is to go home for Tết. Flights, trains, and buses were fully booked the entire month. Officially, Tết runs three days. Unofficially, the world simply shuts down for nearly two weeks. In the middle of it, when banks, the post office, stores, and the market were closed, the holiday break felt tantamount to shutting the electricity off in the middle of dental surgery. Robin would be out of work for two weeks, so we needed to be careful to get by on half his income. Holiday pay wasn't in his contract.

Homie warned me to buy extra water because our bottle delivery service would stop for two weeks. Plus, I would need to shop because the Very Important Market would also be closed for a week. As the date got closer, sidewalk *phở* and *bánh mì* sandwich vendors dismantled their portable kitchens and disappeared from the streets.

Two days before Tết, Mama Hang asked Homie to escort me to the market because she didn't want me to shop alone. This was pickpocket season. Everyone wanted more holiday money and foreigners were the No. 1 target. When we arrived, the market was shoulder to shoulder with last-minute shoppers. The odor, heat, and noise from all the shouting and bargaining hurt my head. Homie helped me find everything quickly. I still needed bananas, but as I passed seller after seller in the fruit sections, I didn't see any. "Why don't any of the fruit stands have bananas today?" I asked Homie.

"No one sell bananas at Tết. It because the word for banana, *chuối,* sound too much like *chuối nhuổi.* The people, when they in business, they so scared 'bout that word. *Chuối nhuổi* mean you business drop."

This was the first sign that Tết was one superstitious holiday.

One misstep in following the rules of the Tết game can ruin someone's entire year. If you are the rule breaker and any bad thing happens to that family, they will blame you. I wish I had learned those rules *before* I nearly caused an international incident. Here is a partial list of the dos and don'ts of the holiday.

- Smile, the gods are watching you. Don't argue or cry. That atmosphere will set the tone for the year.
- Honor your dead ancestors. They will be coming to the party in ghostly form, so put out food, incense, and gifts on the family altar.
- Don't take pills unless the lack of them would cause your death. Then you will have good health in the coming year.
- Don't let a stray cat enter your house. The sound of a cat's meow in Vietnamese is *meo meo*—which has the same sound as *nghèo nghèo* (poor).
- Don't lend or borrow money, or you will have a year of debt.
- Don't take your trash out. It symbolizes brushing money out the door. That's why cleaning is done before Tết.

- Don't show up at someone's house the first day of Tết unless you've been invited. The first person to enter your house on New Year's Day must be someone who has had good fortune.
- Don't enter into anyone's home if you've recently lost a family member. They don't want your misfortune to touch their household.

Homie invited us to his uncle's house on the first day of Tết, the most important day for the family. We wanted to dress up as much as possible, but the heat was making nice clothes prohibitive. Robin wore a short-sleeved buttoned shirt and khaki shorts. I put on my black rice-paddy pants and a light blouse. Jewelry was out of the question. The heat soldered it onto my skin, just one more item on my body to make me hot. We all wore sandals. It occurred to me that I hadn't put on a pair of socks for nearly half a year.

We rode the city bus at about noon with Homie's family for a good hour, at a cost of fifty cents per person one way. Cu Chi is considered a district of Ho Chi Minh City, but is more rural than suburban. The town was one of the most bombed areas in the war and you can still see plenty of evidence by the number of concrete buildings left in ruins. The bus let us off on the outskirts of town, and we walked down a side road for about ten minutes until we turned onto an unpaved lane. Cicadas buzzed and would get louder as the heat of the day increased. Lizards skittered behind stones when we passed. Kai moaned and wiped the sweat off his forehead. He asked, "When we gonna get there?" so many times that even Homie's five-year-old nephew, Kiet, could repeat it in perfect English. Houses along the road were spread apart and surrounded by big yards with concrete cisterns and chicken coops, but no grass. Each house looked stale and dull, caked with brown dust, as this was the dry season. Families lounging on large, covered front porches, stopped all conversation to stare at us as we passed. Young mothers holding babies naked from the waist down waved. The smell of cooking and grilled meats wafted out of each house.

After another ten minutes, we reached Homie's uncle's house, which was full of children and chickens running every which way. Tin tried to tell me how everyone was related to each other (thankfully, he left out the chickens), but after the sixteenth person, I'd forgotten who belonged to whom. The house altar had a porcelain big-bellied laughing Buddha who had struck it rich that day with fruits, red and yellow plastic flowers, coins, incense, and candles. Tin bowed and said a little prayer for good fortune in the New Year.

I was desperate to see what the rest of the house looked like, so I feigned needing to use the toilet. The single-story concrete house was built like all the others on the lane—long, with one room in front of the other. The large open living room had virtually no furniture except a wide wooden dresser where the altar was set. Down a slim, dark hallway was a small bedroom, barely large enough for the double bed in it. A woven bamboo mat served as a mattress on the bed and thin, colorful blankets were neatly folded at its foot. Past the bedroom was a large kitchen, which did double duty as another bedroom with a single bed and a hammock bolted between the walls.

Two women chopping vegetables stopped and stared as I walked through the kitchen to the bathroom. I greeted them with *Chúc Mừng Năm Mới* (Happy New Year) and they giggled and repeated it back to me. More women were cooking with woks over coal grates out on the back porch. Rice cookers steamed and clear, sweetened fish sauce sat on shelves in clear glass jars. The smells were delicious. Behind the kitchen was the bathroom with a squat toilet and a plastic bucket filled with water to flush it. I had to admit, it was far nicer than a restaurant bathroom we'd encountered in Ukraine when we adopted Kai. One evening, when I'd asked for the restroom, the proprietor had pointed out the door to a patch of tall grass. It was raining. I chose to hold it.

Back in the main room, Robin was making everyone laugh with his boisterous attempt to speak Vietnamese. Kai was outside flinging sticks and dipping his feet into a puddle near a cistern. Soon after, he came running back in, chunks of dirt falling onto the tile floor right where dinner was to be served. Immediately, I looked for a broom and spotted a feather-light, short-handled straw one in the corner. I carefully swept the dinner area, moving the dirt onto the porch and then, with a swift swish, pushed it out into the yard. Behind me I heard murmurings. I turned around and saw several of the relatives looking at me, their faces registering shock.

Someone made a high-pitched squeal followed by frantic words. Tin came running over. "Ms. Karin. No! Stop!"

I froze. Had I used the wrong broom? Was it an antique from the Lý Dynasty? More family members began to gather and stare at me.

"Ms. Karin, it a Vietnamese tradition not to sweep dirt out of house at Tết," Tin said with controlled hysteria. "It bring bad luck to house. You sweep money out." I felt my stomach lurch and my face turn red. The uncle came up to Tin, and with great sweeps of his arms said in Vietnamese, "Haha. Don't worry. That doesn't apply to foreigners. Haha. Foreigners in the house bring *good* luck. Yes! Haha. Yes, I will have good luck this year!" I understood him, but his strained smile belied his words and he sounded out of breath.

Great. I had single-handedly caused this already poor family more poverty for the coming year. Homie came up and whispered. "Oh, they so superstitious. It not true."

"But they believe it," I replied. "That's what counts." I felt dreadful. And I knew even Homie wouldn't sweep at Tết, because no matter how much you know logically that something is a superstition or an old wives' tale, there is the teensy-weensy voice inside you that says *let's not tempt the gods, shall we?* I understood that and knew that a centuries-old superstition believed by millions of people…well, it would be nearly impossible to break its spell.

As a kid, I had a weird superstition that began as a game. When walking behind people, I avoided the same footsteps as theirs. I was afraid that if I stepped on the same ground they'd just stepped on, I would become like them. If they had a limp, I would limp. If they were balding, I would lose my hair. I had to keep my eyes on the ground carefully, and if the space was invaded by too many people, I would be hopping and jumping around as if I were standing on a hot plate. I looked especially strange as an adult taking the subway into the city with the same superstition in mind. There I was, spiffily dressed for work wearing high heels, carrying a briefcase and handbag, and yet I was tiptoeing around the imagined evil forces of someone else's footsteps. One day I simply decided to stop. I forced myself to walk in the same footsteps of the person ahead. Every step caused me to wince with pain. Soon enough, though, the discomfort and the ritual disappeared. It's the only Obsessive-Compulsive Disorder behavior I've ever had. Oh, wait, did I turn off the stove?

The start of dinner saved me from more stares and whispers. We all sat on the floor (which, thanks to me, was now clean) in a large oval circle. Traditional foods were set out in large bowls in the middle of the floor, including steamed sticky rice with a filling of mung beans and pork belly wrapped in banana leaves; boiled chicken; deep-fried spring rolls; cold cuts; pickled vegetables; and for dessert, dried coconut and sweetened lotus seeds.

At one point, a salamander lost its suction on the ceiling and fell into an elderly aunt's rice bowl. Without flinching or interrupting her conversation, she lifted it by the tail and flung it outside. I stared at her astonished, and when she stopped talking, I asked, "Didn't that scare you?"

"No, nothing scares me."

Tin told me that this aunt had moved around the countryside during the war, trying to keep her children safe from bullets and bombs while her husband was away fighting. But one day while she was riding her bike, she heard planes overhead, planes that were dropping bombs. Shrapnel nicked her head and another piece lodged in her leg. It's still in there, apparently, held in place by thick scar tissue. Why not get a surgeon to remove it? Well, why bother? It doesn't hurt anymore.

Card-playing and karaoke began in earnest after dinner. Tết is the only time of year the government allows anyone to play cards because it doesn't want its citizens to gamble. I played a popular game at Tết that is similar to bingo, and that helped me practice my numbers in Vietnamese.

We returned home before nightfall to catch the fireworks show the city put on over the Saigon River. We invited neighbors up to watch with us from our fifth-floor balcony, one of the highest vantage points on our alley. The show was every bit as brilliant as those in America, and it lasted a good twenty minutes.

The holiday went on for several more days, and slowly the city came to life again as families returned home from the countryside to start the year rested and refreshed. While some Western holidays seem to be all about amassing as much loot as possible, Tết focuses on garnering good fortune for the coming year—at least for those who don't sweep the good luck out of their house.

CHAPTER 22

Foaming at the Mouth

"I'm so state-of-the-art busy."
(KAI)

LAN HAD GONE HOME TO HANOI for a month during the Tết holidays. Before she left, however, she thoughtfully secured a substitute—a classmate named Nhat who "always got a hundred percent on his English tests and really needed the money." In the afternoon, Nhat took the bus because he didn't own a motorcycle, which caused him to arrive nearly an hour late for his first session with Kai. I opened the door when I saw him on the stairs, looking confused as to why the doors were shut. In a petite Michael Jackson voice, he said, "Hello, I am Nhat. I teach Kai." He came in and dug a toe into the heel of each sandal to remove it, kicking them both into the corner before walking up to me and standing within a do-I-have-something-in-my-eye? distance, which threw off my American sense of personal space. I recoiled a step. He was only chest-high, just a few inches taller than Kai, and had one of those eyes that drifted off to the side so that you couldn't tell who or what he was looking at. In incomprehensible English he blurted... well, obviously, I didn't know what he was blurting. I shook my head, so he repeated it in Vietnamese. I shook my head again. I couldn't believe Lan had recommended him.

"I...love...da...children," he said, now in slow motion. He was looking up at me, or at least I think he was, and continued to froth, "I...tink...children...so...lovely."

My aversion to him was immediate. Was this just a matter of lost-in-translation or was he a creepy pedophile? I know you are supposed to love all God's creatures great and small, and I felt guilty for judging him so fast—but the shrimpy little guy just had a peculiarity about him made worse by the fact that he rarely swallowed his saliva and the corners of his mouth had little bubbles on them.

I told him to follow me upstairs, where I introduced him. Kai sensed his odd personality immediately and reacted by jumping on his bed, throwing his toys at the wall (thankfully, not at Nhat), and singing loudly—all typical Fetal Alcohol Effect (FAE) behaviors that cried, "Stop me, stop me, because I don't know how." The scrawny, bubble-blowing little man expelled a breath. His face registered abject fear. He eyed the door, but made no move. Just when I feared he'd been stricken by paralysis, he bent down to pick up a stuffed dog, shook it in front of Kai's face and pretended to bark. Kai pulled it out of his hands and threw it to the side.

Getting Kai to behave was always a challenge, even for the most experienced sticker-chart-wielding special-ed teachers. Not that fear-producing military tactics worked either. My German-built husband, whose father was an army colonel, often plumbed the depths of his own past to pull up what he believed were foolproof child-rearing techniques, methods handed down, I'm fairly sure, from the Third Reich. In his mind, when a command was given, there was no waffling. In his loudest boot camp voice, he'd bark, "Go to bed NOW! I mean it! MOVE, SOLDIER!" It startled me more than it did Kai, who would simply ignore him and continue doing somersaults on the bed.

Once, on a trip to the Fatherland to visit Opa and Oma, Robin's parents blamed Kai's errant behavior on our poor parenting

skills. They refused to accept that their darling little blond grand-
child had any issues with his brain. Robin's mother specifically
wagged her finger at me one day when I let Kai leave the dinner table early. She clucked, "*Zah* children in Churmany *al-vays* respect
zaher parents *und zay* never *leef zee* table." Point taken, but didn't
she notice how nice and quiet it was now that he was playing in
the other room?

Robin and I were constantly experimenting with both soft-
and tough-love strategies. What worked best was to invoke a
no-nonsense stance and resolve to stay one step ahead of him at all
times. If Kai smelled fear or hesitancy, he'd eat you alive, which was
exactly what he was doing to Nhat.

I coaxed Kai to the table and got him to sit with his workbooks. I told Nhat to read to him and work on math flash cards.
If he needed help, I'd be on the top floor. (And, just in case he
really was a pedophile, I left the door open.) After thirty minutes
of listening to Kai's whoops and hollers, I went back to the room
to stop the mayhem. Kai was foaming at the mouth with exhaus-
tion. Nhat was foaming at the mouth because he had neglected to
swallow since he'd arrived. I told Nhat that study time was over for
the day and he could go. His shoulders, which were now tacked up
against his ears, dropped in relief and his eyes stopped spinning.
He quickly zipped up his backpack and fled down the stairs. But
when he got down to the ground floor, he plopped down on the
sofa and made no move to put on his sandals. Was this a Vietnamese custom that tutors should never teach and run? Was I supposed
to be polite and offer him a cup of tea? I was certain of one thing:
I did not want to entertain him.

He smiled a drippy smile. But he didn't take my hint (one
hand on the door and the other hand pointing the way out) that
I wanted him to leave. In my finest Vietnamese, I said how nice
it had been to meet him and I thanked him for his time with Kai.

He grinned. I waited.

He drooled. I paced in front of the door.

He didn't stand up. I made my move.

I brought his sandals over to him and told him my cat was ready to give birth and I needed to help her cut the umbilical cord. Of course, he didn't understand me, but he sensed my urgency and left.

I shut the door behind him and ran for the phone to call Lan. She was surprised I was making a call to her family's home in Hanoi.

"Is everything okay with Kai?" she asked.

"Lan, you sent someone who can hardly speak English. Kai can't understand him."

She apologized and said she had assumed his language skills were excellent, but, she admitted, she'd never actually *heard* him speak English.

"Would you call Nhat to tell him that we can't use him anymore?"

I realized I was letting her do the dirty work. But she wiggled out of it by saying he didn't own a phone. I would just have to wait until the next day and break the news to him myself.

The next afternoon, Nhat arrived on the back of a motorbike driven by a fellow student he introduced as Huy. I stood in front of the doorway, surreptitiously blocking it so that Nhat couldn't get so far into the house that I couldn't get him back out again.

"Listen, Nhat, your English isn't good enough to work with Kai. He can't understand you. I can't understand you."

"Kai so lovely," he said with a slimy, wet smile.

"Yes, yes, I know. You already said that. Anyway, thank you. And I'm sorry to let you go."

I handed him a five-dollar bill, his pay for the previous day, and waited for him to get back on the motorbike. But he just stood there, smiling. Huy said something to him in Vietnamese, and I watched as Nhat's face crumpled, the bubbles on his mouth finally popping. Nhat turned to look at me—or at least I think he was looking at me.

"Oh, no need me?" Nhat asked.

"No, sorry," I said. I felt terrible. I knew he needed the money. Lan had told me he was from the countryside, which was a polite way to say the person was poor.

Just then Huy spoke up. In perfect English, he said, "Hey, I'll be happy to teach Kai until Lan gets back."

I was shocked. He'd been so silent. But what really astonished me was that he offered himself up in front of poor Nhat, who'd just been fired.

"My gosh, your English is so good. Sorry, I didn't realize...."

"No problem. I'm a fourth-year English-language major."

With perfect boldness, he said, "I'll be here tomorrow at two, okay? And you can call me Steven. That is my English name. It will be easier for Kai to remember."

"Yeah, great," I said, amazed at my luck finding a replacement so quickly.

CHAPTER 23

Kai Goes to Kindergarten

"I dare you to achieve success without a teacher."
(VIETNAMESE PROVERB)

AFTER THE LONG TÉT HOLIDAYS, Homie's nephew Kiet and Kai became best friends, Kai's first real friend. I was so grateful. Not only did Kai have someone else to talk to besides us, but he finally had an all-important peer relationship, which was crucial to his development. Five-year-old Kiet belonged to Useless Brother No. 1 (he was chronically unemployed) and Manicurist Mom. Because Homie had spoken English to Kiet from the time he was a baby, the little kid already had a goodly arsenal of English words. And, because he and Kai played together every day, he was picking up English with astounding speed. However, much of what he was learning were somewhat useless Kai-isms, such as, "I will destroy you," "Oh, man, that sucks," and "Blow it out your ear." Useless Brother No. 1 beamed with pride, though he had no idea what Kiet was saying. Each night the two boys stood on their respective balconies talking across the alley to each other about *Ben 10* cartoons or showing each other their toys. In perfect English, Kiet would say, "Goodnight, have a good sleep."

Useless Brother No. 1 made himself useful two times a day by driving Kiet the four blocks to and from kindergarten. It was difficult for Kai to wait until three o'clock for Kiet's return. It was hard on me, too. Their playtime gave me the opportunity to read, think, and enjoy some good-quality worry time.

One morning, as Kai and I waved goodbye to Kiet, I had an idea that I shared with Tin as soon as he arrived for my lesson. "Here's my idea, Mr. Tin," I began excitedly. (I often called him Mr. Tin because he called me Ms. Karin.) "Because Kai's developmental age is really about five years old, I thought he might fit in well with the kids at Kindergarten No. 12, Kiet's school. Kai could become a classmate of Kiet, and Kiet could help translate the teacher's requests. Could you ask Kiet's mother to call the school for me?"

I could tell he didn't understand me. I had spoken much too fast and used difficult words. Tin had just come off of an all-night shift at the hospital. He put his elbows on the table, propped his face up in the palms of his hands, and looked at me quizzically through sleepy, blinking eyes.

"Listen," I went on, trying to slow down, "I realize there is the language issue at the kindergarten. And I know Kai is older and bigger. But could you ask her to call the school anyway?"

"What do you want she to ask them?"

"Whether…they…would…let…Kai…go…with…Kiet…to…kindergarten."

Tin seemed to wake up and opened his eyes a little wider. "You want Kai go to school?"

I nodded, probably more vigorously than a loving mother should.

"Ah, okay. I will ask my aunt. She call school for you. I not ask Kiet's mother. She don't live in my aunt's house anymore."

"What? She was living there yesterday."

"A very big fight last night with [Useless Brother No. 1]. Did you hear it?"

I had indeed heard the screaming. People in Malaysia heard the screaming. It was at 3 a.m. and Kiet's mom, a beautiful, petite young woman, was hysterical, shrieking at her husband for more than an hour. I don't know what she was saying to him, but I know what I would have said: "Get your butt out of that chair and go find a job!" I sympathized with her. Every day, all day, he just sat, smoked, and drank coffee at the Dragons' TV-Tray Café. Only once did any of us feel hopeful he would ever help support the family. Through a friend of a friend, Tin had helped Useless Brother No. 1 find a job as a waiter in a District 1 foreign hotel restaurant, a coveted job. That morning, we all slapped him on the back and gave him a thumbs-up as he took off on his motorbike, all freshly showered, combed, and dressed up. Two hours later he was back. He had quit. *Waaaaay* too much work, he said.

So on the night of the fight, and under the cover of darkness, the young wife had packed up her nail files, polishes, cuticle trimmers, and scissors, got on her motorbike and went home to mother. From then on, Kiet would see his mother only on weekends. It also meant that the two boys wouldn't get to play together on the weekends anymore. Kai was sad.

The next day Tin had good news—well, good and bad news. Kai would be allowed to go to the Vietnamese kindergarten. That was the good news. The bad news: as long as he behaved. "He must follow the school rules or they will...."

"Kick him out?"

Tin looked horrified. "Oh, no, no! They no kick children. But he cannot come back."

The school's one condition took me by surprise. Were the teachers automatically assuming that Western kids were out of control, rude, and gun-totin'? Had they been watching too many PBS documentaries about violence in American schools?

During Robin's first few weeks of teaching, he had often come home and commented on how every time he entered the classroom, the students would stand up and say, "Good morning, teacher," in unison. They wouldn't sit back down until bidden to do so. It was gratifying, he said, that at all age levels the students were eager and attentive learners, polite and studious. This was what I had always heard about Asian students in general. It was one stereotype that no one rushed to call politically incorrect. Later, however, after I got my teaching certificate, I had many good reasons to throw that archetype off the planet. Vietnamese students weren't *all* so darling. It depended on what kind of school it was.

Outside of the classroom, however, I found the children in Vietnam simply enchanting. They were respectful of parents and grandparents, patient in a waiting room, good at the market, quiet at the post office. I wondered whether such manageable temperaments were formed from infancy or simply part of their DNA. I hypothesized it was because the Vietnamese didn't seem to be in a frantic rush to develop their baby's brain. Dad wasn't flipping flashcards as Baby Hoang was being burped. Mom wasn't stuffing Baby Mai's hands with educational toys long before the baby girl had even discovered that those stubby little digits she was gnawing on belonged to her. The babies in Vietnam were perfectly content clutching a cardboard toilet paper roll while observing the world around them.

How, I asked myself, did they get a three-year-old to sit still in a restaurant with grown-ups, eat everything set before him, and refrain from hurtling his chopsticks across the room? Was it the healthful Vietnamese diet without preservatives, additives, or high-fructose corn syrup? I'd noticed that if the child wasn't eating, a waitress would often come to the table and hand-feed him. Waitresses often grabbed a spoon and hand-fed Kai whenever they saw him balking at eating. I found it so endearing.

I brought the topic up one day to the man who came to repair our internet service. He had been chatting with Kai, and his English was pretty good.

"I notice how really sweet the children are in Vietnam," I said. "They are so polite and well behaved."

"Ah, yes," he said with a satisfied smile. "That's because we beat them."

I gasped and he laughed. "You Americans get in trouble for that, don't you? Here the kids are scared of their parents and teachers. That's why they are well behaved."

Beating wasn't in my arsenal of operant-conditioning tactics for Kai, although I have to admit his conduct has caused me to slap around an innocent cupboard door or two. I'd always considered myself a patient and creative disciplinarian. Sticker charts, positive reinforcement, regular chores (without pay!), and lessons on manners were the techniques that had worked well for my daughters as they grew up. I taught them to be good and kind people first, and knew that those behaviors would build their self-esteem naturally.

But Kai's energy level could short-circuit a power grid, so when he argued, hit, had a tantrum, and was otherwise defiant, the threat of losing out on a Thomas the Tank Engine sticker was just plain sissy. The threats had to be a lot more substantial in order to get his compliance—a year without computer, six weeks in boot camp, ten percent of all his future earnings—stuff like that. (Ten percent of his future paychecks are earmarked as payback for all the plumbing bills caused by at least a dozen toothbrushes he'd flushed down the toilet as a toddler.)

I had no idea how Kai would operate in a classroom sans English and without familiar songs and nursery rhymes. Would he act up out of frustration from not understanding the language? Or would this total immersion experience help him to pick up Vietnamese quickly, something that people always say kids can do faster than adults, especially adults like me whose brains are overstuffed with useless information, preventing them from learning anything new?

We told Kai the good news, then lectured him on and off the rest of the week. We told him we expected good behavior and that he should just follow and mimic whatever Kiet did.

"I pinkie promise," he said as he locked pinkie fingers with Robin and me. Kai wasn't a bit anxious about starting school. He was eager to be with other kids. On Wednesday, we all walked to the school to sign him up and pay the monthly fee ($35), which included daily breakfast and lunch. Kindergarten was from 7:15 a.m. to 3 p.m. with a nap break at the school. The director said Kai could start the following Monday.

Monday morning Kai climbed behind Kiet on the back of Useless Brother No. 1's motorbike and left for school. I watched as they rounded the corner out of sight. For a few moments, I just stood there, unsure of what to do next. I turned and looked around the room. Although Robin was still asleep upstairs, the house seemed empty, silent, and, come to think of it, garishly pink. Why would anyone paint a living room Pepto-Bismol pink?

I was in a pivotal moment in my life. This was the first time in twenty-eight years I didn't have a full-time job or a child under my wing. I'd always been so overwhelmed with life, especially over the past several months with organizing, planning, and worrying about our future on both sides of the ocean. Now I had breathing room. It was too soon, however, to revel in my emancipation. It all hinged on Kai. At any moment he could be expelled from kindergarten for playing piñata with the red paper lanterns that hung in front of the school. I crossed my fingers, but, truthfully, I didn't think he'd last through the week.

That afternoon, when Kai got home from school, he looked happy. I breathed a sigh of relief that there was no restraining order pinned to his T-shirt. In fact, as the week went on, no incidents were reported except one. On Friday morning Homie's mother received a call from the school with a message: "Tell Kai not to pick up the little kids." Kai was Gulliver and they were Lilliputians, and his teacher feared he'd either squash or step on one.

The differences between East and West childrearing practices are vast. A Vietnamese child grows up knowing that the world revolves around her grandparents, parents, and teachers. First and foremost they are to be respected. If not, *slap!* Girl grows up dreaming of working for a foreign company, but she knows she must help out in the family rice-selling business.

At age nineteen, she marries a cute boy and moves in with her in -laws and Grandma, who is in her third year of dementia and loonier than a fruit bat. Whatever Grandma says must be obeyed, because she is the oldest and wisest in the house. Today Grandma has a hankering for bird's nest soup. Girl tries to argue, "But Grandma, that's a Chinese dish. Vietnamese don't eat boiled bird spittle." Grandma shakes her cane at Girl, who must now go in search of a nest.

Within twenty months of marriage she has two children, one of whom is a boy, thank God. Mr. and Mrs. In-Law criticize her every move, and she dreams of the day they die, so she will be the matriarch of the house and will finally get the bedroom with the air conditioner. Sixty years later when Girl dies, she is thrilled to finally meet Buddha in the afterlife. Girl knows her kids will be burning lots of paper money in her name, so she can live in heaven like the queen she truly is.

An American child grows up knowing that the world revolves around him. First and foremost, Boy's self-esteem must always be nurtured. If he scribbles out a self-portrait in which the eyes are where the ears should be, his parents will call it modern art and frame it. But first they'll enter it into an art contest and be completely miffed when he doesn't win. Naturally, they tell Boy he won and hand him a fake first-prize ribbon lest he suffer disappointment and require years of psychotherapy.

As he grows, no value is placed on self-control because it might stunt his creativity. He dreams of the day when his parents send him to a $50,000-per-year private college, directly followed by a career in a large company where he expects a six-figure income and is rankled to find out that his entry-level job pays only $28,900.

He marries, and spends his first year's salary on a muscle car, which means his wife must pay all the bills herself. They get divorced. His rented storage space fills up with so much crap, he doesn't even remember that he already has camping equipment, so when his buddies say, "Let's go camping," he buys it all again. Now he owns two tents, two porta potties, and yet another kayak. When he dies, he's thoroughly horrified when St. Peter won't let him bring his toys through the gate.

As the weeks progressed, Kai's behavior began to frustrate the teachers. They called us when he refused to eat meat. They called us when he remained wide awake during naptime. His kindergarten days were in jeopardy on the days he wouldn't stay in his seat. Luckily, in Vietnam, every problem can be fixed with an envelope stuffed with cash. After these nagging calls, we'd walk over to the school and hand the teacher and her helper about thirty dollars each. Over the next year, my quiet time would prove costly.

CHAPTER 24

New Students, New Friends

"The rich worry over their money,
the poor over their bread."
(VIETNAMESE PROVERB)

NOW THAT KAI WAS IN SCHOOL, I had extra time to take on a couple of private students. One was Mai, a neighbor woman about thirty years old who still lived at home with her parents. She had been one of Robin's students until she asked me if I would teach her instead so she could talk about "girl topics." Her English was excellent, acquired in a college classroom over the course of three years. She wasn't a registered student. At that time, her family had no money for such frivolities. Instead, Mai looked up the class schedule at a local university and simply walked in with the hordes of paying students. When the roster got passed around, she pretended to mark it and passed it on. She also skipped the exams. It was three years before she was caught and got kicked out. Her downfall? She stood out because she was the best in the class. The teacher wanted to know who this remarkable young woman was.

I, too, was impressed with Mai. She was always fashionably well-dressed, stood tall, and was a commanding presence in a room. Her confidence seemed too cosmopolitan for someone of our neighborhood, a characteristic that did not endear her to the average Vietnamese man. Her parents were upset that she was not yet married. She'd been dating a Vietnamese-American man who flew to Ho Chi Minh City often, but when she found out he was married, her heart was broken. He wanted to sleep with her, but she said no. She was not going to lose her virginity and risk getting pregnant with a man who wasn't committed to her. She was smart about not putting all hope in an unavailable man but remarkably naïve about sex and birth control. I became her relationship therapist and was honored she took me into her confidences.

Mai grew up in a tiny house on the next alley over from us with two older brothers and her parents. Poverty had exacted a huge toll on her family. It had caused her second brother, just a teenager in the early '80s, to join the wave of boat people leaving the country. He and another neighbor boy boarded a boat for Thailand. They were never heard from again. One of the biggest dangers at the time was Thai pirates looking for gold, which the refugees usually carried on them. Or perhaps the boat was overcrowded and sank in a storm. Whatever happened, the family would never find out.

Like Homie, she was sent away to live with another family. Her parents worked from dawn to dusk selling shrimp paste, first on the street, later at the central market. They couldn't watch her, so she went to live with a woman in another neighborhood and saw her parents only on Sundays. The woman was stingy with food, and Mai remembers being hungry all the time. Every morning the woman gave Mai 5,000 *đồng* (then about ten cents) to eat breakfast on the way to school. The ever-enterprising Mai stopped at the same soup stand because she had worked out a money-saving plan with the vendor. She could get the soup for 3,000 *đồng* if the vendor left out the meat. With the extra 2,000, she could purchase a snack at school. The snack had to carry her through until supper. But one day the woman saw some money between the pages of Mai's schoolbook and accused her of stealing from her. Mai told her she hadn't, but saved it by leaving the meat out of her soup. Even when the soup vendor confirmed her story, the woman slapped her and said she was forbidden to have her own money.

When Mai turned ten, her mother let her come back home, but she had a choice—either stay in the house all day with the doors locked and never go out, not even to school, or stay outside on the street all day after school. Thieves ran rampant in the skinny, mazelike District 4 alleys, so the house had to be kept locked while her parents were working. She chose school and the street. Neighbors would occasionally give her food or let her watch their TV from the alley. Only one neighbor owned a television, which broadcast one station from 3 to 5 p.m. Crowds of neighbors gathered to watch. She had to push herself under and between feet to be able to see the screen. It was the highlight of her day.

After December 1986, when *đổi mới*, the "socialist-oriented market economy" reforms began, which allowed people to keep more of their profits, Mai's parents' business began to do better (*đổi mới* are really capitalist market economy reforms, but don't tell the hard-liners). Her mother made wise investments, buying two houses for $1,000 each and renting them out. At the time I met Mai, those two investments were worth $600,000 apiece because of their location on a major street in District 1.

Although Mai's family had a thriving business and sound investments, their lifestyle remained the same. They still lived in the same tiny District 4 house and never took vacations or bought nice things. I asked Mai what she did for fun.

"I sleep a lot or hang out with friends in the park," she said. I smiled at her answer. "Hang out" was one of the American idioms I'd taught her the day before.

"You Westerners travel a lot when you have extra money because you know that when you retire you get a pension," she continued. "In Vietnam, we don't get pensions. Government workers get a small one. So we work to save for our old age."

The monotony of such a disciplined life was difficult to imagine. Didn't she want to see the world? Or trade up to a modern apartment in the newer District 7? No. She considered her life quite blessed the way it was. She criticized the American penchant for money, money, money, but from what I'd been noticing, the Vietnamese had a penchant for it, too. The difference—they didn't spend it.

Though I was enjoying my small handful of private students, my own tutor, Tin, was despairing of my progress learning Vietnamese. One afternoon, when the heat was getting in the way of my ability to hear the subtle differences between *củ* (root), *cũ* (old) and *cụ* (old person), I flat out fell apart. "I can't do it!" I told Tin, my eyes filling with tears. "I can't hear it. I just can't hear it. I can't memorize it. I can't pronounce it. I'm sorry, but I must not be smart enough to handle this language."

Perhaps deep down in the recesses of his brain, Tin was saying, "At least you got that one right, lady." But he didn't go there. Instead, he said, "I must not be a very good teacher. I will quit."

I protested, and in my best rendition of a commitment-phobic person, I said, "It's not you, it's me."

My frustration and failure to learn wasn't entirely the fault of either of us. I'd been hearing from some long-term expats that it took them an average of two years to even have a rudimentary conversation. On one blog, I read about a man who said he had lived all over the world and had become fluent in seven languages, including the notoriously difficult Hungarian language. But during his five years' residency in Vietnam, he was never able to pick up the language. That was both heartening (perhaps I wasn't as stupid as I thought) and disheartening (but I was obviously in for a significant challenge).

I let Tin back out of our lessons with dignity though. I told him he could quit as long as he promised to still come around to visit. He'd been hanging out less and less with Homie's family because he and Homie weren't getting along, for reasons they wouldn't share with me.

Still, I hadn't given up on learning Vietnamese. Mai recommended that I take a beginning Vietnamese class for foreigners at Ho Chi Minh University in District 1. Perhaps a professional teacher, who would force us to memorize dialogues, do homework, and take quizzes, was what I needed. Now, finally, I would become fluent!

But first I needed my own mode of transportation. I'd been seeing electric scooters around and figured I could easily ride one. No clutches, no gas to deal with, lightweight, and far cheaper than a motorcycle. Best of all, no "Saigon kiss." The name refers to the burn mark nearly every driver gets when he or she accidentally touches the exhaust pipe with a bare leg when getting off the bike. Robin got one and he still has a scar. I saw plenty of children with Saigon kisses, which was truly sad. It's a searing pain that can take weeks to heal. In parking lots, where motorbikes are so tightly placed together, touching the exhaust of the motorbike next to yours is practically inevitable over a lifetime. Thankfully, neither Kai nor I ever got "kissed."

One day, Homie took me to an electric scooter store and I bought one for about $300. I rode it home, slowly at first, to get used to the traffic, and then I cranked it up to a ripping twenty miles per hour. One charge could last about four hours. The freedom to go exploring and see parts of the city I'd never seen before made it worth the cost. It didn't take up that much room in the living room either.

I arrived early the first day of language class to sit outside in the campus courtyard. While I fought off flies and thumbed through the first chapter of the textbook, some students came up and stood in front of me.

"Eh-cuse me, Madam, you hep us speak English?" one of them said.

I looked up and squinted in the sunlight. Standing around me were three young girls so small and bony, I thought they were fairies and that I was hallucinating from being overheated. "You mean now?" I asked. "Here?" I looked at my watch. "I only have about fifteen minutes before my class starts."

"Fifteen minute okay, Madam." Without waiting for a yes, the three of them sat down on my bench-made-for-two, squeezing me in from both ends.

"Minutessssss," I said, stressing the "s" for their first lesson.

They repeated "minutesssss" and giggled. The girls seemed much too young for college. Their notebooks were covered with pencil drawings of hearts and flowers. Cartoon characters emblazoned their outfits, as if the clothes had been purchased from a children's store. EVERYTHING in Vietnam is covered with Mickey Mouse or other cartoon characters—sheets, towels, clothes, dishware, backpacks, you name it. It makes being taken seriously really difficult. The director of the British International School, whom I'd met at the Ladies Who Lunch and Then Go Shopping Club, said that, in general, Vietnamese students are about four years behind their Western counterparts in maturity. That helped explain these girls. After our short question-and-answer session in English, the bell rang. As they headed toward their classes, I saw two of the girls pull a young man's neatly tucked shirt out of his pants and then run away laughing. Still, they had to be extraordinarily bright to get a place in this overcrowded city university—or have parents rich enough to bribe the admissions officer.

I climbed four flights of stairs to the classroom for foreigners, one of only three rooms with air conditioning. My classmates were mostly Korean men who were in Vietnam to open businesses, and they didn't speak English. Two women from Singapore were fluent in English, so I had someone to talk to at break time. It felt so good to be in school. My brain was enjoying the exercise, and I never minded the occasional morning study interruption from university students taking sincere stabs at speaking English.

One morning, a young man sat down next to me in the courtyard. His name was Quy, and he was a library sciences student from northern Vietnam, who looked like a walking Popsicle stick. He begged me to work with him on English. He had such a gentle sweetness about him, and although I cherished my courtyard time to do my homework, I told him that if he could occasionally help me with my Vietnamese homework, I would arrive every morning at 9:30 and we would practice English before my 10 a.m. class. He thanked me multiple times and never missed a morning, nor was he ever late. His determination was irresistible.

I asked him what his childhood had been like. He told me his parents were rice farmers from a small village south of Hanoi. The postwar years had meant extreme deprivation for his parents. They worked day and night in the fields, seven days a week, yet they were always hungry. Everyone was always hungry. Quy was born in 1987, the same year my second daughter, Talia, was born. While five-year-old Talia took gymnastics classes and played in her tree house, five-year-old Quy cared for the family's water buffalo all day, every day, to make sure the precious animal didn't stray.

"I tell you a funny story about that water buffalo," he said, being careful to correct his grammar or syntax throughout the story. "This buffalo wanted very much to visit her boyfriend in another field. I tried so hard to keep her near our house. But she would not obey me. I put a rope through her nose ring and then tied it to my ankle. I thought that would keep her from running away. But the buffalo only dragged me until she got to visit her friend. I cried and cried because my arm got broken. So I walked to the doctor's clinic and they repaired my arm."

"You walked by yourself to the doctor?" I asked.

"Yes. My parents were far away in the fields."

"How long did it take before things got better for your family?"

"It got better in the middle '90s. Between 1975 and 1986,

our government made many economic mistakes. Everybody was so hungry and no one had money. We had stamps for food, stamps for soap, stamps for cattle feed, which people also ate when there wasn't enough rice. My aunt wanted to make some extra money to buy more food, so she took all her savings and walked thirty miles, crossing over a mountain to another town to buy some clay pots. This town was famous for its pots. She wanted to sell them in our town for a profit. She had to carry those pots back on her shoulders with a shoulder pole with two baskets on each side. At that time you were not allowed to sell anything for profit for yourself. When she was nearly home, the police saw what she was doing and came over to her and broke all the pots. She cried so much. All of her money was gone.

"She never tried to sell anything anymore. But she went to college and became a doctor. Now she is a doctor and she is married, but they have no children. She couldn't have any. But she is raising her niece because the girl's parents are too poor to raise her. She's a very good person."

I thought about my years in high school and my college history classes. Tragedies, wars, famines—such hardships were all so long ago, so far away. It happened to people who were mostly no longer living. But while he talked, it hit me that these experiences were not ancient history at all. I admired Quy for his determination to learn English, which would help his chances of participating in a global economy.

Each day, I couldn't wait to hear more about Quy's family. The next morning, he began with his father's parents. "My grandparents had six children. Grandfather did not allow any of them to go to school because he wanted them to help with the farm work. But my grandmother knew that education was the way out of poverty. She defied him and sent all six to the nearest school seven miles away. They had to walk, which meant they had to leave the house at 4 a.m. The grandfather was not awake yet, so he didn't see them leave."

"But didn't he wake up in the morning and say, hey, where are the kids?"

"He never asked. He knew where they were. If he had seen the kids leave in the morning, he would be obligated to stand by his word and tell them they were forbidden to go. But because he never actually saw them go, he didn't lose face. Their education was never discussed in the family."

This went on for ten years, until all had graduated. The oldest brother was such a bright student, he got a scholarship to study at a university in Russia and is now an investment banker in Hanoi. The next child was Quy's aunt, the doctor. Three more siblings became successful in business. Quy's father, alas, was the youngest and the only one who didn't study hard. He just wanted to go fishing all day. So he became a rice farmer like his father. Quy said his father's family became famous in the area because all the kids had gone to school and did well later in life.

Quy's father was a soldier when Vietnam invaded Cambodia. He managed to stay alive twice, thanks to the call of nature. His troop was sleeping in the jungle. Quy's father had diarrhea, so he went into the forest and wasn't able to hurry back right away. The Khmer ambushed the camp and killed everyone. The next lucky toilet break was when he was playing cards on a small table with his army buddies. He excused himself to go to the bathroom. A grenade fell right into the middle of the table and killed everyone.

Another fateful moment came in the hills of Cambodia. Quy's father and a few fellow soldiers were crawling close to the ground to remain hidden. Near a stream they came upon several solid gold Buddha figurines. The figurines would have made the five soldiers fabulously rich, but they all knew that a soldier carrying gold is bad luck. They didn't want to die. So they left it. Didn't touch it.

Because of his father's army service injuries (he was shot in the stomach and his hearing was compromised from bomb blasts), Quy was now receiving free tuition and board, as long as he kept his grades high, which he did.

Quy's family experienced a sustained, decades—if not generations—long history of suffering, yet his sense of gratitude and belief in good luck propelled him forward. We Americans feel sorry for ourselves if our mother is an alcoholic or our father dies young, and we let those past memories rule and limit our destiny. Many Vietnamese have had to let go of their baggage along the way or it would have become unbearable. Quy seemed none the worse for wear.

CHAPTER 25

Homie's Dad Gets Sick

"Surgery honeymoon"
(SEEN ON A T-SHIRT)

THE CLASS WENT FOR EIGHT WEEKS and my progress was decent, though I still had trouble making myself understood. When I asked for the bill at a restaurant, the waiter pointed to the bathroom because, I found out later, "I want to pay" and "I want to pee" are virtually the same words with only the slightest variance in intonation. At least I was beginning to understand people on the street and overheard two men talking about me. "Did you see the foreigner? Where do you think she's from?" "She looks French."

Now that Tin wasn't my tutor anymore, I studied on my own or with Homie. One morning, though, I noticed Homie's house was all closed up and it was already 9 a.m. An hour later when I looked across the alley again, it was still closed. I'd never seen their house locked up in the daytime. It made no sense.

I sat at my computer trying to finish an article for the *Los Angeles Times* about Ho Chi Minh City's unique coffeehouses, but I couldn't concentrate. I kept jumping up every ten minutes to look over the balcony to see if the door was open. At about 1:30, I looked down and saw Useless Brother No. 1 smoking on the steps. I flew down and ran across. Mama Hang was just inside staring trancelike at her bags of fabric but made no moves to begin sewing. "What is going on? Where is Homie and the rest of your family?" I asked Useless Brother No. 1 in Vietnamese.

"My father is very sick. He's at the hospital."

I felt my face drain. In the past several days, Homie's father had had a fever and Homie was a little bit worried, but said he was taking medicine and would be fine.

Homie heard my voice from inside and came out.

"I'm so sorry to hear about your father," I said. "How is he?"

"They take X-ray. See something on liver. He need surgery tomorrow."

"Homie, I'm so sorry to hear it." A few years before, a dear friend of mine, Pat, also had "something" on her liver. It was a cancerous tumor and she died a few months later, so my fear for Homie's dad was acute. Over the next few days, Homie's house was mostly closed up as the whole family left early each morning on three motorbikes to go to the hospital and didn't return until nightfall. Mama Hang didn't sew, nor did Homie's teenage sister Ngoc talk for hours on the phone pleading with her boyfriend not to break up with her. I asked what I could do, but only received solemn head shakes, so I left them alone. Homie's father's health was a private family affair and I didn't want to pry.

A few days later, Homie invited me to go with him to the hospital to visit his father. He had good news. It wasn't cancer, though they did snip two inches off his liver (and, knowing how the Vietnamese don't like to waste anything, probably added a few fava beans and served it up with a nice Chianti). Shockingly, the surgery left a scar from the top of his chest down to his navel, which his dad was pretty proud to show off.

I rode with Homie on his motorbike to the hospital. Like many buildings designed after the war, it was a Soviet-style gray concrete monstrosity with stairwells and hallways on the outside.

Each hospital room had a door with one small, square window that had louvered glass but no screens. I peeked in each room as I passed and was surprised to see every room absolutely crammed with families and children visiting their loved ones. Female nurses pushed carts full of syringes and pills from room to room and ordered family members out into the hallway as they ministered to the patients.

Homie's father's room was on the fourth floor. It had five beds with two women and three men. None were separated by any privacy curtains. This wasn't as bad as a government hospital, however, where Jade's daughter was a nurse. She'd told me that government hospitals were so crowded that two patients shared a single bed and another patient lay under the bed. Keeping the IV bag lines untangled was always a nuisance.

Homie's dad was lucky. He didn't have to share a bed. Still, all five patients shared one bathroom, which had a toilet and a plastic hose with a water nozzle that came out of the wall for showering. The smell in the bathroom was foul and the floor was wet, so they were careful to keep the door tightly closed. Relatives brought food to their sick family member three times a day because the hospital didn't serve food.

Homie's dad was pleased to see me. He moved his feet to the side and pointed to the end of the bed. "Please, sit. Sit here." The room was stifling hot. A metal ceiling fan, missing one of its three paddles, whirred uselessly above. The conditions seemed so intolerable, I wanted to cry for him.

The two women patients were wide-eyed. They told Homie, "We've never seen a foreigner in a Vietnamese hospital before." Their declaration was followed by the usual, "How old is she? Where is she from? Does she have children? Only one boy? Too bad. She's unlucky."

"How long must your dad stay?" I asked Homie.

"Eleven more days. My mother so tired and so worried. She need to work again. Two weeks in hospital cost us six hundred dollars."

"You have to pay six hundred dollars? Is there no health insurance?"

"No. We must to pay."

I was constantly correcting him on his use of "must to" but not today. His face contorted with worry. Without his ever-present smile, he hardly looked like the same person.

Though the procedure and the two-week hospital stay were only $600, it spelled disaster for a family who lived so close to the edge. Mama Hang hadn't sewn or sold clothes for several days after the operation. Plus, he couldn't be released from the hospital until the bill was paid. Payments on credit or over time didn't exist. When I asked how the family would pay the bill, Homie told me that he'd had a rather clandestine meeting with a woman a couple of alleys over who loaned him the money. They would have to pay it back with ten percent interest within six months. Borrowing from a neighbor or family member was virtually the only way to get quick money. Few ever considered getting a loan from a bank.

"Let me help you. I can give you two hundred now and maybe two hundred next month," I said.

"No, Ms. Karin. That nice you want help me. Don't worry about me. You will get headache. You need keep you money for you family. It's okay, we not starve." And then he laughed and said, "Not yet."

At home, I sat thinking how I could slip the money into his room. I knew he wouldn't take the money directly from me. Though I often sat on his living room floor for karaoke sessions and was treated like one of the family, I couldn't just walk up the stairs and put the money on Homie's bed without being invited up. Instead, a couple of weeks later, I put $650 into an envelope and handed it to Mama Hang with a note to give it to Homie. I suspect she peeked in the envelope because the next morning she was all smiles when she saw me open the curtains up. Her husband's convalescence seemed to take weeks and his fever returned occasionally, but he survived the filthy conditions of the hospital and was happy to be back at home in his lawn chair—watching his wife work.

CHAPTER 26

Two Fewer Problems

"I enjoy convalescence.
It is the part that makes the illness worthwhile."
(GEORGE BERNARD SHAW)

I, TOO, WOULD BE HAVING SURGERY SOON, but in comparison, my experience at FV Hospital was more like a spa treatment. It was May, and Robin was bringing home about $1,800 a month in cash, which came as a thick stack of 100,000-*đồng* bills (about five dollars each). For a change, life was going exactly to plan. Without my need to sacrifice any water buffaloes to the gods, the universe seemed to step in and give me a reprieve from the long stretch of setbacks. If I had a cosmic pen and could write my own destiny, my life would look a lot like it did that spring. We could finally afford little luxuries that we had given up at home because they'd gotten too expensive. We had cable TV (four dollars a month), could and did go out to restaurants nearly every day and went to the movies (three dollars). Bribes were keeping Kai in school, and even though he was coming home marching and singing the praises of Comrade Ho Chi Minh, school was keeping his little mind busy, though he, too, couldn't grasp the language. We had renters in our California house, which meant the mortgage was getting paid. And, I finally had time to write—or at least I had time to sit at the computer with every intention of writing. Oh, yes, and another surprise came: We got a $4,000 tax refund. With a healthy savings account we were on schedule for returning home in a few more months.

Yet, home wasn't on my mind like it had been at the beginning. I found myself falling head over heels in love with Vietnam. I began to experience more moments of euphoria than I'd had in my entire life. Every day I'd throw open the doors and want to run down the street, leaping and yelling, "I can't believe I get to live here!" I wanted to grab people off their bikes and hug everyone. My neighbors were in our lives daily and I loved them as family.

One day, as I sat outside holding Baby Hoa, kissing his chubby cheeks and stroking them with my pinkie finger, Homie walked over and sat down next to me. "Ms. Karin, when you go back to you country someday, everyone in neighborhood say they will sad."

"I will *be* sad, too," I said, putting the stress on his missing verb. "I don't even want to think about that day." I could feel my throat begin to tighten up. The knowledge that we would return home one day was becoming painful. I felt fired up, always kindled by the people in my neighborhood. I'd never felt this alive in the US. Could I carry that energy back with me or would it fizzle as soon as we stepped foot in Los Angeles?

I'd been noticing another peculiar sensation. Without the constant bombardment of advertisements, the money in our savings wasn't calling to me like it would have in America. That is, until one day when I read an advertisement in *Asia Life*, a glossy English-language magazine that targeted wealthy expats in Ho Chi Minh City. *Oh, yeah,* thought I, *there IS something I want.*

One evening, I sat down on our bed where Robin was dozing and said, "We need to talk." He looked at me with concern. We hadn't really had a serious talk since our arrival eight-plus months before, and any conversation that began with, "We need to talk," couldn't be good.

"I have to get something off my chest that has been bothering me for years," I said. Robin stiffly sat up in bed, but relaxed again when I told him.

Years before, in a completely cockamamie act, I had gotten breast implants. Cosmetic surgery was not in my nature. I normally do my best to ignore my body, even to the point of leaving the house without brushing my hair or checking my clothes in the mirror. One time, I wore a T-shirt inside out for most of the day. Another time, I arrived at work in slippers. Thankfully, I had sneakers in my desk drawer for emergencies such as earthquakes or Armageddon.

But this day, a friend and I had been comparing stories about how breastfeeding our babies had left us with these oddly shaped little bags hanging where real breasts used to be. "Let's go get a boob job," she said.

"Yeah, let's!"

We did. But apparently my surgeon didn't believe me when I asked for small breasts. He knew better. He knew what looked good on a woman. When I woke up and peeked under the sheet, they were not small. They were the "big American breasts" of "Two Wild and Crazy Guys" fame (Steve Martin and Dan Aykroyd from *Saturday Night Live*). I hated them. Now, eight years later, they had fallen into my lap and were heavy and uncomfortable in the hot tropical climate. I just wanted to rip them out.

The advertisements in *Asia Life* actively pitched Vietnam as the next new medical/dental tourism destination, cheaper than Thailand and Singapore, but with the same modern technology and Western-trained doctors. I thumbed through glossy photos of resortlike accommodations, the latest surgery equipment, and the smorgasbord of cosmetic procedures with tantalizingly affordable prices: teeth whitening for $30, Lasik eye surgery for $500 per eye, breast augmentation or a tummy tuck for $1,900.

Robin admitted he was going to miss the twins, but he knew that I'd always regretted getting them enlarged.

I made an appointment at the Franco-Vietnamese (FV) Hospital's plastic surgery department and met with a French-trained Vietnamese surgeon. After some bartering, we agreed on his fee, which was one-quarter what it would have been in the States. Plus, he'd throw in a breast lift, too—as if I were buying a new car and they were throwing in free floor mats. The package came with three nights in the hospital. THREE! In America, even hysterectomy patients are pushed out faster. They shove your wheelchair out into the lobby while you are still heavily sedated and drooling. A Post-it note is stuck to your forehead that says, "Please call patient's husband for immediate pickup."

Wow, I thought, *three whole days to myself in an air-conditioned room.* I couldn't think of any place I'd rather be at that moment. Honestly, I don't get why people hate hospitals so much. Think about it: You just lie around in bed all day, food is brought to you, and you can watch a lot of television without the guilt that you really should be doing Pilates or cleaning out the garage. Long airplane trips are similar—a place to suspend all responsibility. But hospitals trump airplanes because they have the added bonus of a morphine drip.

I began practicing my answer to the nurse's question: "How is your pain level, Mrs. Esterhammer?"

"It's bad, nurse…real…bad. Practically a Level Ten," I'd say in my best rendition of a person on the edge of losing it.

"Okay, I'll hang up another drip."

I told my neighbors I'd be visiting a friend in Vũng Tàu, a little beach town about two hours southeast of HCMC. I'd been to the beach town on a previous tour, so if anyone asked about my "trip," I would be able to talk about it with some truth. Mrs. Dragon offered to watch Kai after school for only four dollars per day while Robin worked.

On surgery day, I walked through the entrance farthest away from the emergency department, where Tin would be stationed that morning. But while I was filling out forms at the admitting desk, Tin walked by. He did a double take, and then rushed over to me.

"Ms. Karin, what's wrong? Why you are here?" he asked with such lovely concern in his voice that I patted his hand.

"Promise me you won't tell anyone?" I said, though I was asking a lot of him. Keeping a secret in Vietnam was a Herculean undertaking.

"Of course, I not say *any-ting* to any people."

I whispered to him what I was planning to have done. He politely kept his eyes above my neckline while he dialed up his supervisor to ask if he could escort me to my room. He was given permission. We walked into a large, bright double room, and I was thrilled to get the bed by the window. This wasn't the more expensive elite package that included the deluxe single room, a private nurse, and, later, a private tour of the city in an air-conditioned Lexus. But it was an upgrade from Đoàn Văn Bơ Street. I couldn't help but think of Homie's dad and his hospital room.

My surgery was quick. But it took the rest of the day for the anesthesia to wear off. The afternoon was a surreal blur. I could recall seeing Tin's concerned face bending over me every so often. He looked so official in his suit and tie, and I heard him talking to the nurse to get me more water and another pillow. Early on, Robin came in, but I slept through most of his visit. In the evening, Tin returned to my hospital room with two beautiful mangoes. He knew how much I loved mangoes. I was fully awake and my appetite had returned. Tin cut them up for me, giving me the best parts while he gnawed the fruit off of the stone.

I finally met my roommate that evening. She was an American who had flown out from North Carolina for a breast reduction. She'd already been there two nights and was scheduled to leave the next morning.

The next day, I watched as her bed was stripped and changed, and I wondered what country my next roommate would be from. Minutes later, nurses rolled in a pretty Vietnamese woman in her twenties fresh from breast augmentation surgery. She slept for about an hour and then got up as if all it took to recover from surgery was a refreshing nap. (Damn youth!) She opened the curtains between our beds. Dragging her IV trolley with her, she walked over to my bed and sat down on the edge of it next to my knees. She stared at me. Feeling unnerved, I cobbled together some sentences I was sure I could pronounce correctly. "Hello, my name is Karin. I am from America, but I live here in Ho Chi Minh City, in District 4. What is your name?" She smiled but didn't say anything. More stares and an uncomfortable silence. I handed her my TV remote to divert her attention. She took it, switched on a Vietnamese soap opera, and made herself comfortable *ON MY BED*. I had to move my legs diagonally to accommodate her.

Miss Boobs sat *ON MY BED* for about thirty minutes before a nurse walked in to check her vitals. The nurse didn't appear to think it was at all strange that she was sitting *ON MY BED* and took the young woman's blood pressure and temperature right there, *ON MY BED*. Miss Boobs finally got up to use the bathroom, which gave me a chance to pull the curtain completely around my bed. When she came back out, I heard her stop. She made little puffing sounds, let out a slight whimper, and then got into her own bed. Good, I thought, some peace and privacy. I closed my eyes to sleep. But peace was not to be. She started talking and I had to assume it was directed at me, not the TV. In impossibly fast Vietnamese, her voice sounded like she was on the verge of hysteria, and she panted between sentences. Once again, she got out of bed and I heard the *scritch-screech-scritch-screech* of the curtain rod. I pretended to be asleep, but I could feel her face getting closer to mine, her hot breath on my brow. I opened my eyes and looked at her. Her face was wild with...what? Fear? The wrong medication? Was she hallucinating? Was she wielding a knife? No. Once she saw that I was awake, she sat down again—ON MY BED—this time sitting closer, up by my waist. Her weight on my sheet pulled on my bandages. I struggled to move over to relieve the pressure on my stitches. She said something again and held onto my arm.

I cleared my throat and said, "*Xin lỗi, tôi không hiểu*" (excuse me, I don't understand). I reached around and pushed my intercom button. A nurse came in.

"My roommate is saying something to me, but I don't know what she's talking about," I told the nurse.

The two of them talked for a moment.

"She say she scared. She no want sleep alone. Vietnamese family sleep together. She never sleep alone before." The nurse gave me a look that said, "Come on, the least you can do to make up for the American War is let the poor girl sleep with you."

"Tell her I'll be right here next to her all night, but no, she cannot sleep ON MY BED."

The nurse helped her back into her own bed, and I called Tin. "That's it," I told him. "I'm not staying here one more day. And anyway, I feel fine. Could you tell my doctor to let me go in the morning?"

Tin couldn't stop laughing when I told him about Miss Boobs. "Okay, Ms. Karin, see you in the morning."

Miss Boobs seemed to calm down and stayed in her own bed the rest of the night. In the morning, about an hour after my doctor checked my bandages, Tin walked in with a bag of prescriptions and the exit papers. He had taken care of everything, bless him. I was so happy to see him. Miss Boobs's face registered horror as Tin wheeled me out with my gear. I said a little prayer for her that she would get a suitable roommate—one who didn't mind sharing a bed with her.

I had no pain. Best of all, my surgery results were perfect. The pair were lifted back into the place nature intended them to be and they looked fantastic. I told Tin he'd just have to trust me on that.

CHAPTER 27

Exploiting the Proletariat

"The good leaves protect the worn-out leaves."
(VIETNAMESE PROVERB)

TIN WAS ON MY DOORSTEP the next day. I thought he was checking up on my recovery. But as soon as he sat down, I could see he was upset about something. "My mother lost her job," he said in breathy, staccato words. "She have no job at store now. Today they close store. Not enough customers." He smoothed his pants with his hands over and over as if he were trying to wipe off this new catastrophe.

"I am so sorry to hear that, Tin." I knew she lived with her mother, Tin's grandmother, so at least she and Tin's younger sister had a roof over their heads. But even missing a couple of days without pay would greatly strain the household and could mean his sister would be kicked out of school for nonpayment of tuition.

I asked Tin how much she had earned per month and he answered one million (then about fifty dollars). Even for Vietnam, it was slave labor. "I must find job for her very fast."

It wouldn't be easy. I knew her background. She only had a third-grade education, and because she didn't speak any English, she couldn't work for English-speaking foreigners who paid better. She also had no unemployment insurance, a benefit unavailable to anyone except government workers, and even then you were lucky to get thirty dollars a month for only two months.

I had an idea, but I wanted to run it by Robin, who was upstairs in the office.

"Wait here," I told Tin, after handing him a glass of cold water. "I will come right back."

I'd never considered getting someone to cook, clean, and watch Kai, because I've never been comfortable with the idea of household help. The few times in LA when I was overstressed, overtired, or in my last few weeks of pregnancy and resorted to maid service, I cleaned right along with her. Class differences make me uncomfortable. I didn't want anyone to think I was some pampered professional woman who couldn't scrub her own toilet. It didn't occur to me that perhaps it was okay to equate household help with other service jobs, such as carpet cleaners or painters or gardeners. I'd be giving work to someone who needed it.

I felt stranger still that I would be hiring a local to work for me, a white foreigner, which reeked of colonialism. Comrade Ho Chi Minh whispered snidely in my ear, "Exploiting the proletariat, eh?" Nevertheless, Hanh needed a job and we could easily pay her three times what she earned before. I did need her. Food shopping and cooking were daily time-consuming chores. My lunch that day had consisted of three bites of ice cream, a handful of rice crackers, a mandarin orange, and one cooked beet—in that order. Plus, between school, studying, teaching students, cleaning, and keeping Kai busy in the afternoon, I was writing only about an hour a day. At that rate, I calculated it would take another six years to finish my bestselling novel.

I also couldn't keep up with Kai's muddy footprints on the floors now that we were coming into the rainy season. The heavy tropical showers were great fun for Kai and his friends, who would splash, jump, and even shampoo their hair outside and let the warm rain rinse them thoroughly. I had to mop several times a day. I told Robin about Hanh's job loss. "I know we don't need the luxury of household help, but I think we could afford to hire Hanh." He was as eager as I was to provide a job for her. I ran back down feeling happy, but I was also a bit nervous that perhaps I would be asking her to do a job beneath her dignity, or that I would offend Tin by offering such work to her.

"Robin and I have been needing some household help. Do you think your mother would want to work for us until she can find another job?"

He drew in a breath and smiled broadly. "Oh, Ms. Karin, yes, she will work for you." He didn't bother to ask her, but then, he was the man in the family.

"Would she like a few days off before starting?"

"No, she no need days off. She start tomorrow. What time?"

"Not too early. Robin sleeps late now because he has evening classes. How about 10 a.m. to 4 p.m. Monday to Friday? How will she get here from Cu Chi?"

"She ride the bus."

"Okay, I will pay her three million."

"No, no, too much. Two million."

"No, Tin. I will pay her three million."

Tin smiled and nodded. "Very kind, very kind. See you to-morrow. Thank you. So very, very thanks to you."

The next morning at 6:30 the doorbell rang. I woke up with a start and ran down, wearing only my boxer shorts and tank top. "Please stop ringing the doorbell. Kai will wake up," I hissed as I sprinted toward the door. Hanh and Mama Hang were pressing their faces against the metal grid of the gate, as if trying to melt themselves through it like the T-1000, the shape-shifting assassin in *Terminator 2*.

"You don't need to arrive so early," I said. "We were still sleep-ing." I hoped my Vietnamese came out right. But it must have sounded more like "Sure, come on in," because instead of going back home, they pushed past me like two little tornadoes. Mama Hang, who knew my kitchen well, pulled out a bucket, rags, and cleansers, and showed Hanh where things were. The two of them talked fast, but I managed to extract enough words to know that she was telling Hanh what time Kai would need breakfast and to stay out of Robin's bedroom because he sleeps very, very, late.

Right off, Hanh opened the refrigerator and began pulling out the food to wash the interior. I hardly knew what to do with myself. I was braless under my shirt, sweaty, and in need of a shower, but I wasn't sure if they needed me to stand there and supervise or help them. I felt awkward and useless.

Hanh turned to me. "What do you want to eat today?"

I shrugged.

"Do you want soup today? Or something stir-fried?"

"Sure, anything." I immediately regretted my words. "Anything" could mean snake meat, bull testicles, dog, frogs, even stir-fried maggots. So just as quickly, I said, "Chicken or fish would be good."

Mama Hang put her hand out. "Money. She needs money for the market."

I got my purse and pulled out a 100,000-*đồng* bill. They looked at the bill and then at each other and laughed.

"Too much!" Mama Hang said. "She only needs 30,000 *đồng*."

If she could make lunch and dinner for four people a day (including herself) with $1.50, clearly I had been getting overcharged at the market.

Mama Hang went back to her sewing, and Hanh began taking down all the curtains to wash. I'd never washed them and hadn't noticed they were dirty until she hung them back up clean, a shade lighter. Hanh worked quietly and quickly all day, stopping around 2 p.m. to watch a Vietnamese soap opera and take a nap on the living room floor. She was back on the bus at 4 p.m.

That evening, when Homie returned from work, he came over.

"Ms. Karin, I hear Ms. Hanh work today in you house."

"Oh, my gosh, she's just amazing!" I gushed. "Today, we had purple potato soup, shrimp in a tangy sauce, greens, and rice. Dessert was a sweet soup, with beans, coconut milk, sweet potatoes, and tapioca. She is such a good cook!"

"Yes, she good," he said tentatively, tilting his head from side to side. "It because she learn from my mother. My mother a better cook!" he said with a grin.

The next morning, Hanh was at the doorstep once more at 6:30. Again, as I let her in, I told her to wait until 10 a.m., because 6:30 was far too early. I felt confident she understood my Vietnamese this time because she stared at me for a second and then asked me what I wanted to eat for lunch. After that day, she arrived at eight, a compromise, of sorts.

Having Hanh was blissful. *So this is how the rich live!* The house was never cleaner, the food was never more exquisite. Over the weeks I enjoyed my spare time and so did Robin—except that he slept through his free time. Lately, he'd been sleeping at every opportunity. Day after day he'd go to work, come home, and go straight to bed. I began to fear he had been bitten by something or contracted some sort of rare tropical sleeping disease.

"Do you feel okay? Maybe you should go to FV and see a doctor."

"No, nothing is wrong with me. I just like to sleep."

"Hiring Hanh was meant to free you up to *do* something, not to sleep more."

"Yeah, yeah." And he rolled over.

He'd always slept a lot; this was nothing new, but now in the mornings he'd been sleeping later and later. His German genes weren't goose-stepping in sync with the rest of the world. Germans, according to one British study, sleep eighteen minutes less than the average Brit. The British average is seven hours per night, but the American average is 6.8 hours. Robin was now averaging twelve hours.

Around 11 a.m., Hanh came down the stairs with an armload of folded clothes. She saw that Robin was sleeping, so she set the clothes just outside the door. She looked at me knowingly.

"Robin *vẫn đang ngủ*," she said with a giggle. I rolled my eyes to let her know that yes, he was still asleep and no, I wasn't pleased.

Pretty soon Hanh had lunch ready and I decided to eat alone rather than wake Robin up. Tin came by to give some keys to his mom, so I invited him to join me. He was happy to oblige, especially when his mother was cooking.

"Ms. Karin, [Mrs. Dragon] see my mother here every day. She get mad and tell me I have kicked her rice bowl. That mean I take away her ability to earn money from you. To keep peace in neighborhood, I think you must give my mother two million and give one million to [Mrs. Dragon] so she not be angry."

"No, Tin, I don't want to take your mother's pay away."

"Yes," he said. "You must do that."

"No, that's crazy."

We went back and forth several more rounds. I couldn't believe he wasn't backing down. This was his own mother's livelihood, but I was impressed that keeping peace on the alley was more important than his hardworking mother's income. Finally, I looked sternly at Tin and said loudly, "I will NOT pay her less. I will NOT do that!"

The next morning Homie met me outside and said, "I learned a new sentence from my cousin: 'I will NOT do that!' "

CHAPTER 28

Too Few Classes

"I wish that money will flow into your house like water, and out like a turtle."
(VIETNAMESE BLESSING)

IN THE FALL, the director of Robin's language school began cutting his hours, shaving off a class here, a class there. Her explanation: a sudden glut of new teachers. That might have been partially true given America's rising unemployment rate. We weren't the only ones trying to find work in economically burgeoning Southeast Asia. But I also think she was only being polite. Student surveys at the end of each eight-week course made it clear that Robin wasn't put on the planet to teach. I caught a glimpse why when he invited me one day to observe a couple of his classes.

Robin sat at the teacher's desk instead of getting up and engaging the students. The lessons were not just sleep-inducing, but PhD-dissertation-on-potting-soil sleep-inducing, which was completely incongruous to his real nature. Get him into a room with friends and he was boisterous, animated, and often choke-on-your-saliva funny. That wasn't materializing in the classroom.

To be fair, how do you know you won't be good at something

until you try? "Piece of cake," he'd said when he'd signed up for the monthlong teacher's training program to earn his CELTA, a little piece of paper that assures language schools that you will be able to fill out the hour with more than a game of hangman on the blackboard. Plus, he excels at languages. He speaks German, English, French, and Spanish fluently, and can read Latin—one of the benefits of being born and raised in Germany, where kids start learning foreign languages from first grade. But a talent for speaking didn't translate into an aptitude for teaching a language.

One payday, Robin walked into the house with an envelope stuffed with cash—140 crisp 100,000-*đồng* bills (oh, that they were dollars!)—his monthly income.

"Lookeee…" he hummed as he set his backpack down. He took out a stack of bills, fanned them out and waved them in my face as if he'd just won the lottery. In dollars it only added up to 700.

"Robin, that won't get us through the month," I said, feeling irritated. "Can't you apply for classes at another school and get more teaching hours?"

"Sure, don't worry," he said after a long yawn. "I'll start looking tomorrow." He wasn't a bit unhinged that we were quickly financially backsliding. Robin plunked his six-foot-four-inch body down on the living room lawn chair, our equivalent of a La-Z-Boy recliner. He positioned a small pillow over his eyes, and clasped his hands over his round belly, ready for his evening nap before he went to bed. To him, a nap was like an appetizer before REM sleep.

I'd been sitting at the kitchen table in a tank top and shorts perspiring as I went through a thick stack of mail that Marisa had bundled and sent to us. Under my bare legs the sweat was pooling on the vinyl chair, so I got up to grab a kitchen towel from the counter and returned to the table to tuck it under my legs. I could tell from Robin's breathing that he was nearly asleep. I asked myself: In a global economic meltdown second only in severity to the Great Depression, do you really get to roll over and sleep like a baby?

Kai interrupted my thoughts as he came running down the stairs carrying a red plastic bucket of Matchbox trucks and cars. He rarely went anywhere, even into another room, without his arms loaded with toys. They were his security blanket. In the narrow living room, he carefully maneuvered his little body around his dad's feet so as not to brush up against him and wake him. Kai sat down on the chair across from me and began to line up his cars on the table. Putting objects in neat rows was an autism-spectrum behavior, and of his several behavioral quirks, this was one of the more endearing and practical. I wanted to lean over the table and kiss him on his sweet, furrowed brow, his face frozen in concentration as he placed his cars in a pattern of red-green-red-green followed by blue-yellow-blue-yellow. After a couple of minutes parking tiny vehicles and perfectly mimicking the sound of a truck backing up, he looked at me.

"Who farted?"

I knew what it was. "Oh, damn, damn! Not another flood!" I looked out to see that the water was already eight inches high. "And I forgot to buy food for dinner tonight! Dammit!" I hissed.

Kai giggled. "You said a bad word."

The wafting sewer smell had been the silent-but-deadly alarm warning us that the Saigon River's tide was about to rise up from the gutters and flood the alley. It was the rainy season, and we'd been enduring floods in the alley nearly every evening. After almost a year living here, I guess I'd become inured to the odor. Normally, those first warning smells gave me a ten-minute window of opportunity to run a quick errand while the water was still only an inch deep. But now it covered the lower of our two front steps. It would be at least two hours before it receded.

"Don't walk in the water," a neighbor had warned with a grimace when we first moved to Đoàn Văn Bơ Street. I watched the water rise as it churned and mixed with whatever was on the ground: urine and poop (babies are often diaperless), spit, doggy doo, dead cockroaches, fish bones, plastic bottles, and…OMG, was that a used sanitary napkin?

My Vietnamese neighbors rarely groused about the floods—or any other daily tribulation for that matter. Flood time was just another reason to fire up their karaoke machines and sing heartfelt love songs by their favorite pop singers. The downtime was a kind of "cool, now we get two full hours to party" cheerfulness that I had come to love and admire, but had yet learn to emulate.

Neighbors whose houses were level with the street had already set up pieces of plywood and old rags to keep the water from inundating their living rooms. And when the water eventually seeped in past the barriers, as it so often did, they would simply roll up their bedding, hang the chairs on wall hooks, and set the ubiquitous little Buddhist floor shrines that bring good luck to the house atop metal cabinets. Then the karaoke party was moved up to the second floor.

Newer houses were built a foot higher, so, like ours, only the splashing from passing motorbikes would cause the water to seep under my doorway. After each flood, everyone mopped the tile floors and swept up the scattered trash in the alley. Life went on without complaint. The city's water drainage system had been built fifty years before to serve 1.5 million people. Now there were 7 million—10 million if you included the outskirts. Ho Chi Minh City was Asia's version of an inundated Venice, Italy, minus the raised walkways and gelato shops.

I tapped Robin's foot on the way to the kitchen to rouse him. "Are you hungry?" I asked. I tried to remember if I had any food left in the refrigerator. My do-as-the-natives-do routine of buying food fresh daily, either from roving vendors who peddled the back alleys or from the Very Important Market meant there weren't many staple items on hand. Robin mumbled that he had already stopped for a sandwich on the way home.

"But I'm hungry!" Kai said. "Make me rice."

"*Please* make me…?" I coaxed.

"Please, make me rice," Kai repeated.

I dug through the cupboards—cupboard, rather, which was

the other reason I didn't buy food in bulk. My kitchen was closet-size, though more modern than most kitchens in the neighborhood. Although a great deal of time is spent preparing and cooking food in Vietnamese households, an actual kitchen for such activity is rarely built in. This isn't to say they don't exist in the wealthier neighborhoods in Ho Chi Minh City. Of course they do. But most of my neighbors' kitchens consisted of little more than a plastic basin and garden hose next to a corner floor drain. Then, set on top of a small metal table was a single-burner portable gas camping stove and a rice cooker. And yet, sans granite counters and stainless steel appliances, the meals, which were so often generously shared with us, were consistently and painfully delicious. My kitchen had a counter with a sink but no hot water, and a two-burner cooktop but no oven. Modest and suitable. Who would bake a meatloaf in this tropical heat anyway?

I put a cup of rice in the electric rice cooker, added bottled water and pushed the "on" button. Dinner was going to be meager that night.

As we waited, Kai sat in the doorway with a broken broom handle, poised to nab something as he watched the trash float by.

"Look, I'm fishing!" He lifted out a plastic bag and swung it around like a windmill, catapulting it back into the cesspool. About twenty minutes later, another jab into the water brought up a finger-size centipede.

"Drop it!" I shrieked. "Quickly!"

"Why?" he asked, looking disappointed about my catch-and-release order.

"Because they bite."

"Would I die?"

"I don't think so, but I hear its bite hurts like crazy. Now leave the broom handle outside and go wash your hands. It's time to eat."

I carried our dinner of steamed rice and sliced bananas to the table. The aromatic jasmine rice and tangy, locally grown finger bananas were calming and delicious comfort foods for my frayed nerves. I ate slowly and listened to all the alley sounds: motor-bikes; floodwater splashing against the houses; neighborhood children taking turns with the karaoke microphone, their little voices ear-twistingly out of tune.

After a little while, Robin and Kai went upstairs to get ready for bed. It felt good to finally sit alone, calm down, and remind myself of the simple things that made Vietnam so enchanting—most importantly, the friendships with my neighbors. How quickly they had gathered us into their circle, helping us settle and feel like part of their own families. Their example of cheerfulness despite floods and poverty was helping me learn how to stop and smell the roses without disparaging the aphids that got up my nostrils.

I began to feel better. But about an hour after the dishes were done, the phone rang:

"Karin?" I heard. I didn't recognize the voice but it was clearly American.

"It's Phil, your new property manager. Your house has a plumbing emergency. Your new tenants said their toilet and tub are backed up. I need your okay for repairs."

We were paying him good money to deal with such issues. Why didn't he just call a plumber and put it on our account?

"This is waaaaay beyond rooter service," he said. "There are tree roots all the way into the street's mainline. Three plumbing companies already gave estimates. The cost is about ten thousand dollars."

I didn't want him to hear the fear in my voice, so I forced out a chirpy, "Oh, just choose whichever plumbing company accepts credit cards. I'll get some good airline miles for that, won't I?"

After I hung up, I sank down onto the floor. Tears brimmed and fell, and I let myself slip into self-pity for who knows how long. I finally got up to lock the sliding metal gate for the night. In the alley, the gutters had slurped and chugged back the last of the flood. Neighbors wasted no time sweeping out the debris field in their living rooms and in front of their houses. Cockroaches, however, were left undisturbed, belly-up but still twitching inside people's houses. The Vietnamese have a superstition that if you kill the cockroaches in your house, you will lose money. Choop and Dee's mom treated them as adorable little house pets, often letting one crawl around her hands and between her fingers. How many thousands had I whacked with my flip-flop in hand since we'd moved to Ho Chi Minh City? Perhaps ten thousand? Well, there you go. That was our plumbing bill.

This would clean out the savings account we'd worked so hard to accumulate. We'd been in Vietnam a full year now—our original deadline for returning—and we were far from being able to go home. In fact, now we were stranded.

CHAPTER 29

Job Loss

"Let's begin by taking a smallish nap or two."
(WINNIE THE POOH)

IT'S TRUE WHAT THEY SAY about things getting worse before they get better. A few weeks before Christmas, Robin came home early one afternoon. He closed the door, took off his helmet, and looked at me sadly. "They let me go today."

The blood drained out of my face and my neck felt prickly. "Oh, my God, Robin, what reason did they give you?"

"Too many complaints from the students. They said they couldn't follow me and the class was too difficult."

Without stopping to discuss it more, he headed up to bed. I stayed in the living room on the couch and stared at the floor tiles. My eyes traced each square in an effort to lose myself in the inanity of the activity. I struggled to keep fear from rising up and swallowing me. Contrary to my deepest hopes, he was turning out to be less of a financial help, not more, in Vietnam.

Over the next weeks, Robin's desire to sleep became ever more pronounced. Twelve hours became fifteen to eighteen hours a day. I ping-ponged between worry for his mental health and my own feelings of rage. In my best Glenn Close voice, I hissed, "I'm NOT gonna be ignored, Robin. Get out of bed and get a job!" I begged him again to see a doctor. "I feel fine." Well, then, could he talk with a shrink, because oversleeping is often a sign of depression. "I'm not depressed." I called the Australian clinic in District 1 anyway, because that's what all good enablers do, and was told, *yees* (they're Aussies, *remeeember?*), they had a clinical psychologist on staff. I told Robin that despite the fact the shrink came from a country situated upside down on planet Earth, I'm sure the guy was level-headed and could be of some help. But before Robin agreed to go in for his first appointment, he got a job again, which worked just as well for getting him out of bed and was far cheaper.

Because Vietnam was taking inspiration from China's success in the global marketplace, which meant English was becoming ever more essential to getting ahead in business, the city had language schools every ten feet. It was really not that hard to find employment somewhere. I shouldn't have worried so much.

But instead of feeling celebratory, Mr. Murphy of Murphy's Law fame queried: "I wonder how long this job will last?" His new job gave him almost as few hours as the last, so to round out his hours, he advertised for a few private students at twenty-five dollars per hour. One was a wealthy restaurant owner and his wife who invited us to eat at his restaurant for free. Another was a Korean business executive who was studying Vietnamese and English. He offered Robin as many beers as he could guzzle per lesson. Needless to say, he was Robin's favorite student.

Still, Robin's mood had hit bottom. He called me from inside the bathroom one afternoon. "Why did you buy this brand of toilet paper again? I don't like it. It isn't perforated and just rips apart."

"Yes, but it also doesn't have the wasteful cardboard cylinder in it. I'm helping to save the planet's trees."

He'd been complaining mightily about everything lately— the heat, the traffic, the noise, and one chain-smoking neighbor's incessant guttural snortings followed by the hacking up of brown-ish green loogies right into the alley. (This same neighbor once invited Robin over for barbecued rat. Too bony, said Robin, who would try anything, including—once—cobra.) He also hated our mattress, the floods, and the bugs. But most of all, he hated teaching, and said so often. I was sure he would lose this new job, too, especially if he wasn't willing to push himself to become a better teacher. But what other jobs were available for a foreigner?

I decided to get help from the Ladies Who Lunch Because They're Bored. On a Thursday morning, I dressed up and headed to the Rex Hotel for the weekly meeting. Seeing the group as a source of support made it easier for me to graciously handle any table banter involving such honest-to-God misfortunes as the caterer who arrived late or not getting upgraded on a flight. In truth, as the morning went on, it was an unexpected pleasure to relax into conversations with other English speakers. With my Vietnamese friends, I needed to be more aware of choosing simpler words, speaking more slowly, and refraining from idioms. The Ladies Who Have No Worries meeting gave me a chance to step out of my cultural classroom and relax back into mostly familiar Western sensibilities.

I walked around the room looking for…oh, I don't know, loose diamonds? money? Until I spotted Kricket, the Nike lady from America. I sat down next to her, hoping we could pick up where we'd left off so many months ago. Would she remember me? "Now about those Nike Airs in size seven for seventy percent off…." Instead, we talked about our kids and their adjustments to life in Vietnam. Her nine-year-old daughter was struggling in her Mandarin Chinese class, a requirement at her international school. Kai's latest struggle, which I didn't share with her, was more basic: keeping his hands off the little spray hose common in Vietnamese bathrooms—which was traditionally a substitute for toilet paper. Whether at restaurants or at home, the temptation to play with the water was too great for Kai. "Look, Mom, it's raining!"

Two women from England joined our table and we exchanged pleasantries. When I told them I lived in District 4, one of them asked where it was. "It's just across the Saigon River from District 2," I said. And then I added proudly, "There are no expats, so I'm really getting a chance to experience the culture there."

"Culture?" one of them said, nearly gagging, as if I'd just fed her a spoonful of dung beetles. "I have *no* interest in learning about Vietnamese culture."

That was my cue to move on. I sat at various tables and asked several women if their husbands could find my husband a job. Anything. Filing, data processing, coffee runs. Their response: Unless he was an engineer, software developer, or in international finance, their husbands had nothing to offer him. The unskilled jobs went to the English-speaking Vietnamese whom they could exploit for fifty cents an hour. He'd be better off teaching.

I gave up and decided to leave, but before I did, an announcement was made for upcoming excursions. The Ladies Who Have Absolutely Nothing to Do occasionally put together cultural outings or shopping tours, but none had ever sounded worth my precious time. On this day, though, one caught my attention. It was to a national "wilderness" for a hike and picnic lunch. The bus would leave from the hotel at 10 a.m. and return at about 3 p.m. I'd still have part of my day left to get some work done. I signed up, along with eleven other Ladies Who Lunch and Then Go Hiking. It would be nice to escape the city. I pictured a lush, cool forest with picnic tables and shady trees.

CHAPTER 30

A Walk in the Park

*"When it is dark, there is not enough light
to see properly, for example, because it is night."*
(ON A SYMPATHY CARD IN THE ENGLISH-LANGUAGE SECTION
OF A BOOKSTORE)

THE NATIONAL WILDERNESS PARK was near the border, where signs
warned that within 500 feet you would fall off Planet Vietnam and
make a hard landing in Cambodia. On hiking day, I boarded the
bus and sat next to a Canadian member of the Ladies Who Lunch
Because They Have Pristine Karma, and we chatted up the usual—
how long is your contract here, what district do you live in, do you
like it, isn't the food just divine? She was a picture of Weltschmerz,
having the look of someone who has seen too much of the world
and would just like to eat a hamburger and once again be able to
wear long sleeves and socks without looking like an overdressed
mental patient in the heat.

The ride took nearly two hours and when we arrived, the lush,
cool forest I'd envisioned—and, indeed, lusted after—had only a
few pencil-thin trees. The rest of the vegetation in this jungle, or
park, or whatever it was called, only went up to one's knees. We

got off the bus and were met by not-so-friendly natives of the bug variety that seemed to glom onto the sweatiest parts of our bodies. Suicide squads of bugs drowned themselves in my cleavage. The hike hadn't even begun and I was already miserable. Worse, I had to pee. Urgently.

"Are there any outhouses in this park?" I asked Perky Troop Leader Julie. She didn't know. *Wait, Julie the troop leader doesn't know? Hasn't she been here before?* She turned to ask the driver. With a laugh, he pantomimed squatting behind a tree. I pantomimed right back: What tree, pray tell, would hide me? I imagined my lily-white derrière glinting in the sun, looking like a signal lamp on a ship and flashing signals to confused villagers miles away.

I watched a German woman venture out to find her own patch of vegetation to relieve herself. She looked like a giant cat in a shallow litter box and was seemingly oblivious to the fact that she wasn't hiding her privates at all and the whole world could see her, including the bus driver, who pretended he wasn't looking, except he was. I've had dreams like this before. You know the kind, where you have to go to the bathroom and there are no doors on the stalls or you find yourself in the men's room? The German woman pulled up her pants and headed toward the trail. Even if I had that wonderful European lack of shame about showing the naked body, like she did, I'd still suffer vapor lock and be unable to go.

I looked around and saw a house down the road from the trail-head with lots of kids and a scrawny dog on the porch. I was just certain they'd love to let a foreigner in to use their toilet—if they had one. Even a hole in the ground, if it's discreetly hidden behind some bamboo, would be better than a foot-high patch of shrubbery. I ran to the house. In Vietnamese, I politely asked to use their toilet and waved a 10,000-*đồng* bill (fifty cents) in front of them. A young girl smiled and beckoned me in. The younger children followed me down a dark hallway to a little closet with a....yes! A real toilet! The kids waited just outside the door for me, talking and giggling. Before I left, and out of pure gratitude, I handed them another fifty cents.

The hikers hadn't gone far and I caught up with them quickly. The walk was sweltering and the trail ugly. Forty-five minutes into this misery, Perky Troop Leader Julie announced it was lunchtime, so we set out the picnic right there on the trail and sat down in a long row, a configuration hardly conducive for chatting. But it was either there or some scratchy foot-high bushes likely filled with snakes, ants, toads, shrub beetles, and who knows what kind of animal excrement.

After lunch, we continued on down the trail for another thirty minutes until we ended up in the backyard of a villager. A little old man looked up from his garden, startled to see twelve foreign women staring back at him. No one made a move. I waited for Perky Troop Leader Julie to say, "This is Huong and he's going to give a tour of his home and explain what it is like to live in the countryside." But Perky Troop Leader Julie said nothing of the sort. We stood, silently, hungrily waiting for some kind of cultural exchange to give meaning to this miserable walk.

There had to be some little prize at the end of this hike through the hottest, buggiest, scrawniest jungle that would make all the time and effort worthwhile. But no, the frightened man wasn't part of the itinerary, and it was now obvious that Perky Troop Leader Julie didn't expect to end up in someone's yard. In fact, I suspected she didn't know where we were. If it weren't for the fact that we could see the trees for the nearly nonexistent forest and in the distance was our bus, we would have been hopelessly lost. I wanted to sit down and cry. I wasted my precious writing time for nothing—no waterfalls, no picnic area, no forest service boxes that point out the flora and fauna. We got back on the bus scratching our bug bites, mopping our faces, and sitting silently. I vowed no more nature trips in Vietnam.

The day would have been all for naught, except for one useful conversation. I sat next to a woman named Maggie from Australia. As we commiserated that the hike had been a colossal waste of time, she told me that not all the activities and outings sponsored

by the Ladies Who Lunch Because They Have Nothing Else to
Live For were this much of a disaster. She told me her favorite outing was a weekly trip to an orphanage in the Go Vap district. The
work was as simple as holding babies, playing with them, and feeding them. In short, a blissful afternoon if you like babies, which I
do. I immediately pictured myself sitting in a rocking chair with
an armload of squishy, squeaky, marshmallow-soft babies. I asked
Maggie again, "So, the Vietnamese actually let foreigners come
into the orphanages?" She assured me they did.

What a difference from when Robin and I adopted Kai in
Ukraine. That orphanage had been strictly guarded, a gated com-
pound with bars on all the windows. I wasn't sure if the extra security was to keep people out or to prevent the babies from escaping.
No one but staff was allowed in. Each day for two weeks, while
waiting for a court date to finalize Kai's adoption, we went to the
orphanage to start bonding with him. In the lobby, a woman in
a white medical coat would hand him to us. We could play with
eighteen-month-old Kai there in the lobby or go outside on the
front porch, but we couldn't go behind the scenes. Once, though,
when someone inadvertently left the door to the baby room open,
I poked my head in and saw a dozen crying babies crammed together in one playpen with no toys, and no one to soothe or hold
them. Because the orphanage couldn't afford diapers, the babies'
clothes were wet up to their armpits. Three chunky caregivers sat
off to the side talking and laughing as if the babies weren't there.
It was a sad picture that will haunt me always. Now, right here in
Vietnam, I could turn that memory on its head and make my con-
tribution to the cause of crying babies the world over.

CHAPTER 31

Orphanage

"Funny Center"
(A CHILDCARE CENTER IN AN UPSCALE DISTRICT 1
DEPARTMENT STORE)

I'D ALWAYS WANTED to do volunteer work but never had the chance when I worked full time. The idea of helping to give institutionalized children some much-needed human contact sounded so gratifying, and I knew this was what I needed to get my mind off the family finances.

On a Tuesday morning at 8:30 a.m., Maggie's personal driver picked me up, along with two other Ladies Who Lunch Every Damn Day. We arrived thirty minutes later at the Go Vap orphanage. The SUV stopped in front of a chipped, dilapidated, gray concrete building with thick chain-link fences around every possible opening but the sky. It looked and felt like a prison until we opened the gate, which was unlocked. A security guard was texting and didn't even bother to look up as we walked right in.

About 250 children, ages one week to young teens, were housed in the three-story complex. An interior open-air courtyard offered benches and some once-colorful but now sun-faded and cracked vinyl play equipment. I looked up to the covered roof deck and saw hundreds of dingy cloth diapers on clotheslines, flapping like Tibetan prayer flags in the breeze. The sounds of crying babies and squealing kids rushed out of every door as we headed up the stairs to the infant room. Thirty chrome cribs stood in neat classroom-like rows. The turquoise room looked like its last paint job had been in 1962. Everywhere rust stripes from leaky metal window casings streaked the walls. Christmas decorations hung from the ceiling, not because it was Christmas, but because they were stimulating and colorful for the babies.

Maggie introduced me to the room's four caregivers, none of whom had any idea of what she was saying. (I always find it amusing when English speakers talk to non-English speakers as if they absolutely should understand them. They don't try to speak slowly or use simple words.) We all nodded to each other. Nobody asked to see any baby-holding credentials or my passport, which Maggie had suggested I carry with me. We headed to a large porcelain sink to wash our hands with slivers of slimy bar soap slowly melting in a watery pink plastic saucer.

"Well, then," Maggie directed me as soon as I was finished, "just pick up any baby, get a bottle from one of the workers, and start feeding." The bottles had name tags so no baby would go hungry or get fed twice. We spread out across the room and picked up the crying babies first. The mouth nearest me was a one-week-old baby girl wrapped tightly in a flannel blanket, which had a small hole in it. One tiny foot had escaped through the hole, and her toes formed a perfect row of petite peas. I picked her up and petted her head of silky black hair that stood straight up. She latched onto the bottle nipple easily, took a couple of long draws, and promptly fell asleep. I wiggled the nipple and managed to get a couple more ounces down her before I picked up another baby and then another. For the next hour it was feed, burp, change diapers, return to crib, feed, burp, change diapers, and return to crib. The babies calmed down the second they were picked up. Alternatively, most

wailed mournfully when they were returned to the crib. I wished
I had more arms. After the feeding frenzy, we held the crying ones
and sang silly songs to the others.

The underpaid staff workers (Maggie told me the pay was only
fifty dollars per month) weren't terribly enthusiastic about their
work or sympathetic toward the babies. They dressed and diapered
the babies like factory workers assembling toys—fast and not too
delicately. They weren't mean, just impassive. Or perhaps they had
simply become immune to wailing orphans or the babies' heart-
breaking circumstances.

As I held a fussy baby, gently swaying him for a long while, a
surly worker grunted at me, grabbed the baby out of my arms, and
shook her head as she put him back in his crib. I glanced over at
Maggie, who had seen it.

"Did I do anything wrong?" I asked.

"No, not at all. These workers act like we are in their way. But
we tell ourselves that we are here for the babies, not for the caregivers. If they want to act annoyed, let them."

When it was naptime for the infants, the four of us moved on
to another room where babies ages seven to eighteen months old
were housed. One by one we carried the tots out of their cribs and
put them together on a large, soft mat surrounded by good-quality toys that had been donated by foreign charities. It wasn't easy
keeping the babies on the mat. They spread out like cockroaches
reacting to light. Twenty-five little bodies headed out the door,
disappeared under the tables, or crawled over each other. Tiny feet
kicked heads and slimy fingers poked eyeballs. I never knew human beings this small could be so dangerous in large numbers.

The babies were randomly dressed in frilly pink dresses or in
T-shirts with baseball caps or rocket ship designs, without heed to
gender. In Vietnam, pink was not considered a girl's color (indeed,
I'd seen plenty of grown men wearing pink hats), nor was blue
necessarily a boy's. It wasn't until I changed a given baby's diaper
that I knew the sex of the tot.

A baby seated on the mat near Maggie began to cry. His toy had just been rudely swiped by Sumo Baby, a rotund little guy who was out for his share of anything he could get his chubby hands on. Maggie picked up the sad baby, who was wearing a blouse with pink puffy sleeves, and sat down with him.

"Oh, baby Phong," she cooed to him, "you are dressed in drag today!" He stopped crying and smiled at her.

"Do you ever see babies get adopted out?" I asked. Maggie had been volunteering at the orphanage for about a year.

"We do," she said. "Not often enough, of course, but we do see couples from Italy, France, Australia, and Britain. Right now, Americans are barred from adopting here, but that will change. The laws change often depending on which country is in or out of favor. And," she added with a laugh, "that favor often depends on who is forking over the most money."

I, too, had heard that adoptions were closed to Americans after a wee spat that had occurred in late spring 2008. American Embassy officials had accused the Vietnamese Department of International Adoptions of corruption and baby-selling. It was reported that orphanage directors would approach pregnant women in the poorer countryside and offer them $100 to $300 for their babies. For foreigners adopting a baby, the costs could total $20,000 to $30,000, a pretty good return on an orphanage's investment. But the Vietnamese denied it and said, basically, "Okay, until you take that back, you Americans can't have any more of our children." So while the two countries slung insults, the babies waited for families. At least I could hold them in the meantime, and doing so was such a joy.

Back at home, even Kai's incessant chatter and his loud toy firetruck sirens couldn't sully my mood. The orphan babies were still fresh on my mind. I could even smell that wonderful baby smell on my clothes. I couldn't wait to go again. Excitedly, I told Homie and Tin about my day.

"I had so much fun. I think Vietnamese children are so cute. The babies have beautiful dark eyes and those chubby little cheeks.

Ooh, I could just eat them up," I cooed.

Homie looked at me. "Eat them? What do it mean?"

"It's just an expression. Don't the Vietnamese say something like that when they see a little baby?"

"No, we don't eat our children," he replied with a grin.

Tin loved the idea of "charity work" and wanted to help, too, so the two of us began going on our own twice a week and did so for the duration of my time in Vietnam. The caretakers were friendlier toward him, perhaps because he was a man—a good-looking man—which gave us more freedom to hold onto the babies longer.

Over the next few months, I discovered a lovely benefit from volunteering. I felt strangely safe. Instead of feeling as if I couldn't control my world, volunteering gave me the reigns to take happiness into my own hands. It felt like the first time I went downhill skiing and, as we stood perpendicular to the slope, my instructor told me to put my weight on the downhill ski. It seemed so incongruous. Every part of me wanted to lean into the uphill ski to keep myself from toppling headfirst down the mountain. Facing my losses and fears, I was pawing, flailing, and hugging the hill. Holding babies kept me grounded, with my weight on the downhill side.

More volunteer work showed up on our doorstep. Three families from another alley had discovered us and wanted their kids to learn English. One evening, as the three of us were heading out to dinner, Robin opened the front door and saw a small crowd gathered around Homie, who was standing with them. They were asking him questions and pointing to us. When he saw us, he walked toward our door and the crowd shuffled over with him.

"They want you teach their children English, yes?"

"Sure, we'd love to," I said.

Homie continued. "They want you teach the parents English, too, yes?"

We both answered yes. Helping people learn English who couldn't afford classes had been on my Vietnam to-do list anyway.

Tuition at the city's twenty-some English-language schools, where native-born speakers were hired, was prohibitive in cost to all but a small percentage of people. Yet the people who most needed at least rudimentary English skills were the people who made their living from tourists—taxi drivers, cyclo drivers, food vendors, salespeople on the street peddling sunglasses and trinkets—in other words, people like my neighbors.

I told Homie I would work with the little kids. Robin would take on the adults, who would be less likely to run in fright because of his uncanny resemblance to Fafner, the giant, in Richard Wagner's *Der Ring des Nibelungen.*

Homie cupped his mouth with his hands and lowered his voice. "You give them good price, yes? They very, very poor."

"Oh, we'll do it for free," I offered.

"No, you need earn money," he countered. He recommended fifty cents per lesson for the kids and one dollar for the adults. "You get ten kids, you earn five dollar. See, that a lot of money for one hour!"

I nodded. Robin, who was as tenderhearted as me, quickly agreed to that price.

On Tuesdays, the adults sat on our couch or floor poised with pencils and notebooks in hand to start with the basics: "Hello, my name is Bao. What is your name?" "My name is Phuong. How are you?" "I am fine." Robin's adult students were eager, expectant, courteous. If Homie or Tin happened to be nearby, they would come over and help translate for Robin.

On Thursdays, I taught the kids. They, too, sat shyly on the couch, dutifully repeating all the words in unison. They were so quiet and so good. *Hey, teaching is easy.* But after the first week, they must have noticed that I didn't wield a ruler or a paddle, because all hell broke loose. In perfect gender-predictable behavior, the boys ran around, pushed each other off the couch, and played monkey-in-the-middle with a little girl's hair scrunchy. The girls, however, were much worse. They wanted to sit in my lap.

Their shiny little black eyes bore into me, and I was smitten. We put music on and danced, drew pictures on the white board, and basically got nothing done. Then, one Thursday evening, not one child came to class. I stood by the doorway and waited a long while before giving up and heading up to bed. Obviously, I was *sooooo* not a teacher. I was perfectly fine with that. I loved children. I could have adopted the whole lot of them. But teaching them made me too nervous. I found out later the parents decided that homework was a better use of their kids' time.

CHAPTER 32

Tin Gets Sick

**"When the pain has passed,
one forgets the medicine."**
(VIETNAMESE PROVERB)

THE AUTUMN RAINS WERE FEROCIOUS. The thunder literally rattled the walls and windows. It was odd that the power never went out during such violent storms. The VietNam Electricity Company regularly attended to the great clumps of black cables hanging between the houses. From above, the whole city looked like it was draped in a web of black licorice laces. Power outages were neatly reserved for the hottest days, never when the rain brought a cooling wind. I loved the rain and spent great swathes of perfectly useable time watching it pour off everyone's vinyl awnings and make little rivers in the alley. As Kai ran in and out of the rain, Hanh was always right behind him mopping the floor.

One morning, between swipes of the mop, I noticed she kept taking a tissue from her pants pocket and wiping her eyes and nose. She'd stop and stare at the floor, lost in thought, then rattle herself back to reality and push the mop again.

"What's wrong, Hanh?" I asked. She waved her hand and

turned away, but then turned back and said, "Tin is sick. Something is in his neck. He must go to the hospital."

I took her hand and held it tight. "We will get him the best doctor. Don't worry."

My stomach was in my throat. I ran upstairs to get my phone and called Tin, not knowing if he was on duty at FV or at home sleeping off a graveyard shift. He answered right away. His voice was quiet.

"Tin, your mother said you are sick. What's wrong? Did you talk to a doctor at FV?" I held my breath waiting for his slow, quiet reply.

"Something grow in my *tyroid*. I feel it. It very hard and grow fast."

"My God, Tin, you've got to see an FV Hospital doctor. Go see an ENT. Don't worry about the fee. I will pay for it."

"Very expensive, Ms. Karin. No, I go Vietnam doctor. He do X-ray. He say it look like cancer. I go surgery. Take it out."

His speech was steady but halting, as if each word slapped him as it came out of his mouth. Yet he was bearing it bravely.

"Tin, please, I'm very serious. Go see an FV doctor."

"Okay, maybe I ask. Maybe they check me free. I don't know."

"Yes, yes, go. Where are you now?"

"I at work."

"Good, go now, please, Tin. Do it for me, do it for your mother. She's crying right now."

"She crying? I call her. Thank you, Ms. Karin, for you care and you worry 'bout me."

I ran upstairs to my computer to google "lump in throat," "symptoms and types of thyroid cancer," and "life expectancy for Stage Four cancers." My mind leaped from "nodule in throat" to a vision of me sitting at his funeral wearing a black veil decimating a 250-count box of Kleenex. I tried to tell myself it was probably just a swollen gland, but I have no control over my mind, and like a naughty child, it handed me a macabre picture and I took it. Tin had once told me I was like a second mother to him. Well, he was my second son. Homie was my wonderful, adorable friend, but Tin was my *son*. And no mother should ever lose a child.

That evening after Tin finished his shift, he stopped by. I nearly pulled him off his motorbike and dragged him into the living room by his collar.

"Show me!"

"It here," he said, pointing to a spot on his throat. He guided my fingers to his neck, and I felt a stone-hard lump the diameter of a nickel.

That was no swollen gland.

"When is your surgery?"

"Five weeks"

I shook my head. I've never worked in a hospital, and I don't know the intricacies of scheduling surgeries, but I will never understand that when a doctor suspects the lump is malignant and you need a biopsy or surgery, that the hospital wouldn't do everything possible to get the person in ASAP. I've already mentioned my friend Pat, who was told she had a tumor in her liver. She chose the best hospital in Los Angeles and called the best specialist, but it took a month before she could get an appointment. Then, it was another month before they could schedule her for chemo treatments. In those sixty wasted days, the tumor continued to ravage her good cells while the maggot bad cells multiplied like flies. I was so angry. I still am.

I also couldn't understand why the hospital he worked for didn't offer him a health insurance program that allowed him to see the doctors there. Wouldn't they want to help their own? Couldn't he befriend someone in the ENT department and then say, "Hey, by the way, could you just feel this lump here and tell me what it might be?"

"Sure, stop by my office at the end of your shift." That's what I imagined, what I wished for. I wanted Tin in a clean bed with crisp, white sheets in a cool, light-filled room with a spotless bathroom. I wanted him in a hospital with low nurse/patient ratios.

I wanted to speak English to his doctor and ask him questions, to make sure nothing was overlooked. I wanted to cut up fresh mangoes for him and give him the best pieces, and I would eat the stringy part around the stone.

I refused to let a child of mine go to a government hospital where he might draw the short straw for who gets a bed and who ends up on the floor. I vowed to pay for Tin's surgery. I would put it on a credit card first, but I'd need to pay it back quickly. That meant I would have to take a CELTA or TEFL (Teaching English as a Foreign Language) course and get a job teaching so our income could double.

CHAPTER 33

Teacher Training

"Catch the bear before you sell his skin."
(VIETNAMESE PROVERB)

THOUGH ROBIN HAD TAKEN a CELTA course, which is more prestigious than TEFL because it was developed at the University of Cambridge, I signed up for a TEFL course that was closer to home. Having observed Robin slog through copious pages of homework into the wee hours of the night, I knew what I'd be in for: frequent exams, memorizing the phonemic alphabet chart, learning classroom control strategies, developing lesson plans for varying levels, and student teaching. Ten or fifteen years ago, backpackers could travel the world teaching English as they went. They didn't have to have any type of certification or know anything about the science of teaching. They needed only to be an English speaker. Already, just the little bit of teaching I'd done at home had made me anxious and exhausted.

All my kids' best teachers were the ones whose vibrancy was electric. They bounced around the classroom and could think on their feet. They had voices that projected, energy that would exhaust mice, and they could whip up a windstorm with their enthusiasm alone. I admired that personality. But I wasn't born that way. I could be perky when called on to be so, just as I could laugh at someone's unfunny joke, but doing so wore me out and I could only pull off this personality reversal for a few hours at a stretch before needing to run off to a quiet room to recharge.

The TEFL class started with fifteen students, but within a week seven dropped out, six because it was too much work, and one Brazilian man because, oops, he really didn't speak much English. From my end, the homework load was a bear, and I was so happy I had Hanh to care for Kai and the house or I couldn't have survived. The worst part of the course was game-playing. I hate games because I can't understand the instructions. One example: "Okay, everybody line up and face your partner. Now, the first person who picks up a card with the word *pickle* stands to the side and your partner moves down. Now the next person sits down and draws a picture of a pickle. Whoever can guess the word gets two points and the other team will get three points, but only if they can write and say two words relating to pickle. Then the person at the head of the line will pass the word to the person across from him. Okay, now the two in the front will stand facing outward and only they can look at the cards."

Get it?

No? Me neither. This is exactly how game directions sound to my ears. My brain ceases to function at "face your partner." This is why, when I was a kid, I hated going to birthday parties. While the other kids were playing games, I sat in the corner near the snack table, licking the icing from around the edges of the cake and then carefully covering up my finger trails before the candles were lit. I just wanted to hurry up, eat the cake, go home, and read a book.

I ask now: Who decided school needs to be fun? Whatever happened to good old rote memorization? It has worked just fine for centuries.

If it weren't for wanting to help Tin, I would have quit. The class made me so anxious, I could barely eat breakfast or lunch, and I was losing weight. I kept telling myself that the course was good for me. It would force me to organize my thoughts, stay focused, and help others. After the first week of classroom work, we got into vans and drove to different public schools to practice what we'd learned. The night before each class, I spent hours drawing flash cards and planning games.

At every school, I got good marks on my preparation, enthusiasm, and clarity, but low marks on my games. I wouldn't have wanted to play them either. Regardless, at the end of the four weeks, I passed the course. Now I could start looking for work. Though I continued to beg Tin to let me pay for his surgery at FV, he was set to go into the government hospital in a week. He firmly refused to take my offer. "I thank you again for you worry, but I go cheaper hospital. I not want you pay." Later he sent me an email:

[sic all] *"Thanks for you helpful, i dont know how to perform my feeling with your help, I am so happy, but I have to recognize one important thing that is when get a trouble, I need the help I never receive any helpful from my relatives. of course I never waiting their helpful. but also i thanks god give so many good friends like you. some time i know we are difference country, difference language, difference culture…so many thing is difference. But now we have one same point is we are living the same country, the same street Also I want to say Thanksgiving to you for all of thing you had been helped me, so many Thank."*

Hanh took the day off for Tin's surgery and graciously called me that afternoon to say the operation went well. Tin wouldn't let her tell me which hospital he was in. He was probably afraid I would kidnap him. Still, he had to wait three agonizing days to get the results. The next couple of days, Hanh was quieter than usual as she worked. I was a mess and couldn't concentrate on anything. I just sat at the computer and googled questions like, "Why doesn't Victoria Beckham smile?" and "Why are Michael Jackson's kids white?" I also watched a kitten get a flea bath on YouTube along with 1.3 million other viewers. Every cell in my brain knew I was wasting valuable time. But I was too anxious about Tin to do anything about it.

On the fourth morning, Tin arrived with Hanh on the back of his motorbike. I flung open the door. "It not cancer," he said. I nearly flew in the air with joy and gave him a hug. He showed off the stitches in his neck. A potential tragedy was wiped off his life's record. He'd had enough misfortunes. It was his turn to be tragedy free. Now he could get back to being the head of the family.

Even though my efforts to get a teaching certificate didn't help Tin in the end, I was glad to start earning and begin to fill the savings account once again.

CHAPTER 34

New Teaching Career

"If you are going through hell, keep going."

(WINSTON CHURCHILL)

I GOT HIRED RIGHT AWAY by an educational employment agency that sent teachers to schools all over the city. My first school was a kindergarten in the outer reaches of HCMC. "Your driver take you to a kindergarten. Maybe ten children. You teach one hour, okay, madam?"

"Sure, but aren't four- and five-year-olds a little young for a whole hour of English?"

"No, madam. Parents want to start children very young now. It is good for the brain."

Most of my TEFL lesson plans were for older children or adults, but, I reasoned, at least we could toss a ball around and sing songs.

The drive took about ninety minutes and when I arrived, I felt the familiar discomfort of eyes boring into me as I passed through the doorway. A group of parents was seated at the back of the classroom to watch. The children were still outside at recess, which gave me time to glance at my lesson plan, look around the room, and mentally configure how much space I'd need for certain games. First I would start out with the ten kids in a circle on the floor. Then we'd go over greetings and colors and maybe the names of school items. I'd brought a few of Kai's toys with me to teach names such as "car," "ball," "monkey," and "doll."

The classroom attendant stood at the back door and rang a little bell. I watched in horror as they began to trickle in. These weren't five-year-olds. These weren't even four-year-olds. These were babies holding bottles, sucking on their fingers. These were screeching, crying, hair-pulling babies! They couldn't yet speak Vietnamese let alone understand English. One little boy toddled in, took one look at me and threw himself down, crying hysterically and pointing at me. "He's never seen a foreigner," the teacher said apologetically. "He's scared."

Great.

More and more kids marched in. I counted ten, then twenty, then thirty tots. The teacher and two helpers corralled them into two circles, the inner circle on the floor and the outer on tiny little stools. One attendant saw my shock and quickly pulled out some flash cards of colors and handed them to me. The tykes immediately recognized the cards because when they saw the first one, they screamed in unison, "blue, blue, bluuuuuue!!!"

I was relieved that at least they knew colors. I went through the stack with them and then looked at the clock. I was sure I'd already used the full hour. But only five minutes had passed. I looked over at their parents, who stared back at me. Everyone was waiting for my next act. One young high-school-age helper walked up to the circle with a hairbrush and began brushing and rebraiding every little girl's hair. I decided to get a toy from my bag that would correspond to the color they had been repeating. I pulled out a lanky brown monkey, one of Kai's favorite, if not beloved, stuffed animals. The word for monkey in Vietnamese is *con khi* (con kee), which sounds similar to English, so I knew it would be easy.

"Monkey...brown monkey!" I articulated slowly. The tots

screamed as I waved monkey's little hand, and all thirty babies ran up to me. They wanted monkey. They wanted to kiss monkey. They wanted to hug monkey. They wanted to yank monkey's arms apart and hit their classmates with monkey. I dove into the crowd, rescued monkey, and lifted it above my head and out of reach. That was their invitation to practice their rock-climbing skills on my body. Tiny tots began climbing up. They grabbed onto my shirt and nearly pulled down my pants. In one hand I held monkey high and with the other hand I held up my pants.

The teacher pulled out her ruler and screamed at them to sit down. She whipped the ruler in the air—*swoosh, swoosh*—and they scrambled back onto their little stools. Okay, monkey was not a good idea. Next, I got out a ball. "Ball," I said above the din, "blue ball." They all jumped up again, this time with deafening screams. Two children hung from my forearms like iron filings as I tried to hold up the ball. Once again the ruler came out. My heart was pounding so hard against my chest, I thought I heard it say, "Get me out of here! Now!" Newspaper headlines flashed before my eyes: "Foreign Woman Killed by Marauding Toddlers. Her Last Words: 'They Looked So Innocent.' "

I glanced at the clock again. Thirty minutes to go. I'd never walked away from responsibility before. That was one lesson my dad instilled in me. I'd once walked out of a bad movie and twice out of a bad relationship, but I'd never walked off a job. Now, it occurred to me, I could leave, walk out, and no one outside of this classroom would ever know. It wouldn't mar my résumé or even show up on LinkedIn or Facebook. I could just head for the door, hop on a motorbike taxi, and go home. It would be my little secret. I looked at the babies and then back out at the street, which was beckoning me with comforting hugs.

Alas, my inherent cheapness won out. The agency had provided a car for me and it wasn't there yet. I didn't want to use my own money to get home. I persevered by singing "Head, Shoulders, Knees, and Toes" with the kids until my voice grew hoarse.

At the end of the hour, I picked up my bag of toys and walked out of the classroom with my head held high. I hadn't quit. I'd pushed on. I was proud of myself for sticking it out. I did, however, twitch in the back seat of the car all the way home.

CHAPTER 35

Drinking Witches' Brew

"Goat's Nipple and Wild Alive Animals"
(MENU CHOICES AT A RESTAURANT)

THE AGENCY CONTINUED to send me all over the city for substitute teaching jobs. By being a substitute I forfeited my chance to follow a class, measure progress, or really get to know the students. On the other hand, no one would tire of my games and songs. Occasionally, the agency sent me out to pretend I was a teacher. These jobs were my favorite. They needed a token white person to hand out awards and stand for photos with "my students," so parents could show off to their neighbors that their child learned English from an actual white person.

Weeks went by, but my nervousness in front of the classroom never waned. I lived for weekends, so I could crawl into a cave and calm my exposed nerves. It was spring again, the hottest season, so Robin, Kai, and I would occasionally treat ourselves to a swim at the Rex Hotel. We always took a few neighbor children with us for Kai to play with. For five dollars apiece, we could swim for the day in a large, clean pool and order drinks poolside. After one Saturday swim session, my ear wouldn't clear. I had the sensation of being underwater and the pressure from it was giving me a headache.

That afternoon, I told Homie, who told Mama Hang, who told Tin, who told Hanh, who grabbed a basket and immediately set off for the market. Within fifteen minutes she returned with what looked like ingredients she had just raked up in the backyard. Twigs, leaves, and a tree branch covered the kitchen counter. Hanh chopped, hacked, peeled, and began to boil the white woody cores in a huge pot of water along with some sugarcane stalks. After simmering the brown liquid for about an hour, she strained it, poured it into a big steaming mug and brought it to me.

Travel Channel celebrities, such as Andrew Zimmern, who hosts *Bizarre Foods*, get the big bucks for being intrepid eaters. Viewers love to watch them eat bugs, worms, wild-boar testicles, or congealed goat's blood in some exotic country. These TV guys may make faces, but they never vomit.

But I'm not one of them. I have an overactive gag reflex and retch on cough syrup. "*Uống này* [drink this]," Hanh said firmly. "This is good for you." She stood and waited, watching. It was too hot, so I blew on it, though not too vigorously. I was hoping she would get tired of standing there and walk away. She looked at me as if to say, "*Oh, you big baby! Swallow it already.*" I meant to drink it. The month before, some Chinese herbs I'd been given brought me back from the brink of a cold. So I knew these ancient remedies had validity. I just needed a few moments to brace myself.

I took a sip. It tasted a lot like the inside of a shoe, but thankfully it wasn't bitter. I took a few more sips. Hanh seemed satisfied and left me alone. I breathed deeply to keep nausea at bay. Strangely enough, about thirty minutes later, my ear made a little snap, crackle, pop sound and some air moved through the ear canal for the first time in hours. The clog was gone. Hanh was happy and told me that I needed to drink two more large cups of the tea before bedtime. There was a lot left in the pot.

That evening, Homie and I sat outside. While he drank coffee,

I drank the last cup of Hanh's tea. Homie looked at my cup. "You drink it all? You feel better?" he asked.

"Yes," I said between swallows, trying not to breathe through my nose so I could avoid the taste. "My ear feels a bit better."

"Good. It's a very good medicine for teenagers. When you eat too much greasy food or spicy food, you get pimple. So now the pimple in your ear dry up. That good."

I choked. Ever so slowly, so that the last few swallows of medicinal tea would remain in my stomach, I leaned toward him and said, "Um, Homie? It wasn't a pimple. I had water in my ear."

He squeezed his eyes shut. Then he opened them wide but didn't look at me. He began to stir his coffee vigorously.

"Homie," I said, a little more animated this time. "You told her I had a pimple in my ear? And now I've just downed a half-gallon of acne medicine?!"

"Oh, Ms. Karin, I so very sorry!" Homie said, putting his hands over his eyes. "Sorry, so sorry!"

I started laughing. He peeked at me from between his fingers and started laughing, too. I said goodnight and went up to the office to tell Robin about the dangers of translation. He smiled halfheartedly and then, completely off topic, announced he wasn't going to teach anymore. He was going to put all his efforts into reviving his CD-producing business. That was that.

I was too shocked to argue. He'd never been so definitive. I'd always hoped he could continue his business because it made him so happy, but I didn't trust that we could depend on it. He looked dejected and, like a good $175-per-hour shrink, I asked him to tell me what he was feeling. He said he felt trapped. We couldn't go back home because there was no job to go back to. And, besides, California still had a 12.5 percent unemployment rate. We had begun to talk about possible solutions, but conversation was difficult. So many questions with no certain answers impeded our ability to formulate sentences. We just sat silently, stuck in our own thoughts. Kai had been playing video games at the computer.

He stopped and turned around to look at us. "Don't you guys have anything more to talk about?"

"Nope, we're all out of conversation," Robin replied.

"Well, then, next time talk slower."

The next morning, I felt weak, disheartened, and abandoned. I began to clean out closets and drawers because nothing brings me back to life more than getting rid of needless crap. While Robin slept, I attacked his pile of papers and books from all his teaching jobs to cull out anything I could give to Quy, my university friend, or to neighbors. Later, I called Quy to stop by and pick up some English-language workbooks left over from one of Robin's schools. Wanting first dibs, he left his house immediately and arrived at my door in fifteen minutes. I set out the stack of workbooks for him on the kitchen table and while he perused them, I poured two glasses of iced tea for us. When he asked why I was giving them all away, I broke down and cried. Thoroughly embarrassed, I sopped up my nose and said, "Robin quit teaching. He keeps losing his jobs. Now we will never get home. We don't have enough money to start our lives again in America!"

He couldn't have been more concerned for me than if it had been his own family. "Oh, Ms. Karin, I am so sorry for you. Keep trying," he said reassuringly. "You will find a way to get home. You must not give up."

Quy continued. "My parents never gave up. When I was born, my parents lived in a one-room house made of scrap-metal pieces and cardboard, and the floor was only the earth. They lived there ten years before they could save enough money to build a real house out of brick and tile. Sometimes they only had cassava roots and a little bit of sugar to eat. We didn't always have rice. But, they persevered and they finally got a house."

I sat at the table stirring the ice around in my tea glass, watching how quickly it melted, tiny air bubbles coming out of it. Hanh walked by the table and noticed that the water from my glass was pooling onto the glass tabletop. She grabbed a towel, wiped the bottom of the glass, then set it back down on a little piece of cloth. But I was so absorbed in my self-pity that it took a moment to realize that—ding, ding, ding—*a maid is wiping condensation off my glass, and I am fussing about not having enough money!*

"Oh, Quy, I am so sorry. I have no right to complain when your parents suffered such hunger and poverty. I must look like such a spoiled brat."

I knew his story was not meant to one-up me. He was only telling me about his parents to illustrate that I could still have hope and not give in to despair. I was so ashamed I could hardly look at Quy. I wanted to run out into the alley, throw my body down, and offer myself up as a speed bump.

"Ms. Karin, that was a different time. Our country is stronger now. I understand that you need money to live. Of course. Do not be embarrassed."

Instead of counting my blessings, I'd been discounting them. All I could do now was toughen up. I had no other choice.

CHAPTER 36

Going for the Big Bucks

"Bicycle Love"
(ON A TEENAGER'S T-SHIRT)

WITH ROBIN RESTARTING the CD business I was sure would doom us to eternal poverty, I was relieved to get a call from the agency to teach every afternoon at a private high school for twenty-five dollars per hour in air-conditioned classrooms. "A teacher just quit," said the woman on the phone. Her voice sounded apologetic for assigning me to this particular school. I assumed she was alluding to the long drive because it would be about forty-five minutes to get back home in rush-hour traffic. For five hundred dollars a week—in cash—the trade-off would be worthwhile. No more rooms crammed with sixty kids, sometimes sitting two to a chair, and no more screaming toddlers. My days of teaching in poor, government-run schools—where fans whirred in futile, lopsided attempts to move the humid air—were over. Within thirty minutes, a courier dropped off the workbooks so I could prepare.

I couldn't believe my good fortune. We would finally be able to grow our savings quickly. I was also hopeful that a steady job in the same school would end my stage fright. I'd gotten so many compliments on my teaching skills and I really wanted to be able to enjoy teaching. If I could get to know my students over a whole semester, I reasoned, I'd be more comfortable.

On Monday morning I woke up early after a night of fitful sleep. Running on nervous energy, I dressed quickly and organized my lesson plans, packing them neatly in order of my classes. The first class was Level Three (out of four), which meant the students probably had a good grasp of English. The second two classes were Level Two; they'd be working on "Who is in your family?" and "What is your favorite food?" This was a relatively easy level to teach and my favorite. I picked up my tote bag and looked up at the clock. Sigh, big sigh. It was only 9 a.m. I had three more hours to try to ignore my nervous stomach.

My nausea that morning was more aggressive than usual. I knew I should eat breakfast, but the most I could swallow were a couple of salty crackers and some sips of water. Every cell in my body was on tactical alert. I passed a mirror and noticed that my blouse and skirt hung more loosely than ever before. During the last several months of teaching, I'd lost ten pounds. My normal weight, which resides on my five-foot-six-inch frame, had always been around 115 pounds—maybe 120 pounds around holidays. Kai thought it fun to run his cars over the bumpy road of my spine. Even skinny Quy suggested I might die soon and that I looked like a teacher from a concentration camp.

Hanh was upstairs doing laundry, so I headed down to the living room, turned on the TV, and sat nervously picking at my calloused heels. CNN and BBC, the two premium channels that only foreigners were allowed to subscribe to, helped me keep my mind off of teaching.

Noon came just as the last layer of the epidermis on my heels was picked clean. I put a bottle of cold water into my tote bag, stepped into my shoes, and went out into the dirty sunshine where Dragon Man was already waiting to take me to the school. I had hired him because I didn't want to take the chance that my electric

bike would be too slow or run out of juice mid-trip. We arrived at
the school at 12:30. As I got off, he looked up at the faded pink,
five-story concrete building, read the name of the school out loud,
and, still straddling his bike, walked it closer to the gate to look
through its wrought-iron grid. I thought I detected a wistful look
on his face. Sympathy washed over me. Had he had the opportunity to go to such a school, life might have dealt him a better hand.
He turned, looked at me, and cackled. It was first time I'd heard
him laugh—or seen him smile, for that matter. Come to think of
it, it was the first time I'd ever seen his teeth. Dotting his grin were
dark abysses where incisors and molars used to be.

"*Tạm biệt* [goodbye]," he said, still cackling. "See you at five."
He revved his engine and made a fast departure.

A sullen security guard opened the gate and closed it behind
me. That a guard was even at the school didn't ruffle me. Security
personnel were everywhere in Vietnam—schools, grocery stores,
outdoor markets, building sites. What threw me was that the
school was weirdly silent. Had I arrived on a holiday? I turned and
gave a quizzical look to the guard, who pointed me in the direction
of the office. I walked across a courtyard only to find the office that
he had pointed to was locked—and dark. I cupped my hands and
peered in through a small window in the door. I could just make
out a man sleeping at his desk, his head against the chair back
and his mouth wide open. When he reached up to rub his eyes, I
stepped away from the window, hoping he hadn't seen me looking
at him. A minute later the lights went on. Again I peeked through
the window and saw a dozen shirtless boys lying in neat rows on
thin bamboo floor mats. They began to stir, stand, roll their mats,
and put their white uniform shirts back on. The whole school
came alive with shouting, laughing, squealing (teenage girls), and
eardrum-bashing announcements over a crackling PA system.

Just minutes before 1 p.m., a tall, brown-haired man, his tie
slightly askew, walked toward me. Oh good, another Westerner.
But he wasn't smiling, and even seemed annoyed.

"You got here early, I see," he grumbled. "You don't need to. Waste of your time. The whole school naps between twelve and one." I detected a New Zealand accent and I wanted to ask whether he was from the North Island or the South Island. But he didn't look like he was in any mood for chitchat.

I cleared my throat and replied, "I don't mind waiting. I wanted to be on time."

"You taking over Ethan's classes?" he asked, while bending down to inspect a patch of dried food spilled on the knee of his gray pants.

"If Ethan is the one who quit last Thursday, then yes, I'm the new teacher." I held out my hand, "I'm Karin."

"Oh, yeah, okay, I'm Ryan." He shook my hand quickly, without making eye contact, and returned his attention back to his knee, scratching the food off with his thumbnail. "So, they give you the room number?"

"Yes, 5C. Where is it?"

He looked up and pointed to the gray concrete staircase that wound around the outside of the building. "Top floor."

I headed for the stairs, looking back to see if Ryan was following me up. Though the warning bell had already rung, he was still studying his knee, apparently not feeling any compunction to rush to class. As I went up the stairs, the air-conditioned classroom was singing to me. By Floor Two my blouse was sticking to my skin like wet newspaper. As I reached the last step and saw Room 5C in front of me, my throat went dry. My esophagus began to roll up like a paper party blower. I couldn't swallow. In the classroom no one was seated. The boys were teasing and shoving each other. They pulled chairs out from under the girls, who screamed and slapped back at the boys.

"Good afternoon, class!" I said, boldly amplifying my voice to avoid a nervous crack in its sound.

The room was small but bright, with walls of six-foot-tall windows on two sides. Several wood tables and thirty-odd chrome-and-vinyl chairs were pushed in equal numbers to either side of the room, leaving a narrow middle aisle. I stepped up onto the teacher's platform, which was a foot higher than at the other schools where I'd taught.

The eighteen kids begrudgingly flopped down into their seats, but they weren't looking up at me. I wrote my name and "from America" on the chalkboard, then swung around, eager to meet them. The boys had flocked to one side of the room and the girls to the other. They sat in obvious poses of boredom and defiance, chins leaning on hands or heads down on the tables. The girls sat in groups, one reading a teen romance novel while four others read over her shoulder. I could have undressed and no one would have noticed.

"Hey everybody, get out your books!"

I waited. A moment of hope flashed as a short, skinny boy pulled the English reader out of his backpack and slammed it on his desktop. He promptly lay down on it.

I spoke again. "Did you all finish reading 'Beauty and the Beast'?" Silence.

With a jaunty "you can't intimidate me" air, I jumped down off the platform and walked among the desks.

"Come on, come on, open your reading books." I tapped on each table with my pen, and when half a dozen students opened their books, I cheered my small victory and decided to move ahead with this little group of eager learners.

I called on a few students to take turns reading aloud, but the text seemed beyond their level, which made me feel better because it was beyond mine, too. The textbook *English 3* had a British publisher. How was I supposed to explain "you're talking codswallop" and "the old gaffer was too knackered to budge"?

I climbed back up on the platform, and began acting out the whole story. I cowered as the frightened father. I growled as the ferocious beast. I acted as the brave heroine. I drew pictures and wrote down vocabulary on the chalkboard for the palace, the magical rose, and the dark forest. When the scene called for a horse, I galloped into the aisle. When Belle danced with the Beast, I waltzed with the air. And then I swooned as the Beast turned into a handsome prince. I finally had their attention—all eighteen students. They stared at me, mouths half open. *Damn, I'm good!* See, these kids just needed more creative lessons, that's all.

I stepped back up onto the platform, still breathing heavy from the theatrics, but elated with my success. *I am teacher. Hear me roar!* And then the most unexpected thing happened. They went back to ignoring me.

When the bell rang I stepped out into the corridor to watch the students change classrooms. Ryan walked by, and a look of snark-asm crossed his face.

"Hey, huh-huh, yuh have fun in there?"

Sure, as much fun as washing my face vigorously and accidentally jamming a finger up my nostril. I smiled and decided to let him think I had it all under control. But the subsequent classes were similar failures.

After returning home that afternoon, I turned on the BBC and wound myself into a fetal position on the couch. Robin came down the stairs.

"You look awful. How did your classes go?"

"They were horrible."

"Now you see why I hated teaching. If you aren't born to do it, it can't be done."

I roused myself from the couch and called Andrew, my TEFL teacher. "You took a job at a private school?" he asked incredulously. I could hear him muffle his laughter. "Private schools aren't for the studious or the wealthy like they are in America. They are for the kids who got kicked out of government-run schools. You've got the dregs, kiddo. Those are Vietnam's delinquents."

Lovely.

"Listen," he continued. "You just have to go in strong, don't show fear. Threaten them that you will call their parents. They are afraid of their parents."

I tend to think that every challenge is really a prodding from destiny, that God puts us into situations in which we can help change the world. The Universe wanted me to become a teacher and to love the unlovable, to reach the unreachable, to make a difference in the life of a child. The high-income windfall was the Universe blessing me for carrying out my mission. I walked into the school the next day even more determined. Then, at 5 p.m., I quit. The agency didn't seem surprised. I got assigned to a much safer public school.

CHAPTER 37

Betrayal

"Better to die than to live on with a bad reputation."
(VIETNAMESE PROVERB)

LAN, KAI'S TUTOR, had moved back to Hanoi, so through a friend, I found a new home tutor to work with Kai. She was a pretty twenty-three-year-old woman whose name sounded like Swan. She had a Western sensibility about her and spoke excellent English even though she'd never been in the West. She was the least traditional Vietnamese woman I'd met in Vietnam. Her hair was short and bobbed, and she always wore jeans, a T-shirt, and colorful heeled sandals. Swan could have passed for an American, and I was beginning to think of her as such until she told me her story.

She was the only child of parents who had low-paying government jobs. From the moment she popped into the world, they sacrificed mightily and saved every extra cent to be able to send her abroad for college. Their goal for her was an American university, but her visa was denied repeatedly for unknown reasons. Instead she went to a private English university in Japan.

Freshly back with a degree in journalism, she could only find part-time work, with the youth section of a Vietnamese newspaper.

Swan was delighted to be able to earn extra cash working with Kai. She was bright, energetic, and able to keep Kai on task for whole ten-minute segments.

One Monday after her session with Kai, she asked me if she could interview me for an article about foreigners' thoughts about living in Vietnam. Sure. Absolutely. Gushing about Vietnam to anyone who'd listen was one of my great joys.

Without her prompting, I started right in, cooing, "I love living in Vietnam! I love the food, the people, the culture, and, of course, the cheap prices. Our experience here has been so happy."

She smiled but wasn't taking any notes. Swan tapped her pencil on her notebook impatiently and said, "No. I want to know what you *don't* like about living here."

I hesitated. I couldn't think of anything. "Really," I said, "the only negative I can think of is the oppressive, smothering, sticky heat. There are times I am so tired of sweating, I just want to sit down and have a good cry."

"That can't be fixed," she said. "I think our country needs to make some changes. So, from a foreigner's perspective, what would you suggest?"

Her question made me uncomfortable. I'd pledged from the start not to rail on the Vietnamese government. Nor did I want to bring up uncomfortable topics such as the poor treatment of animals; the pervasive, if not dangerous, superstitions that the Vietnamese live by; or the need to bribe authorities to get anything accomplished. It wasn't my country or my prerogative to criticize, and I never understood why some of the foreign teachers I'd met did so openly and inconsiderately right to the locals' faces.

Swan kept pushing though. I looked up at the ceiling again for more ideas. "Well, okay, here is one. It's so loud here. Motorcycles, honking horns, construction, crowing roosters, barking dogs, karaoke, vendors announcing what they are selling. In America, we call this noise pollution. Any big city has it, of course. But in Vietnam, people sing karaoke with their microphones cranked up so high. And they sing well past midnight. In the States, the police would be called in to break it up after 10 or 11 p.m. Nobody gets mad about it here. Sometimes I just want to yell, 'Hey, go to bed already!' "

Swan laughed. She wrote fast and seemed pleased.

She set her pencil down. "Now, may I take a photo of you?"

"Sure," I said.

She took a couple of shots, made a few more notes, and then picked up her bag. "This story will be published in the paper on Sunday."

Six days passed and I had mostly forgotten about the article. I stopped in on Sunday afternoon to visit Jade at the pharmacy. Instead of flashing her usual smile when I walked in, she looked serious.

"Ms. Karin," Jade dropped her voice to a whisper. "The neighbors…they very angry, very angry about you story."

"Story? What?"

She held up a copy of Swan's newspaper article. There I was, a thumbnail-size photo of me smiling next to a long, two-column story with Swan's byline. Knowing it would take me hours sitting with a dictionary to read it, I asked her to translate it. She had only read a few paragraphs when my heart seized up.

"Oh, no, no, no! Jade, my God, no!" I felt myself begin to unravel. My heart pounded so loudly in my ears, I couldn't even hear her speak. I interrupted: "Jade, I never said that. Oh, please, tell them, tell everyone. Swan wrote that. I didn't say those things… no, not like that." Or had I? I squeezed my eyes shut and tried to remember the interview. What were my exact words? I couldn't remember. These were my neighbors, my "family." Yet the story implied that I thought Americans were more civil and better educated than anyone on Đoàn Văn Bơ Street.

I was so distraught, I grabbed the paper out of Jade's hands and ran out of the pharmacy. In the alley, I noticed how my neighbors turned and pretended they didn't see me when I passed. I shut the door, pulled the curtains, and sat with my head in my hands, crying and shaking. Why would Swan put words into my mouth? The article made me sound arrogant. Didn't she think my neighbors would read it? *Everyone* reads the paper here. I wanted to run up and down the alley begging for forgiveness. My tears turned to frustration that I didn't have the language skills to defend myself. Besides, who would they believe, a spoiled Westerner or one of their own? It was in print, after all, so it must be true.

Still clutching the newspaper, I began to pace in the living room. How could she be so cruel? In America I could sue for libel, but here, my only recourse was to regain their trust—or save face and move. I heard a knock. *Please, let it be Homie or Tin.* I swung open the door. It was my landlord Vinh with lease papers in his hand.

I had forgotten he was coming over for my signature. We had told him we wanted to stay a third year. I'd been so excited. This would be the year I became fluent. I'd get more time to see Baby Hoa and his new baby brother, Benh, grow up. Suddenly, I wasn't so sure I should sign it.

"Vinh, did you read the article? My neighbors, they hate me now. They won't look at me," I said tearfully.

Vinh looked confused and concerned. He hadn't read the article. "Ms. Karin, you neighbors like you so much. They tell me so."

"Not after this newspaper article." I briefed him on the story and what the neighbors' reaction was. "Read it. Tell me how it sounds."

We sat on the front steps. As he read I stared at his face, trying to interpret any change in his expression. Nothing. He finally looked up.

"Is it bad?"

His expression finally changed. His lips were tight. "Yes, it is bad."

I burst into tears again and pleaded. "Vinh, you must tell them I didn't say that, the writer did. I love my neighbors, you know that."

"Yes, Ms. Karin," he said, looking grim. "I will tell them."

He suggested we put off signing the lease until this blew over. He was sure it would. His head hung. He needed the rent, which was double what he could get from locals. The rent was his two sons' tickets to a foreign university. The fact we were even living in this neighborhood had been a miracle for him. A miracle helped by the fact that he was friends with the district's police chief. He shook his head and said he'd call me later.

I locked the door and sat in the living room staring at the wall until I heard Homie's motorbike. I ran out to him. Yes, he'd heard about the newspaper story. "I going to talk to you about it. Neighbor don't understand why you say bad things. They help you, give you things, teach you cook, teach you talk Vietnamese, watch out for you house when you not home. No, they don't have education. They poor, but they good people."

That sent me over the edge. "I know they are, Homie!" I clutched my stomach, which was twisting and stabbing at me. "I didn't say those things. Swan wrote lies. You must believe me. You know I love my neighbors. I would never say they were inconsiderate and uneducated!"

Homie nodded. "I know that not sound like you, Ms. Karin. Don't worry. Soon they forget."

"No, they won't forget!" I said. I couldn't stand to be outside anymore. I turned and ran back into the house and locked the door.

That night in bed I tossed and turned, unable to understand why she had done this. And then, suddenly, it came to me. She was suffering from reverse culture shock. She'd just spent the past four years in Japan, a country full of people who craft origami birds and flowers with crazy precision. She had lived where her neighbors spent hours designing pebbles into sculpted Zen gardens. They walked around the house in those funny socks with the little pocket for the big piggy toe (you know, the one that went to market). She had just left a country where waiters kneeled and bowed at your table, and where some of the world's best appliances and cars are made. Swan probably returned to see her country in a new light, at least when the electricity was on. The only way she could complain and criticize safely in a Communist country was to make me her mouthpiece.

I got up the next morning and called Swan. "Would you please write a letter of apology to my neighbors. Tell them I was just speaking in general, not personally. Tell them I honor and respect them; they are my family."

"So, you want me to lie for you?"

I was furious. My head was reeling. "It's not a lie!" I shouted.

She arrived in the afternoon with letter in hand and a stick up her butt. I made copies and then we stopped at each house on both sides of the alley. At each house while she talked to the neighbors, I smiled contritely, bowing awkwardly. When they didn't react with "Oh, never mind. We forgive you," it occurred to me that her letter and apology might not have been all that sincere. Indeed, as I perused the letter I saw no *Tôi xin lôi* (I'm sorry) anywhere on the page. I took the leftover letters and sent her home, telling her that Homie and I would finish later. When Homie got home from his workout, he read her "letter of apology" and was angry. The letter said that the "editors" made the article sound a little preachy, but that the content still stood. It obviously didn't clear my name, and Swan wasn't taking responsibility for it. So, I fired her.

I hid at home with the curtains drawn for another two days. On the third morning, Homie pounded on my door. "Come on, we go get breakfast. You feel better."

"You *will* feel better," I repeated to him. Even in my distressed state, I couldn't let an auxiliary verb slip by.

I walked out into the alley and tried not to look at anyone. We walked to a *phở* vendor and when she didn't throw the bowl of hot soup at me, I relaxed. As Homie and I ate quietly, a woman from a nearby alley saw me. She trotted over smiling. "I want to say thank you for that story in the newspaper. You spoke the truth. The Vietnamese are too loud. I get so mad at some of my neighbors. I cannot sleep or even think sometimes. I hope now they will think about their behavior." Homie began to translate, but I understood her. I wanted to get up and hug her. We both thanked her. After that, she greeted me warmly whenever I walked to the market. It felt so good to have an ally.

We finished our soup and walked back home. Mama Hang whispered something to Homie and then he repeated it to me. "My mother say she not sing karaoke anymore."

"Nooooo! If I don't hear her sing soon, I'm going to move to another house," I said. It was my only leverage. Of course I didn't want to live anywhere else in the city, but I refused to stymie anyone's life. He told her my threat. She smiled and promised she would sing again—and he would, too—at midnight!

Homie rewrote the apology letter and together we passed it out. As we stood in each doorway, my neighbors read the letter and then smiled at me and said, "No problem." I was back in their good graces.

CHAPTER 38

Going Home

"When eating a fruit,
think of the person who planted the tree."
(VIETNAMESE PROVERB)

WHETHER IT WAS GOOD KARMA for holding orphan babies, teaching English for fifty cents an hour, or making frequent pay-in-advance donations to the Dragon family (who now owed us two years' worth of free motorbike parking on which we would never collect), two remarkable events took place that shortened our third year on Đoàn Văn Bơ Street.

Robin secured a license to release the heretofore unreleased full score of *Rain Man* and the out-of-print *Red Sonja*. Ardent film score fans had had the two films on their wish lists for years. We watched together as the orders arrived, one, ten, fifty, and upward totaling 2,000 of each. Within a few weeks, and after his production expenses, we had the $10,000 cushion in our savings to go home. The second event, which happened almost simultaneously, was that the Federal Reserve cut interest rates to near zero and our adjustable-rate mortgage dropped by $1,000 a month.

One morning, we sat at the white board and drew a line down

the middle of it, the US on one side and Vietnam on the other. We went through the pros and cons of living in each country. Vietnam won in most categories. But Kai needed to continue his education in an American school. And, of course, I missed my girls.

That was the morning we knew that our time in Vietnam was nearly over. We decided we would return home a few days before Christmas and start 2011 in America.

We called Vinh, who was disappointed we wouldn't finish the third year, but graciously let us out of the lease. I went outside and told Mrs. Dragon, who strangely grabbed my wrist as if to hold me hostage. Then she let go, ducked into her house for a few moments, and brought out an iced coffee. Free, for you. Especially for you. I realized I never did get to hear about her life and find out whatever secrets she had wanted to tell me alone, without Homie translating. Such a loss. I'm sure it was a worthy story. Maybe another time.

Across the alley, I told little Choop and Dee about our move as they stood holding their baby brother (whose nickname was Pig because he appeared to get the bulk of the family's food supply). They reached up to hug me and looked tearful, turning quickly to run back into their house. But half an hour later they came back out with crayon drawings for me of hearts, houses, and flowers, the artwork of little girls everywhere.

Over the course of the next few weeks, we doled out most of our belongings to various neighbors, but sold the motorbike because Homie refused to take it for free. I gave my electric scooter to Tin's sister and the black padded adjustable desk chair we'd bought to Jade, who squealed as she sat down and twirled around and around in it. Mama Hang got the shiny new refrigerator we had purchased the year before, and Hanh got a wad of cash to keep her going until she could find another job.

A day before the move, Robin, Kai, and I sat at a *phở* stand across from the Renaissance Hotel along the Saigon River. We'd only recently discovered this vendor, who made the best chicken *phở* we'd ever eaten. I looked at the river between bites, trying to stop my tears from dripping into the soup. "I can't believe it's over," I told Robin. "The next time we come here, we'll be tourists." I wanted to somehow liquefy Vietnam, store it in vials, and shoot it into my veins as needed for an occasional jolt of elation.

That evening, Homie's family threw us a goodbye party at their house with way too much food, including buckets of grilled shrimp. Mama Hang and Hanh had been cooking all day and as we sat on the floor in a circle and ate until we couldn't eat anymore, we traded thank-yous and we'll-miss-yous. Various neighbors dropped by to say goodbye or to simply stare at us one last time. Robin and Useless Brother No. 1 moved the party outside to the steps, chugging back several more Tiger beers. Kai and Kiet played upstairs, so Homie, Tin, and I ran upstairs to our roof one last time, settled into lounge chairs, and looked up at the stars. We listened to music coming from a neighbor's house, traditional pentatonic funeral melodies played on oboe, zither, wood blocks, and a two-string fiddle made from a coconut shell. It was haunting. A Buddhist monk was chanting for an old woman six doors down who had died the night before. The ceremony would go on for three more days with almost nonstop music. The Vietnamese say her ghost will hover, so friends and neighbors can gather to ask her for blessings that she will carry back with her to heaven. In return, family members write her name on fake money and then burn it so she can buy nice things for herself on the other side. The bills are very real-looking euros, dollars, and Vietnamese *đồng*. Once, I stooped down to pick up a fifty-dollar bill, thinking I'd hit pay dirt. "Drop it," Homie said. "It's unlucky. That money for the dead."

Homie began to reminisce. "I remember when you arrive in Vietnam." I closed my eyes and thought about my first shy meetings with the neighbors and smiled to myself. He continued, "You at the pharmacy a lot! You alway have diarrhea!"

EPILOGUE

Back Home

"I want to take a picture of it in my brain."
(KAI, AS THE PLANE TO THE STATES TOOK OFF)

WHAT'S LEFT AFTER YOU LOSE EVERYTHING? As I discovered from living with people who struggle on a completely different level than most of us in the US—lots. My story is a tribute to how Vietnam changed me. I learned that spending an afternoon people-watching is good for your health, that it's okay to reveal your age, and that a sumptuous feast is best eaten on a tile floor because afterward you can nap next to your plate. I have since stopped hurrying conversations along when speaking with children and old people. I've quit lusting for a bigger house, a newer car, or another exotic vacation. Has life become stagnant and unproductive? Not a bit. Just more precious.

The first morning back in America, we woke up early. "Listen," I said to Robin.

"What?"

"Nothing. I hear absolutely nothing."

My first reaction to reverse culture shock happened at the grocery store. *A clove of garlic is one dollar? Just two weeks ago I got it for five cents at the Very Important Market.* I was appreciative, though, of the quiet suburban streets, happy that cars stopped for pedestrians, and positively giddy about seeing green grass again.

We couldn't yet afford to live in our house, so our tenants stayed on, and we found a one-bedroom apartment in a building that was a dead ringer for a Motel 6. Between dumpster diving and thrift stores, we found furniture, pots and pans, and small appliances within a month. Our new home felt cozy and I was content. Robin's business kept rolling and I found work as a communications specialist. Kai was happy to be back in his old school.

We'd been back barely a month when Homie decided he wanted to come to America to earn the big bucks. He'd found an agency that, for a hefty fee, helped place foreign workers in Western jobs on an eighteen-month visa. He had a job offer to work as an assistant chef at a restaurant in Maine for nine dollars an hour. Huge money to him. They would pay for a shared room. But… Maine? Really? Did he even know where it was? How would he survive the snow? He'd be so alone and so cold.

He called us from Vietnam. "I go today for visa appointment at US Consulate. I so scared, Ms. Karin. I must to pay $140. If they say no, I lose that money. I must to pass! I must to pass!" I hung up and waited for the news. A few hours later the phone rang. "I not pass. My dream not come true." I was heartbroken for him.

Once again, the ghost of Grandma must have stepped in to grant his wish. Homie felt a nudge and then an urgent pull to take a detour and stop at a nearby coffeehouse before going home. Seeing a Westerner sitting alone at a table, Homie smiled his lovely smile and started up a conversation. The man was as charmed by Homie as we had been upon meeting him. But this chance meeting was more fortuitous. The man was a supervisor at the US Consulate who was at the coffeehouse on his lunch break. He pulled strings and within a few days, Homie got his visa.

We paid for Homie's plane fare, so I purposely found a flight that stopped in LA en route to Portland, Maine. We were over-joyed to see him walk out of the international terminal at LAX. He stayed with us for a week, and we all slept on our apartment floor on mattresses like, as Homie noted, "fish in a can." On our first walk with him, he was nearly sideswiped by a car when he stepped out into the crosswalk at a red light. We yanked him back onto the curb and told him that in America one must wait for the green light. He was so jubilant seeing Americans, he said hello to nearly everyone we passed on the street.

I took him to thrift stores to buy warm sweaters, jackets, wool socks, and boots. At the end of the week, he hugged us goodbye and spent the next eighteen months freezing his butt off in Maine. He proudly sent money to his mother so that she could take one day off a week. He also bought himself a watch, something he'd never had. Now he works in Macau, the Las Vegas of Asia, as a chef.

Unemployed Brother No. 1 is still sitting in his lawn chair, smoking and watching life pass by. Mai is heading her parent's shrimp paste company. Quy won a full scholarship to a university in Australia to get his master's degree in business information systems and will get married soon. Lan got married and now has two baby girls.

Tin is still working at FV Hospital and now has a special boy-friend in his life. Robin had been right about him; he really didn't want to date girls. His mother, Hanh, found work at the Very Important Market selling clothes.

"I miss Vietnam," Robin said one day. "I loved living there."

I was confused. "How do you know?"

"What do you mean, 'How do you know?'"

"Well, you slept through most of it."

I, too, miss Vietnam. What I don't miss: smelly floods in the alley, frequent all-day power outages, loud karaoke singing, the ants that swarmed Kai's cookie crumbs within seconds of his dropping them, always feeling sticky and sweaty, people staring at me, the rooster crowing at 4 a.m., Dragon Man's hammering, and Hatchet Lady's chopping.

What I do miss: all of the above.

Acknowledgments

I<small>T TAKES A VILLAGE OF EDITORS</small> to raise a writer. I am forever indebted to *Parched* author Heather King for agreeing to be my writing coach, mentor, and muse. You yanked and pulled the words out of me and understood me better than I did. And now I can brag to everyone that you are also my dear friend.

I enjoyed arguing with Al Watt from LA Writer's Lab at our Saturday morning writing group. I am grateful to editors Nomi Isak Kleinmuntz, Treva Silverman, and Alicia Ramos for helping me find my voice and my commas. I especially want to thank my agent, Betsy Amster, for her patience and invaluable guidance. A special thank-you goes to Prospect Park Books publisher Colleen Dunn Bates for taking a chance on me.

Finally, to my loving family: Everything of value in my life is because of you. Thank you, Dad, Loriann (sister), Mark (brother), Marisa, Talia, and Kai. Extra thanks to you, my sweet husband, Robin, for constantly inspiring me and making me laugh. And to my kitties, Strubbel and Princess Petunia, for keeping my lap warm while I wrote. Adding gggggggggggggg 4444444444 //////////////////// to my manuscript when you sat on my keyboard was mighty generous of you.

About the Author

KARIN ESTERHAMMER's travel writing has been published in the *Chicago Tribune, Los Angeles Times, Baltimore Sun, Christian Science Monitor, Orlando Sentinel,* and *The Standard—China's Business Newspaper.* Her diary-style article in the *Los Angeles Times* about the move to Vietnam elicited more letters to the paper than the travel editor had seen in a long time. Karin has also had essays published in the *Chocolate for a Woman's Soul* series, and she once won the grand prize in a romance-essay contest for Harlequin Books. After their years in Vietnam, Karin and her family are once again living in Los Angeles.